LIFE
in
OPERA

Truth, Tempo, and Soul:
Encounters with Stars,
Innovators, and Leaders of
Today's Opera World

Maria-Cristina Necula

AMADEUS
PRESS

An Imprint of Hal Leonard Corporation
New York

Published in 2009 by Amadeus Press
An Imprint of Hal Leonard Corporation
7777 West Bluemound Road
Milwaukee, WI 53213

Trade Book Division Editorial Offices
19 West 21st Street, New York, NY 10010

Every reasonable effort has been made to contact copyright holders and secure permissions. Omissions can be remedied in future editions.

Printed in the United States of America

Book design by Michael Kellner

Library of Congress Cataloging-in-Publication Data
Necula, Maria-Cristina.
  Life in opera : truth, tempo, and soul : encounters with stars, innovators, and leaders of today's opera world / by Maria-Cristina Necula.
      p. cm.
  Includes interviews with performers, producers, and others, and essays by the author about her own experiences in the operatic world.
  Includes discography, videography, and web resources: p.
  ISBN 978-1-57467-179-7 (alk. paper)
  1. Opera--Interviews. 2. Necula, Maria-Cristina. I. Title.
  ML1700.N43 2009
  782.1092'2--dc22
                          2009036960

www.amadeuspress.com

Contents

PART 2 Author's Corner

Preface

It all began at home. My academic home. After studying singing for three years in Europe, I returned to the United States, and guided by a blend of nostalgia and curiosity, I paid a visit to my alma mater, Purchase College. That visit triggered my involvement with the Purchase College Alumni Association board of directors, and soon thereafter I discovered that the great American baritone Dwayne Croft had also been a student at Purchase. Thus I found myself in a propitious constellation of factors: a renowned singer and fellow alum performing at the Metropolitan Opera during those very days, an alumni magazine hungry for news, and my love of writing. The decision to interview Mr. Croft for *Purchase Magazine* was instantaneous.

So I scoured the Metropolitan Opera calendar and on the day before one of Mr. Croft's *La traviata* performances, I headed straight for the stage door, armed with a letter that highlighted our connection as Purchase alumni. The next evening, impressed by Mr. Croft's noble rendition of the elder Germont, I showed up at the stage door again and was pleased to find out that he had indeed put me on the backstage list in response to my letter. Nervous beyond belief, with no previous interview experience or any publications to my name, I walked down the corridor beyond the secure backstage door. As I turned in the direction of the dressing rooms, a fabulous fur coat suddenly materialized in front of me. It took me a few seconds before I realized that Dwayne Croft was inside that coat. He had come out of his dressing room to meet me. We spoke briefly and shared a moment of Purchase-related anecdotes. (Little did we both know then that seven years later, he would be invited to return to Purchase to receive the Presidential Distinguished Alumni Award during the May 2008 commencement ceremony.) We agreed on the interview time and place.

The place was a café in the vicinity of Lincoln Center. The time was breakfast. I sat down facing a true gentleman who boosted my interviewer's debut by ordering me a delicious omelet. Tape recorder rolling, I was instantly captured by Mr. Croft's use of language. He spoke like a writer and made the interview easy to capture.

It was an auspicious beginning, as this interview's journey did not end with its publication in the *Purchase Magazine*. One day, in search of a laryngologist, I wrote an e-mail to the late CJ Williamson, the founder and first editor in chief of *Classical Singer* magazine, asking her to recommend one. E-mails followed back and forth, and I mentioned the Dwayne Croft interview. She asked to read it.

Two months later, my interview with Mr. Croft became *Classical Singer*'s April 2002 cover story. It was my first step on a fascinating seven-year journey through the world of opera—a journey I began as an aspiring singer who loved to write and ended as a writer who loves to sing.

I have divided this book into two parts. Part 1 consists only of interviews, most of which were published in *Classical Singer* magazine between 2002 and 2008. The interviews with Diana Damrau, Natalie Dessay, and Anna Netrebko appear here for the first time.

While all my encounters with the interviewees have been unforgettable, there are a few stories related to some of these encounters, that I felt were remarkable, surprising, and worth telling. In part 2, Author's Corner, I share these stories as well as two interviews that became articles, plus a tribute to the Bucharest Opera House, the place where, as a child, I fell in love with opera.

My goal in bringing the words of the interviewees to paper was to stay as close as I could to the natural flow of our conversations. I strived to maintain their manner of expression as unedited and unaltered as possible, even when translating the few interviews I've conducted in other languages.

It is my hope that this book will offer a wide perspective on life in the lyric universe, from the stars and leaders that define and advance the operatic art form today to the creative individuals that nurture opera's future and enrich its present.

Here's to the fans of the many great artists featured in this book, to the lovers of opera, to aspiring singers and their teachers, and to the curious reader who may want to discover a new world. Last but not least, here's to all those who work behind the scenes, in every capacity, making an essential contribution to bringing the magic of opera to the public.

Maria-Cristina Necula
December 2008

Acknowledgments

I would like to express my deepest gratitude in memory of the late Carla Wood, a.k.a. CJ Williamson—founder and editor-in-chief of *Classical Singer* magazine, a lovely singer, and great mentor to many. CJ gave me my first chance to be published as a writer, and her enthusiastic support was a guiding light on my path from interview to interview.

Many thanks go to Sara Thomas and David Wood, respectively editor-in-chief and publisher of *Classical Singer* magazine, for their kind permission to use my *Classical Singer* interviews for this project.

Along this book's journey, I've encountered a few publicists and agents. I particularly want to thank Sean Michael Gross from 21c Media Group for being so professional, considerate, and responsive. I would also like to acknowledge the late Edgar Vincent—a true gentleman—for his prompt and elegant manner in facilitating my encounter with Plácido Domingo. Sincere thanks go to Connie Shuman, President of Shuman Associates Inc., for having made a few of these interviews possible.

Thank you a thousand times to my agent, Paul Feldstein, for his positive outlook and encouragement, for believing in this project and carrying it through to Amadeus Press. I also offer my thanks to John Cerullo at Amadeus Press for making *Life in Opera* a reality. In addition, I'd like to acknowledge Jessica Burr and Iris Bass at Amadeus Press for their excellent work in editing and bringing the book into its final form.

Closer to home, I wish to express my love and gratitude to my parents, Maria-Ana and Nicholas, for their all-encompassing love as well as for their support and patience through the countless hours of voice lessons and vocalises I went through to find my way here.

I would also like to express my appreciation and pride of my alma mater, Purchase College—the never-ending source of knowledge and experiences that have shaped my life from the moment I stepped into its classrooms up to my present work with my fellow alumni. Many thanks go to Purchase College president Thomas J. Schwarz for his encouragement and advice. Thank you also to the voice department chair, tenor Jacque Trussel, and his opera students for making my Italian-teaching experience a rewarding one, and for keeping me in tune with the aspirations of young singers and the challenges they face in conservatory opera programs.

I am forever indebted to the voice teachers who have enriched my life, thus making an essential contribution to the *raison d'être* of this book: the great tenor and friend Ramón Vargas; the wonderful soprano Victoria Bezetti and her husband, baritone Mircea Bezetti; the magnificent diva Virginia Zeani; pianist David Maiullo; the late Greek mezzo-soprano Antonia Kitsopoulos (1928–1994); and the late Cuban soprano Carolina Segrera (1905–1998). My heartfelt gratitude extends to the Bucharest Opera House, where the fierce determination to "go on with the show" despite the challenges of the Iron Curtain era made it possible for me, as a child of ten, to get to know and fall in love with opera.

And most of all, thanks to all the amazing personalities who took time out of their lives to talk to me. It has been an honor to serve as their pen, capture their words from the recorder to paper, and transmit these conversations out into the world.

LIFE in OPERA

Part 1
The Interviews

Dwayne Croft

Recorded December 2000 in New York City. An edited version was published in the Fall 2001 Purchase Magazine. *The present version was published in* Classical Singer *in April 2002.*

How did you decide to attend Purchase College?

I was in the middle of my senior year in high school, thinking of taking a year off to study privately, but I then decided that once I did that, I would probably never go back to school. I had heard about Purchase and liked that they offered the possibility for me to study privately in New York with a teacher of my choice. It was the only school I applied to. The professors were all professionals, and worked in the business, so I was really excited about it.

Did you live on campus?

Yes, from 1979 to 1983. I made a lot of friends there and had a good time.

Were there any professors or colleagues that had a special influence on you at Purchase?

One of my favorite professors there was Myron Fink. He was not only extremely gifted at teaching but a great musician as well. Another favorite of mine was Robert Fertitta, who accompanied my recitals and with whom I became good friends.

How did you discover your vocation?

I'd been singing since I was five years old. I decided to be an opera singer when I was about fifteen. When Glimmerglass was founded in Cooperstown, I became involved in the chorus and really fell in love with opera. My family was absolutely supportive. They knew I was musically inclined—I also played the trumpet for twelve years—and they never discouraged me.

There are so many methods and approaches to singing out there. How did you know what was right for you?

KARIN COOPER

It took me a while to figure it out. Attending the Purchase Conservatory from 1979 to 1983, I was singing as a tenor and I didn't discover until my senior year that I was actually a baritone. I had a teacher who was very strict with me and made sure I didn't sing too heavily. All throughout college I struggled to find my voice, singing very lightly to get my tenor voice to work. By my senior year, I knew more or less what I was doing, but I didn't have any high notes. In that last year at Purchase, I went to a different teacher, and kept on studying yet doing very little singing. I was working at other jobs so I could afford to take a voice lesson at least once a month. Then I finally went for a vocal consultation with Marlena Malas and she switched me to baritone. One year later I got into the Met Young Artist Program. I'd been working for so long to be a tenor and to have to switch was very upsetting, but it ended up being the best thing I could have done.

Do you believe there has to be the right chemistry between teacher and student?

Oh, yes! It's a personal relationship. I need someone who is encouraging, someone who is not putting me down, because that has such an adverse effect on singers. We need nurturing, we need to be calm because it's stressful enough to be a singer. The last thing you need is somebody who makes you afraid to open your mouth. You find your voice by just letting go and not being afraid to make sounds whether they are good or bad. You find it when you get encouragement . . . I have a great relationship with Marlena Malas. Unfortunately, I don't see her very often but we talk on the phone.

What is important for a young singer in taking the next steps after college/conservatory?

Most young singers out of college are not ready to jump into an operatic career. So, it's important to find a way to keep studying. A possibility is going for a master's degree. I got a job and tried to study as much as I could. It was a struggle. For seven or eight years I was doing everything but singing. Once in a while, I'd have the chance to sing a small tenor role with Eve Queler or at Glimmerglass in the summertime. But that was the extent of my singing. Of course, every singer has his or her own particular circumstances and financial situation. If you don't have a lot of money, you will need to work and struggle to keep studying and perhaps get into some kind of program that can help you. I was very fortunate to get into the Met program at twenty-eight, because they took care of me. Suddenly everything was free. I was singing and coaching every day and I didn't have to work in anything but singing anymore.

At your high professional level, do you still need a voice teacher?

I think one always does. There are times when you might have a little trouble and you need to tune up, therefore you should continue taking lessons. It's something I've been thinking of going back to, especially since I am doing all these new roles. I also coach a lot.

You are married to soprano Ainhoa Arteta. Is it difficult to balance family life with all of the commitments you both have? How do you manage?

We knew it would be complicated and now it's even more so since we have a four-month-old baby. We're traveling all the time, trying to set our schedules so that we do not spend too much time apart. It can be stressful and difficult, but it's worth it because we are crazy about each other, so we try to make it work.

How do you deal with stage fright?

I get nervous in a good way. It's a positive energy. Lately . . . the more I perform, the more relaxed I am. On performance days, I just conserve my energy. Luckily, being nervous never shows in my body or my voice. It's always something I feel in my stomach. But I feel very comfortable at the Met. Making my debut there, singing small roles and working my way up to big roles, my confidence grew. Then, when I started singing leading roles, and realized I could do that, it was a huge confidence builder. Suddenly I felt like I could sing anywhere without being so nervous.

How do you choose your repertory and how do you know when you should move on?

It's a natural progression. I want to have Mozart and Rossini roles in my repertory because they keep me in good shape. I've always liked singing *The Barber of Seville*. Eugene Onegin is another role I love and want to perform as often as I can. I just started singing some Verdi, my first role being Rodrigo in *Don Carlo*. I've recently done Germont, I'm going to do Falstaff this summer, and I don't have any plans to go further with Verdi for a while. The other Verdi roles are really big steps . . . I've had some major steps in my career. Deciding to sing Pelléas at the Met with James Levine and Frederica von Stade in 1995 was one huge step. I remember accepting the contract three years before, not knowing if I could even sing the part. That was where the Met helped me again. They knew I could do it, they coached me on it, and they wouldn't have let me perform had I not been ready for it.

What steps do you take in preparing a role?

First, I translate it. Then I listen to a recording of someone I respect. If it's an Italian opera, I make sure I listen to an Italian singer singing it, then I coach like crazy. I listen to the recording just enough so that I can start coaching the role. I like to make the role my own, finding what the composer wanted, learning the words, the music, adding the dynamics. It's a long process, depending on how much time you have. I used to have a lot more time to learn things.

What do you do to keep yourself in good vocal and physical shape?

I don't exercise constantly, but that is something I highly recommend to any singer. It's just so hard to keep a regular exercise routine when you're on the road. Vocally, if I am healthy, just singing every day in rehearsals or coachings keeps me in shape.

Do you ever take long breaks from singing?

Yes, especially since I have a family. This fall I was supposed to sing Marcello at the Met, but I wanted to be with my wife and my newborn baby. They were very understanding and released me from the schedule. So, I took a month off.

In performance, are you conscious of your technique or do you just allow the characterization to take care of everything?

When I'm healthy, I am not conscious of my technique. I take a deep breath and just let my voice go. This approach has also been helping me to become a better actor. My favorite performances happen when I really feel I am the character and I don't have to think about the difficult phrase or high note coming up. Obviously, when I was learning how to sing, I had to think about technique. Some teachers do not believe that a singer should be so concerned with technique, but when you're first learning how to sing, you are trying to coordinate so many different things that, until they become second nature, you have to concentrate on each one. All through college I was struggling with coordinating these factors. Once I switched to baritone and got into the Met program, it became a lot easier to understand technique.

If you had to choose another profession, what would it be?

Sometimes, I think about how I've got these two little vocal cords and how my whole life depends on them. If I didn't sing, I would definitely work in the opera field, in a company, directing, coaching, teaching.

What piece of advice would you give a young singer, something you wish someone would have told you when you were starting out?

I knew a lot of professional singers when I was in college because I was singing in the chorus at Glimmerglass. I received a lot of good advice from them. I would say: "Know your voice, know what repertoire is good for you, do not sing anything too soon." People tend to think that they can sing big operatic arias when they're in college. They shouldn't. The idea is to have a long career and be a healthy singer. The Met program saved me at a time when I was getting offers to sing things that were too heavy for my voice. Naturally, it's tempting when you're being offered money to take certain roles. My main advice is to go slowly and get a solid technique. It sounds really simple, but some young singers think they know their instrument and they believe too soon that they are ready. True, every singer is different; some mature earlier than others. However, I heard voice students performing arias that they shouldn't have been singing in college and having huge wobbles in their voices at nineteen. They were finished before they even got out into the world. One thing is true for everyone: find a teacher you can trust, who will suit your individual needs. When I was trying to decide whether I was a tenor or a baritone, I went to two different vocal consultations. The first person I sang for told me I was a tenor and that I would never have a career as a baritone. Then I sang for Marlena Malas and that was it! A lot of it has to do with luck as well. But if you have a talent that people recognize, then it's knowing how to be smart, to protect it, to be careful, knowing what's right for you and, when you are ready, being conservative and trusting your instincts. It's very simple: if it hurts you, it's wrong for you.

José Cura

Recorded March 2005 in New York City. The first part of this interview was published in Classical Singer *in January 2006. The continuation* dates from October 2008 and appears here for the first time.*

Did you grow up in a musical environment?

I grew up in a musical environment, but not in an environment of musicians. My mother had no prejudices when it came to music. She would switch from Beethoven to Sinatra without any kind of discrimination. That kind of openness toward music is hard to find today. At first, I knew only that there is good or bad music; it didn't matter if it was pop or classical. My mother encouraged my open-minded view because my house was always full of good music of all kinds. My father used to play the piano for pure pleasure, having taken piano lessons, like many kids in the fifties.

When you began focusing on composition and conducting at the age of twelve, were you aware that you had a voice? Did you like to sing?

I was singing since I was twelve or thirteen, in several groups: quartets, octets, et cetera. We did jazz [and] spirituals, among other styles. Then I sang in choirs, old music like Palestrina, for example. So I was always singing, but never in an operatic way. Yes, I was completely dedicated to composition and conducting; that is still my vocation. Of course, there can be a difference between vocation and profession. If you are lucky, your vocation is your profession. But I only started to sing lyrically when I was twenty-one or twenty-two. I had problems; I couldn't find a proper teacher.

What kind of problems did you have?

I think most singers know that to find the right teacher is a great problem. Certain people say, "Oh, today we don't have any good teachers!" But these people also say that there are no good singers—so they are actually transferring the invented problem of not having good singers to saying that there are no good teachers. Well, let me tell you something: There have never been just good teachers or just bad teachers! You might already know that an extremely good teacher for somebody can be an awful teacher for somebody else.

COURTESY OF CUIBAR PRODUCTIONS S.L.

The voice is not an instrument where you can easily "see" what is going wrong. Singing is a very empirical thing, so you never really know what is happening, unless there is an extremely rich and harmonious human communication between the teacher and the student. If the teacher is able to go inside the student's being and give him or her a couple of clues about what to do or how to do it, then that teacher is the right one for that person. If you find a teacher who has a good chemistry with you, who understands your body and your voice, and on top of that is also a great technician, then of course, you are in heaven!

Personally, I had many problems, until I found somebody who, for one year, dared to "dig" inside my body, my cords, my larynx. This was when I was twenty-six or twenty-seven, in Argentina. Before that, every other teacher I had tried was damaging my voice badly.

When you found the right teacher, did you do a great deal of technical work with him?

Well, we worked for a year. I have always been a rebel in my life, self-taught in almost everything I do. I always wanted to carve my way, in my own style. But this teacher helped me discover and understand my instrument. He didn't change it; he didn't try to shape what was the rough prototype of my voice into an artist. So, from there on, I took charge of my own instrument, and kept asking myself, "Now that I understand how it feels, what do I have to do, what do I have to keep feeling? How do I have to mold my understanding of the voice into the musician that I am, in order to continue on my own path?"

Of course, when you do things alone, it takes a lot of time. It's very dangerous, and you hit your head against the wall again and again! I was lucky, because I was always surrounded by great musicians, and by people with great ears who said to me, "This is not good; check it!" or "I don't know what you have to do, but this doesn't sound nice."

It's interesting, when you read the reviews of my career from the start to today, you understand that in the beginning, I was developing myself within the process of performing. I was trying to identify with my own way of expressing and my own body.

In the early reviews, for example, you read a lot that "Cura doesn't have a technique." And I always thought, "Wait a minute, you cannot handle such a career as I have had from the beginning, and still be able to speak after singing a Samson or an Otello, if you don't have a technique!" In a couple of years, you would be out, completely aphonic and unable to sing one note.

On the other hand, I am happy to attribute to the lines of those reviews [that said] I don't have a technique, the fact that I have my own technique!

I think that singers can learn a lot from you when it comes to facing unfair reviews.

The ideal for a singer is to have his or her own technique. Singers are not like instrumentalists. A singer is an entity in himself or herself. You cannot apply the same resources to everybody. That is the main challenge of being a singer, and of growing from rough material to a professional. And that is also the big challenge of finding a good teacher. It's not only about knowing where to place the notes and how to do scales.

But it's hard not to get trapped in that! Don't you think that a teacher needs to make a singer aware of physical things that may inhibit the best result from that singer?

Yes, but in moderation!

What happens a lot is that we forget the fact that singing is a natural thing. In order to sing, you have to breathe; in order to live, you have to breathe. Singing is a natural process that you need to develop, not invent.

So, you're saying that the natural act of singing is already present in each singer, but it's more or less disguised, and the work involves uncovering this natural gift rather than "building" it?

Exactly! For me, the key is this: We cannot invent singing, because there is nothing to invent. You need to develop what is inside the person. It's like when you are an athlete, and you have a trainer who trains you how to run as fast as you can, to break the records and be one of the top athletes. He is not teaching you to run in the basic sense of, "One leg goes in front of the other one!" That's a natural motion. We don't have to invent that. He will teach you how to train your muscles, how to articulate your knees, in order to obtain the maximum result from that which is a natural thing for a human being, like running, in this case.

That is why teachers fail when they take somebody and they try to invent a voice. No! As a teacher, you have to take your time to understand what is there. Just start with that and try to get the best out of what your student already has!

What was your existing core, or your starting point?

I've always been an athlete, even close to being a professional, before the beginning of my career. My starting point was to understand that there is a direct relationship—not to say identical—between the body that you use for sports and the body you use for singing. It's the same body. When you sing, you use muscles, blood, tendons, bones, and fluids—all the things you use when you go to the gym or when you play a tennis match.

A singer is not somebody with a crystal bird in the larynx, so [that] you can push a button and all of a sudden the voice comes out! No, it's a physical thing. That's why many things have to do with the cycle of glucose and lactic acid, things that people wouldn't normally think about.

For example, there are singers who don't understand what is going on when they start vocalizing, and after ten minutes, they get hoarse and can't speak anymore. Then they take a short break—and they can sing again, and they have no idea why. It's very simple. You just burned the glucose in the muscle and you have lactic acid as garbage, and the liver needs to clear the lactic acid and add glucose again.

The same happens when you do push-ups, for example, and after the twelfth push-up, you can't move anymore, because all your muscles are burning. But if you stop for five minutes, the lactic acid is replaced by glucose, and then you can do ten more push-ups like a miracle. The body is just doing its job.

It's the same with singing. Once you see this relationship, once you understand that it's very much about muscles and blood and physicality, you will face the fears of having to sing with a completely different mind.

People say, "I have to warm up my voice." You don't warm up your voice, because the voice is an intangible thing. You warm up the muscles that produce a sound [that] you call "voice." You warm up those muscles in the same way an athlete would warm up his body for a competition, trying to put into motion the circuit of glucose and lactic acid, so that the energy will be there. Once you understand that, your whole life as a singer changes.

In the beginning, you sang in Teatro Colón in the choir. How did that experience develop you as a singer?

I think that every singer who wants to be a soloist has to spend some years singing in the choir. That is some of the best training you can get. You learn how to be onstage. You learn about makeup, and costumes, and how to walk, how to follow the conductor. You can take some risks with your voice and experiment a little, because whatever happens, you are covered.

If you are a tenor in a big choir where there are twenty to forty tenors, you can try diminuendo, crescendo, and some things that if you were alone you wouldn't dare to try, because you might be afraid your voice will break. So you can use the choir as a territory of experiences for the future. Not to mention that by singing in the choir of a big opera house, you have the chance of sharing the stage with great artists. You are there when they sing, and you see what they do. You learn how they breathe, and how they move their mouths. You are in rehearsals, you see their problems, you watch how they struggle to obtain a result, and you learn how to fix certain things. It's a really great experience!

You made your operatic debut in a few small roles, until the bigger role of Jean in *Miss Julie*, in March 1993. Is that where your career started taking off?

Well, yes. It's a weird thing, that a career takes off with a completely unknown opera that I've never repeated since. Some people who saw me then started to think about the possibility that "maybe this guy could be somebody interesting to follow."

You were thirty at that time.

Yes. You've been counting the years. *Mamma mia!*

Do you think it's better for a singer to start a little later, rather than throwing themselves out there at twenty-two or twenty-three?

It's not about when you start . . . it's about what you have inside your head to deal with your life and your career, which has nothing to do with when you start, or with age. This is like getting married. If you feel that you have to get married at twenty-two, even if everybody says that you are too young, then you get married at twenty-two. I got married at twenty-two! I've been married for twenty years—I have three kids and I am the happiest man. So, it worked!

On the contrary, I started to sing very late, and that worked, too! It depends on when it comes. The train passes in front of you, and if you don't jump on it, maybe there won't be another train. But it has to happen at the right time. There are no rules. You just have to keep your senses on alert and be ready to jump if the occasion is there. And be intelligent enough to understand if you are up to the challenge of a certain occasion or not, because that can also be tricky.

When I did my debut in *Otello*, I was thirty-four, and that was a daring thing to do. There I was with Maestro [Claudio] Abbado, live in front of the world, and I thought, "I cannot lose this chance!" So what I had to do was to sing Otello like a thirty-four-year-old guy. I couldn't intoxicate my interpretation with interpretations of forty-five-, fifty- and sixty-year-old tenors who have great experience with the role and whom I couldn't compare to. Because if I did that, by the end of the first act, I would have been kaput! So I created a very lyrical Otello, based more on stage presence and acting, rather than the volume of the voice. Many said, "But this is not Otello, this is too lyric." It was lyric, of course, but what can you do when you are thirty-four?

It was your own interpretation.

It wasn't a set interpretation that I will keep forever. It was a guy of thirty-four taking this risk in a role that is emblematic for a tenor; a role that is very dangerous and very difficult, and which you are mature for when you are forty-five.

It's about taking calculated risks and surviving to tell about it. And that created a very nice image: The first tenor in the history of opera to make his debut in *Otello* at thirty-four in a live broadcast, which is absolutely daring and irresponsible!

Every tenor I know made his debut in *Otello* in a more or less hidden way, to be sure that they could cope with the role—and when they knew that they could do it, the second [*Otello* production] was more in the open. I went for it at thirty-four, and I did it in my way at that time. So what was at the time a surprise for critics, now it is understood as a demonstration of intelligence, to have done it like that and then to live and be here to speak with you about it!

You manage your career yourself through your own management agency. Did you have an agent when you started?

When I started I had agents like everybody—until I discovered certain traits in some of them . . .

Like what?

I will not go too much into detail because it's not necessary.

Actually, it would serve as advice for singers in terms of what to watch out for when they have an agent.

Singers have to [make sure] that the agent is honest. At the time, I was getting fed up with the image they were trying to create of me—"sex symbol of the opera"—something that is very nice at first glance, but then you understand that it is superficial. I didn't spend thirty years of my life to become a musician and only be considered because I am kind of good looking, for goodness' sake! That is frustrating.

You are very good looking! And don't tell me that doesn't help at all!

Yeah, okay, but that is still frustrating. You are a woman and you know how it feels when people consider you because you are pretty, and they forget that you may also be intelligent, by the way. And that's the case with a lot of good-looking women, and men. So, it took me several years to convince people of the fact that I was a serious musician, and that nothing that happens onstage or in my career is a result of coincidence, or chance, or the good luck of a purely gifted person, an overnight sensation—the typical media formula. On the contrary, it's the result of thirty years of hard work!

Of course, thank God I have these talents, but I've worked very hard to develop them. If, on top of that, I am considered to be good looking onstage and be a good actor, that makes me happy, too. It's the cherry on top of the cake, but it's not the cake!

Then how do you see the importance of looks for this career?

Honestly, I think that if you look good, it is better. Not to the point that the looks will make your career if you are not a good singer, because then it is not better, it's worse. But from my own experience, I can tell you there's no way to sing roles such as Samson or Otello only with your good looks, because you won't get to the end of the second act. Okay, you are good looking, but go onstage and show me what you can do! And then you will know the truth about a singer.

The paradox of opera is that for one reason or another, great voices don't always go with great looks. You can make a very good actor out of a good-looking guy, even if he's not good from the beginning. But you cannot put a voice in a good-looking guy, if the voice is not there.

This is where you need flexibility. If you have a great voice in front of you, the voice comes first. But there is another important fact to consider. I say this to everybody who has a great voice: Be careful not to rely on the fact that you have such a great voice, so that you do nothing more. Do not use that excuse to neglect the way you look, to start eating like a pig, to not dress properly, or not act well onstage! Because then you become a bad artist, you just become a voice, and you break the idea of the integral performer.

An integral performer is not somebody who is pretty. It's somebody who is professional enough to obtain from his own body as much as his own body can give. And each one of us has to find his or her limit. There's no way everybody can be good looking, or smart, or fit. That's not the point. What you have to do is just face yourself in the mirror and be honest with yourself, and see what you can improve. Then you try to improve the way you look, and you get to the point when you know you tried your best and you are happy with yourself. But when you use having a great voice as a pretext to ignore the remaining aspects of what is to be a professional whose body is the instrument of work, then you are not a complete professional and you are giving a very bad example.

It's not about how you look, or how pretty you are compared to somebody else. It's about you, in honesty with your instrument, with your body, with yourself—not trying to be the best, but as good as you can be! Of course, there are medical problems [that may be] difficult to deal with and have an effect on your looks, but in a normal situation, an ideal artist obtains from his instrument the best he can in every way. That is an artist's responsibility.

When did you decide to start your own management company?

In 1999, certain things happened. I had a couple of very disgusting legal situations with people who wanted to obtain the most from me without doing anything. So I decided to cut with everybody and to be my own man. This cost me three to four years of nightmares.

From 1999 to the beginning of 2004, I [was] under the harshest of . . . attacks from many different sources: people calling theaters to convince artistic directors not to engage me, and journalists being paid to write that I was history, that I was a falling star. But we persisted very hard, and we created my own production company with a branch for my own management . . . In 2001, we created my own record company. We have three records now in the catalog, and they're very successful.

A few months ago, we added two new branches: one is productions/special events. Our company is open for theaters or international organizations who want to engage us to create and produce shows for them.

Today, a lot of things are changing; subsidies are being taken away from theaters, and business has changed a lot. Record companies now are not doing as well as they were years ago. Certain agencies are selling their buildings because they cannot pay the rent anymore, and they are moving into small offices.

In the actual picture of how show business is reshaping itself, I am very happy to say that my company is among the pioneers of what is probably going to be the new way of doing show business. After four years of struggle, we are now successful and very happy with our work. We have expanded and moved into new offices, and we are building our own recording studio.

Between singing, conducting, managing your own company, recording, composing, do you even have time to sleep?

Well, I have a group of people working with me and for me. I don't do everything! For example, I don't manage the careers of the singers on my roster. I observe and I am consulted when somebody new is going to be part of the company. I've conducted a great deal in the past, and finally, I am coming back to what was supposed to be my vocation: to be a conductor. The singing was an accident in my life—a very happy accident—but not the reason why I became a musician.

This year I am conducting a lot, and making my debut in four or five new symphonic works. I'm conducting Rossini's Stabat Mater, Puccini's *Messa di Gloria*, [both] Kodály's and Bruckner's Te Deum, Brahms's Fourth Symphony, Verdi's *Vespri siciliani*, and Puccini's *Madama Butterfly*.

Do you have time for any hobbies?

Actually, I've always been interested in photography as my hobby, as my way out. I am a pretty good photographer. I don't say that I am the Richard Avedon of the lyric panorama—but pictures can also be interesting to understand what goes through the head of the photographer. So in my case, maybe it could be the ultimate way for my fans to comprehend certain things. Now I have a Swiss publisher who has approached my company to ask for the possibility of releasing a book of my photographs, whenever I am ready for that. It's a big step!

Do you compose for voice?

My favorite thing is to compose for voices and orchestra at the same time, mainly choral symphonic music, probably because it's the most complete of the ways you write music. You have the best of all worlds: the orchestra and the voice, all together in one.

What is your philosophy of life in general?

One thing I can tell you—and this has been my challenge since the beginning—trying not to be overwhelmed by the fact that because I have been given several different talents, there is the danger of becoming mediocre in all of them. [I'm] following [the dictum of] Einstein, who said, "If you look for different results, do not always do the same things!"

Well, you know the expression, "Jack of all trades, master of none!" How do you avoid that?

By working very, very, very hard and giving time to each of my talents, sometimes giving more importance to one of them in a certain period and putting the other ones aside, and so on—alternating. On the other hand, if you discover that you have several talents and you put most of them aside to concentrate on one, at the end of your life, you will feel very bad. You will know that you gave up your other gifts, just for the fear of not being able to face them all . . . at the same time! Or what's even worse, you gave them up for the comfort of not having to work double or triple in order to maintain all of them at the same level.

But if people do so many things at once, then how can they become excellent at something?

If you only do one thing and you want to be perfect just in that one, the "bad news" is that nobody is perfect. The very bad news is that there is always somebody who is better than you. So at the end of your life, you will turn around and you will see: "Okay, I have not been perfect as I wanted, because it is impossible, but I've given up a lot of other chances because I was a coward."

I am not trying to pontificate here. What I am saying is that each individual has to make his own decisions and take his own risks, and forget about what other people say when they judge your behavior. Just go for it, and be responsible for your achievements and for your mistakes.

I prefer to suffer today the attacks and the criticisms of people saying that I am doing too many things, rather than just doing one thing, and at the end of my life, having to face God and explain to him why I have put aside all the other talents he gave me. If I have to deal with somebody's judgment, I prefer to deal with human beings rather than with God!

How do you balance all this activity and your family life?

My company is very close to my house, so when I am there, I am in both places at the same time. The company's general administrator is my wife, so we are always working together for the company.

I am making many sacrifices to be in my house as much as possible. For example, last week I did my last performance in New York on Saturday. I took a plane on Sunday—I went to Madrid for five days, which is not around the corner exactly—and then I took a plane back to New York to finish the remaining performances. That is exhausting! I sang the performance two days ago with a big jet lag. But, well, that's the price you have to pay if you want to be a good parent, and I happily pay it.

What do you do for that? Try to be as healthy and as fit as you can, and to have the most reliable technique possible in order to face those demands. Not everybody is capable of identifying with what I do, because sometimes it is extreme. But it's working very well, because my family is great and we're very united. I am not a father who brings up his kids by telephone.

How do you prepare for roles?

Studying a lot, as usual.

Do you read related materials, too?

Yes, of course, depending on the role. There are certain roles . . . you can really dig inside psychologically, like Don Carlo, Canio, Samson, or Otello. There are other roles, like Calaf in *Turandot*, for example, where if you have a nice presence and you sing well, it's already enough. You can maybe find two or three colors, but it's not such a rich character in terms of psychological background.

Then, if the character is very physical—like the Samson I am doing now, for example—I try to be as fit as I can to avoid accidents onstage, like twisting my back, for example, when they kick me around.

You are by far the most physical Samson I have ever seen.

When I am waiting to go onstage, between the millstone scene and after the Bacchanale, I am actually stretching and warming up as a dancer, to be ready for this very physical scene.

What kind of sports do you do right now?

I have no time for sports right now. I just try to do some push-ups sometimes to "keep the blood going." Life in hotels, airplanes, and rehearsal rooms—which are almost always located three floors or more below ground level—is not the easiest thing to deal with if you want to stay more or less fit.

Any words of advice?

I would not say "good luck," because I don't believe in luck. I believe in being prepared. Luck is to be in the middle of the desert dying of thirst and all of a sudden having a short shower on your head. That is good luck! But if you don't have a glass to gather the water, you lose the water. The glass has to be prepared.

Many people think that they didn't have a career because they didn't have the luck. Some say, "Oh, Mr. Cura, he's very lucky, he's been at the proper time in the proper place."

No, no, no! Wait a minute! I moved from Argentina to Europe in 1991. I worked for two or three years in restaurants—my wife worked with me, washing dishes—and we did many things that a lot of people wouldn't even think about doing. We had a very hard life. We lived in a garage for one year because we couldn't pay the rent, and we heated the garage with a small fire, with me gathering wood in the middle of the night!

In 1990, one year before going to Europe, I was singing in commercial centers in Argentina, with my hat on the floor for coins! So don't tell me about pure luck, because that is garbage! It is all about hard work! And then, be sure that through your hard work and preparation, the moment when you have that short shower on your head in the middle of the desert, you [are carrying] the biggest glass possible to gather as much water as you can.

That is my advice. Don't live on dreams, don't live thinking that one day somebody will knock on your door and say, "Hey, you're the greatest on the earth, we are waiting for you—come!" That doesn't exist. [That happens] only in movies—unless you do certain things that I don't wish anybody to do, to make certain compromises at certain levels in order to start a career, compromises that could go from economical to physical ones. I know many of those situations, but I also know that all of them who started their careers by compromising lasted two or three years, and they were gone.

The advice of someone who's been onstage for thirty years—fifteen of them professionally—is: Do not compromise! Just be as good as you can. And know where your limits are!

All the time I hear people saying, "I am the greatest artist on earth, but because nobody knows it, nobody gives me a chance." That's not true, because if you put many of those who say that onstage to do a solo, they can't open their mouths for being too afraid or too unprepared. I am generalizing just for the sake of giving you an example, of course, but the problem remains.

Everyone can be great in the shower! My advice then? Speak less and do more!

*During the past three years, you have expanded your work even beyond singing, conducting, and composing. You have created and starred in your own show, *La commedia è finita*; directed *Un*

ballo in maschera; and your photography book, *Espontáneas*, was just released. How do you feel after having conquered these new territories, and how does the expansion influence your singing and conducting now?

I do not think I have conquered anything . . . [I've] just [been] digging in new aspects in my holistic conception of career: the broader your experience in related, complementary disciplines, the strongest the feeling of confidence and interaction when the time for performing comes.

How did the idea for the show—*La commedia*—come to you?

La commedia è finita was born after a fairy tale. [To learn more, visit www.lacommediaefinita.com]

As a singer, did you feel you had more of an advantage directing singers than a theater/opera director would?

Advantages or disadvantages are only related to being a good professional or not. The fact of [whether you are] a singer or a conductor at the time of stage directing a show only enriches the experience. If you are a good stage director, you may turn out to be even better; but if you are a bad one, being good in those other things will not fix it...

What does it mean to you to see [your] book published?

It is a weird feeling to see your pictures, which are like your kids, out in the blue. I really never thought about making my hobby public. I love the feeling but I kind of feel that I lost my hobby from the moment it went on sale . . . I will have to find myself a new way out for my almost inexistent time-out!

Have you thought of doing exhibits of your photos in galleries?

An exhibit has been done to great success—allow me to proudly say it!—in Cortona last summer. I hope a new one can be done soon.

Do you teach at all?

Not privately, as I have no time to assure a follow-up with the student, but I do many master classes. It is very rewarding to feel part of the development of the future generations of performers! I have done master classes in Indiana (Bloomington), Yekaterinburg, Nancy, Italy, Argentina, and UK, where I am actually the patron of the New Devon Opera, vice president of the English Youth Opera, and visiting professor of voice [at] the Royal Academy of Music. It's beautiful to see all these talents and I'm ready to fight whoever insists that there are no voices today as there were in the past. There are great voices out there, and we just need to find them and help them.

When you teach a master class, what is your approach?

I don't have an approach in the sense of a previously conceived plan. I take the temperature, so to speak, of the student(s) and I adapt myself to what I feel they need. Every person has different dilemmas and therefore needs different advice. I usually say, "Here I am; I am all yours! What do you want from me?" And an ominous silence follows until somebody breaks it, and off we go!

Is there something coming up for you in 2009 that you would like to mention?

My return to the Met with *Cavalleria rusticana* and *Pagliacci*. *Cavalleria* was my debut opera in New York, so now adding *Pagliacci* to the formula is a very nice and challenging perspective. In January, I will record my *Sonetos*, a song cycle after Neruda's poems, and hope to release them both in CD and in printed scores. In November 2008, I will add a new role to my repertoire: Boito's Nerone.

What role do you identify with the most? And is there a quote from the libretto of that role that you really feel close to you or like?

I do not identify with roles, but there is a quote I really like in *Otello*: when Iago is asked to sing the praises of Desdemona, he answers, "Me, singing? Oh, no, I am only a critic . . ."

Diana Damrau

Recorded August 2008 in Vienna, Austria. Published here for the first time.

**One of your earliest musical memories is from when you were
four years old, singing along to Grieg's *Peer Gynt*.**

Oh, you're really well informed!

**And your grandfather played music from *Der Freischütz* for
you and your brother . . .**

Yes. He would play the Wolfsschlucht [Wolf's Glen] scene when we
went to bed, so we could walk up the stairs to the bedroom to the music.

Was that your first contact with opera?

Yes. Günzburg—where I was born—doesn't have an opera house; it's
a small, small town. My parents are not really opera fans and musicians.
So they only went once a year to the opera house in another city for New
Year's. That was it. And I was longing: "Oh, I want to go to the theater,
I want to go!" They would say, "No, no, you have to grow up."

**You saw Franco Zeffirelli's film of *La traviata* when you were
twelve.**

Yes. Then I had to wait three more years to get to the sacred place of
opera and see a live performance.

What was the first opera you saw live?

The Magic Flute—a really terrible production! I hated it. But my love for
opera grew. I was fascinated. I wanted to learn how to sing and find out
if I can do this. I mean, it's not only the voice and technique, it's also the
personality; everything has to be together so you can do this quite difficult
profession.

**So when you saw the Zeffirelli film, what was it that really
struck you?**

It was the whole thing. And Stratas. The character of Violetta. I
remember when she walked through her house, and the furniture was
already covered, and they were already carrying out her stuff. You could

TANJA NIEMANN

see her face . . . and the music . . . ooh, I get goose bumps just talking about this. And then . . . the story, first of all, is world literature! Then the visual—like real life! And then the beautiful music, and the words, and the voices, and these wonderful artists! It really blew me away and I said, "This is the most beautiful thing on Earth!"

Wasn't it amazing that twenty-three years later, you sang with Plácido Domingo, and to top it off, you sang the brindisi from *La traviata* at the 2006 Soccer World Cup in München? Were you aware of how symbolic that moment was?

Oh, absolutely! This was really a special moment! It was the sixth of June and we had six degrees Celsius! It was so cold! We had to stand on this platform and the wind blew, and we saw, like, an ocean of people in front of us. I felt like being somewhere on a cloud in space. It was not Earth anymore. And then dancing and singing with Domingo! In the rehearsal I thought, "My God, hopefully I can sing because I was, like: aaaah!" We did Brindisi and then I had to sing "Glitter and Be Gay." I just thought, "Please, voice, don't freeze!" and concentrated on technique. Also [Zubin] Mehta accompanied for the first time this aria, which is quite tricky with the rhythm and also the rubati in the first part. He stood behind me diagonally thirty meters away, back to back, and I was facing this huge space and just saw some TV screens. We said, "We have to do it through telepathy."

Your first teacher was Carmen Hanganu—I saw the name and thought, "She must be Romanian!"

Yes. She sang in Bucharest and Kronstadt [Braşov] at the opera houses. She was a star in her time—a lyric-coloratura soprano. When she was very young, she sang Marguerite, for instance. But she also sang Konstanze and *La traviata*, and even Mimi and Butterfly. She showed me some TV recordings from Romania where she sang *The Merry Widow* walking down the stairs in a mist with a huge hat and great costume! She ran away from Romania and ended up in my hometown. It was a miracle. It was gift from God, really!

How did you start taking lessons?

My aunt was a choir singer in München. Through her and her husband, I had received this recording of "Morgenstimmung" at four; she is a very special person in my musical life. So I asked her, "When do you think I should start taking singing lessons? There's this opera singer in my town and I'd love to learn how to sing," because singing heavy metal did not work at all. My voice wanted to go somewhere else; it just didn't sound right!

You were trying to sing heavy metal?

Yeah, sure! "Smoke on the Water." Really strange!

Was that your favorite type of music?

Well, as a teenager . . . everything was! We had a jazz-dance group and we danced. So I approached the stage more from a dancing and acting point of view than from opera singing. The classical came later. We danced [to] Michael Jackson's "Thriller" at parties and I did choreography with my friends. I still can dance the beginning of *A Chorus Line*—step, push, step, step, touch, kick . . . again . . . step, push, step, step, strong arms!

What was a lesson with Carmen Hanganu like?

I studied the piano with her, too. I started voice lessons at fifteen. First we did a [voice] lesson every second week, just breathing and vocalises. We began with Mozart's "Veilchen" and Schubert's "Ständchen" ("Leise flehen, meine Lieder"). These were the first real classical songs I learned and also performed. We had a concert of our *Musikschule* where she taught, a special music school of the town of Günzburg. [Ms. Hanganu] declared, "We need more hours. You have wonderful talent here; she can be opera singer later!" And the town realized it and gave me an extra twenty minutes. That was a good start. After a while she told me, "Yeah, you can do this as a profession. But you have to study. You have to get diploma in *Musikhochschule*."

Ah, you do the Romanian accent so well!

I *love* it! She's such a wonderful woman! She gave me a great basis in all the styles. We did French songs and early French arias. We started with Mozart arias like Zerlina's, and she said, "You can act a little bit. I know you can act!"—using "Batti, batti" with different expressions. So she worked right away with my talent of acting and expressing. And she really encouraged me. She said, "You have to sing on every possible occasion. Okay, so you make mistakes. When you are onstage, you have to forget what you learn in the room and concentrate on expression. We know what goes wrong, but you have to do the show!" This was a very good foundation to start. And then I sang in church—lots of weddings! I loved singing in the church with organ—oh, it's beautiful!

What was the most challenging thing about your voice?

Actually . . . we built it up. So it was never about jumping to a level that was too extreme or too difficult. It was gradual. Like building a house: you can't start with the highest thing, you really have to go step by step. What I have found difficult—because I'm singing with emotion—was to sing Olympia when I learned it. This [requires] absolute control and you have to sing like a machine. Then my subconscious would say, "Okay, concentrate, put it here and there!" and I couldn't relax and just sing it. You can't move, you can't have much expression in the face. Forget it! At the end it went well but it was really a challenge. Actually . . . the first challenge onstage was Eliza Doolittle because as a high soprano, when you have to belt and sing in the first octave, you can really hurt [yourself].

So you know how to belt.

Well, I learned a little bit. I never trained it. I sang my natural belt and not higher. I didn't want to force. Because *My Fair Lady* is a classical musical, you only have to use some belting sounds in the first part, and then never again. So this was like, "Hello. Okay, I'll have a look how it works, and then . . . thank you! Whew! Rest!"

Did you do it in English?

No. German. They do it with a Berlin accent. I had so much fun in this role! Oh, my God! Well . . . and then the next challenge was to sing the Queen of the Night parallel with [Eliza].

Parallel? My God!

Yes, in the same season. But the bosses in the Würzburg theater [Mainfrankentheater] saw how fragile the whole thing is. They said, "Okay, can you do it?" I said, "Yeah, I will try. The Queen of the Night is actually where my voice is going, but we need to have these two roles really separate from each other. So one month I can sing five performances of *My Fair Lady*, then give me two weeks of rest and then put on some Queen of the Nights so they are not in touch with each other, so I can really concentrate and not stress out the body and the voice completely." They were very careful.

When you were making this switch in concentration from Eliza to the Queen, did you use any images, any principles?

Actually not. I went with the character, with the music, and I had to separate the two from each other also in my brain, because when you're thinking like Eliza Doolittle and you have to sing Queen of the Night, forget it! You really have to get into the music and the character and forget everything around it. It's just *Magic Flute* that night! And that day, and the days before. It's like in sports, in athletics, when you do the Zehnkampf [the decathlon], the ten different disciplines; you separate these from each other. Actually . . . for Eliza I learned how to belt and scream. There was so much dialogue, and you have to speak a stronger dialogue in the theater when there is music. You really have to pronounce and know where to put the speaking in order not to hurt yourself, so that you don't start screaming the wrong way, and then the voice is gone for the rest of . . . the career! Well, and then I found out that the dialogue of the Queen of the Night before the second aria is important. It's quite long and she gets really, really angry. So you can't speak like you sing, thinking, "I don't dare to speak because I have to sing these high F's." So I took the Eliza Doolittle technique for speaking and screaming and I jumped into the Queen of the Night's angry dialogue!

That is great! Who would ever think to find such a connection between Eliza Doolittle and Queen of the Night?

Yeah!

Is your coloratura ability natural or was it trained?

I think it was a natural ability. Also my voice was very high. Frau Hanganu could tell that my voice was going to be a coloratura soprano. I couldn't do all the high notes when I started. I mean, I couldn't even sing Adele. The training started from the middle part of the voice, which comes naturally. And then we expanded slowly. It's also a process of understanding, of images, of what the teacher is hearing and manages to teach you so that you get what she means. You have to work from the feeling and the hearing. There are some teachers who would say, "This young singer has a strong voice, no technique, well . . . but she can sing the high F, okay," and after half a year she sings Queen of the Night. And then two years later, the career and the future life as a singer are dead. It happens a lot. Teachers have to be very careful. They have a lot of responsibility with a young singer. This is a young human being that has to grow and to experience a lot that he or she can express. As a singer you have to gain confidence in you and your singing. You have to get to know your voice. Sometimes when you sing, you think: "Wow, this is great!" You have the sound around your head—it's huge—and then people tell you, "Well, that wasn't great! The voice didn't carry." Then sometimes you think, "Yeah, maybe it was okay," and the teacher says, "Yes, yes, yes, that's it!" And then you don't understand it. It's a long process of learning.

And every day you feel different.

Oh yeah, absolutely! Now I even feel it more than when I was studying!

You mean, you feel the subtle everyday differences more now?

Yes, yes. It's really, really hard work with yourself. With your psychology. You always have to be nice to yourself, to your voice. Sometimes I compare my voice to a horse. If I'm hitting a horse, the horse doesn't want to do what I want. I want to go over this obstacle; it doesn't help hitting the horse because it gets nervous and it will never jump. So you have to be confident and say, "Okay, I'm calm," and relax. It's all muscles and the voice reacts with the emotions you have. When you're scared, everything is tense. You can even hear it in the speaking voice: it gets hard, and then it's not possible. So you always have to convince yourself, "This is easy. This is a very interesting phrase; this is a nice phrase, it's a beautiful phrase!" while a part of you is thinking, "Oh shit, I'll never be able to do it!" You have to fight with yourself. Then at the end when you win and it works, it's great! It's a great success, but it's hard work!

After Carmen Hanganu, you studied with Hanna Ludwig.

Yes. I participated in a master class in Salzburg with Edith Mathis and she said, "You have to meet my teacher. She helped me a lot, and she was an icon in her day." So for me Hanna made the connection with the body and the voice. She taught me about phrasing. We talked a lot about building up a character and playing with the language, with the subtleties. She made me aware of lots of things I already felt inside. She also shared her experiences and her stories about opera and life in the opera world, and that was very, very interesting. It completed the whole picture. After I finished my studies, in 1995, I often went to her when I had to study new roles, so at that time it was never constant work; we did one-week sessions. I would stay one week in Salzburg and we'd work every day, because I had to sing in the opera house and I needed very concentrated [lessons]. I only had my limited time and I had to fill it with as much as possible.

Do you still see any of your teachers?

No. Well, I see them in private; I keep in touch.

Do you still study with anybody?

Well . . . I think it is good to have the ears of the people who know you. They come to the performance and say, "Hmmm . . . I have the impression that your voice has changed a little bit" or "Why are you doing this?" giving little tips to keep me on my path. But it's like with children: You guide them, and then you have to let them go. You can't stay with them forever. You can't sing for them; they have to learn it themselves.

You can't live their life for them, that's what I mean . . . it's the same with singing teachers and their students. Also, for your own strength, you need to actually depend on yourself because you're alone. You're always alone. You wake up alone in the morning with your voice and you say, "Hello, stranger! Oh. What happened to you?" And then you have to find out how to solve the problems by yourself. What if I would call my teacher in every little case of emergency: "Aaah, help me, what is this?" No. You have the help of your teacher now and then, you have what you have learned, you have your wisdom [that] is growing day by day, by experience. But you have to learn to help yourself. And then . . . okay, good, this is for the daily life. But now that I'm studying for Lucia, I'm going to talk to Edita Gruberova about the role. As you know, I have lots of recordings at home. I listen to how the others approach.

Some singers say they don't listen to any recording when they are studying a new role because they don't want to be influenced. You would rather listen to everything you can find. Tell me about that.

√ Listening can't hurt. Never! You can have great surprises. It's not that I'm copying anybody. You can't copy. Every singer is an individual. It's one instrument that exists only once ever. It won't help to sing along. It's just listening and seeing: okay, how is she building up the phrase, which cadenzas does she use, what are the tempi; sometimes, with Strauss, for example, how is the orchestration, where do I need to give more voice to help build up the whole evening for my energy?

Have you heard of the Romanian soprano Virginia Zeani?
Yes.

I think you will be able to sing all soprano Fachs [voice categories; _Fächer_ in German] throughout your life, like Zeani. What strikes me is that, like her, you follow a very healthy transition in progressing from one Fach to the other. She started with the same progression—very gradual, from coloratura to lyric coloratura, and moved toward the Verdi roles. Is this kind of step-by-step progression something that you got from your first teacher, Carmen Hanganu?

Yes. This, and also being aware that you only have one voice and you can't buy a second one. If it is destroyed, you can't get another instrument. I love singing, and I want to do this profession as long as possible. You never know where it's going to go, but I want to have a healthy voice.

That is the Romanian school of singing: teaching young

singers this kind of discipline to follow the right steps, the healthy path for the development of the voice and not rush.

Yes.

But then you see some students at twenty-two singing dramatic arias.

Well, you never know. When you look back . . . how old was Birgit Nilsson when she sang the heavy roles for the first time? There are natural voices. You can't make a big voice sing small and light from the beginning—this is also not natural. You have to work with each instrument like it is. But what comes out artistically . . . that's why the best years of opera singers are between thirty-five and fifty, because you're grown completely as a human being as well. Look, you have models who are thirteen years old and look like thirty-eight, like real experienced women. They have no clue what they're doing, sorry! They look like vamps and they are thirteen, fourteen! What is this? Okay, they will get there when they're older, then the whole thing is complete. But this is only the picture—you have only one side. We have the picture, the language, the singing ability—which is the picture in my comparison—all these components; it's much more complex. Experience, growth . . . you learn. I think it is a slow process.

You are going more toward bel canto now with Lucia at the Met.

Yeah, but this builds up from Adina, Norina, Rosina, Gilda.

Any plans to do Bellini?

Yes, *Sonnambula*, *Puritani*.

Norma?

No! I don't know . . . Not yet. Far away . . .

At the Met you sang both the Queen of the Night and Pamina in one performance run. That was the first time anybody's done that.

Yeah, okay, but it's not an aim.

How was it for you to hear your role—Queen of the Night—being sung to you?

It's strange . . . I think it's just the situation from another point of view. But I experience it as I stay in Pamina. I'm not the Queen of the Night at that moment; I am Pamina.

Any thoughts about doing crossover?

Nothing is planned in that direction.

Would you like to?

I sang songs a lot . . . like Cole Porter . . . during studies to gain experience how to sing and act in front of audiences. I did these musical evenings mixed with operetta. So I know quite a lot of this repertoire. In Hong Kong I did a recital with everything: gospel a cappella, "Somewhere over the Rainbow," then a song from *Yentl*, "I Feel Pretty," "Love Is a Many-Splendored Thing" but also Richard Strauss songs and Norina's aria at the end. That was nice.

I read somewhere that for your recitals you have secret themes.

Sometimes. It's just like on my Schubertiade CD, it's "Schumann and friends." Some people think, "Huh? Polish songs by Chopin? And then French songs?" I wanted to show variety and use more languages, but I could only sell this program to the organizer [as] "Schumann and friends," and they said, "Oh, yeah, cool! We'll do it!" And then they saw: "Polish? French? Help!" And I said, "Relax, relax! It's all one thing." The other recital—the CD of the Salzburg Festival—was songs of the late Romantics, but cycles. Sometimes I have my nature thing—"*Hommage à la nature.*" There are lots of possibilities. And sometimes I really step out of categories. Because the cosmos of lieder is a real cosmos.

You call them mini-operas.

Yes. Sometimes they are like little operas because these are stories and situations that are complete.

You have a lot of debuts coming up in 2009: Donna Anna, Lucia, Manon, *Schweigsame Frau*, and Marie in *La fille du régiment*. Wow!

Yeah, it's great!

Are you finished studying these parts?

I'm still working on them. Some of them I haven't started at all.

You work very much. You do a lot of song literature, too, and oratorio. Do you ever take any time off and stop singing completely?

Yes, because the body needs to rest. The concentration on my voice, sometimes I really have to forget it.

Are you a fast learner?

Yeah, thank goodness!

For your *Arie di bravura* CD, you went through fifty kilograms of handwritten scores from the Austrian National Library. How long did it take you to pick the material from that?

I had to work and to travel. I took some music with me and looked through it, then I needed to listen to the songs several times to make the right choice.

Did you play them for yourself?

No! This is impossible! It's hard to read. It's orchestra scores, with old musical keys—so it's like math. I had help from two great pianists. They are geniuses. They sit down and say, "Okay, well, it's a little bit tough but okay," and then they start playing and you think, "Where is the problem?" So they played it for me, and I made the first selection. At the end I had about twenty-five arias never performed in our time. Then the selection became smaller and smaller. It was about one year of work.

You discovered Salieri in Würzburg singing in the world premiere of his opera *Cublai, gran Khan dei Tartari*. What was it about his music that was an instant attraction for you?

Well . . . it is beautiful music! First of all, I was angry of the picture we have of Salieri, that he was possibly the murderer of Mozart and he was jealous . . . the bad story, the movie. I listened to this music and thought, "My God! No, he can't be that bad." Then I started reading about him, and he appeared more often in my schedule: "Oh, another Salieri, and another Salieri, well, great, I have to do something with that!" I wanted to show that Salieri's music, some of it—I mean, Mozart is the genius, you can't touch him—has wonderful qualities and it can survive next to Mozart.

I found that there were some, let's say, "twists" in the coloratura in Salieri's arias on your CD, that have a different "flavor" than Mozart's coloratura, though in many ways the coloratura is similar . . .

Yes, it's similar but [Salieri] has his own musical language. It's a challenge. The arias I chose are quite difficult. I especially chose the high ones because now my voice still has the abilities [to sing them] and maybe it's going to change in a few years so that I won't want to do the *sopracuti* the whole time, and I'll use more the lirico qualities.

For the aria "Numi, respiro" from Salieri's *L'Europa riconosciuta*, you do a high G.

Yes.

Wow! What's your vocal range?

What I've sung onstage is from the low G [below middle C] to a high A flat.

So spanning one half tone more than three octaves.

I also tried a high A, a high B, and they came. But then I said, 'Okay, come on, relax, we don't need this ever! So it makes no sense to push your voice and train this high. You can touch them when they're there.' But I also know singers who sang a D above high D! That is for really special literature and there's not much of it. And I think you can't hear it [for] that . . . long.

Going back to Salieri, do you think that if Mozart had not existed, Salieri would be part of the staple repertoire today?

Possibly. I'm not sure. The world goes as it goes, and everything influences everything else. It's really hard to say. They kept playing Mozart's music after his death. Only a few things get immortal. Nowadays with all the possibilities of recording, we manage to find all these treasures and keep them with us, like with documents. You can listen to an opera of Vivaldi nobody knows about. Only some will survive. But sometimes it's also the taste of the time, and the choice of one special publisher. There are so many factors you can't tell why something happens. Even personal taste. When some operas are played—which are really not good—but certain people love them—they are played. And other treasures are not found because nobody's looking for them. For instance, Righini . . . Who has heard of Righini before? And the two arias [from the *Arie di bravura* CD] are amazing! It's beautiful music. So there are treasures we don't know and we have to find! We still can.

Going back to education: Some singing teachers have no idea of the repertoire. They just stay with the common arias you can use later for auditions. Okay, this makes life easier. But sometimes these arias don't fit the voice or the abilities of that singer at that point. You have to search for the right aria, and there are lots of them that provide various difficulties, lots of possibilities, changes in tempo, recitativi. It doesn't always have to be Norina for an audition. You can also sing *Linda di Chamounix*, for instance. One has to get in touch with the possibilities in music, and be open. That's also why I searched for the Salieri arias because there's not only Mozart who has written this kind of arias. Salieri's arias are great for a coloratura soprano, even just for studying, or maybe singing them in a concert; why not? It's hard to get to the material, but anything's possible.

For me it's been rare to hear Mozart performed with such passion as you put into it. Usually when I've heard Mozart, the feeling is more restrained, but I really love the way you sing his arias, with a lot of feeling.

Yeah, it's also a risk. Maybe it's because singers don't want to take any risks because you can hear everything in Mozart's music, like if you lose the position the voice maybe, just for the sake of expression. For me, when I'm onstage, it is not only singing—it's the whole thing. And then I have to take risks sometimes. It's not clinical.

You're planning the four roles in *Hoffmann*.

Yes, in three years.

So you'll be spanning all these Fachs in one night.

Well, I'm not·going to sing the mezzo version at the end. There is a version for soprano. Gruberova did it, Sumi Jo, Sutherland, Sills.

I read that you like to ride horses and that you spent a weekend in the Sahara riding six hours a day and sleeping in a tent.

Yeah. Sometimes I really like to go back to nature. What an experience! No toilets, no showers; you just used the possibilities that were there. The silence there . . . but mobile phones work, so I switched mine off! Actually I was studying for *Die Ägyptische Helena*. I was in the area and I slept in a tent, so I was experiencing the whole setting for the role. Now next Saturday I'm singing at Bryn Terfel's festival in Wales, and I'll get the Scottish flavor for Lucia there! You have to be always open and aware of these things.

When you were in the desert, did you sing for pleasure, in all that space?

I started humming in the tent and [the others] said, "We can hear everything." And I thought, "Oh shit, okay, no, relax, Diana." Nobody in this group knew about opera. They sang their Berber songs in their Berber language, with drums, and I sang for them [the] *Traviata* Brindisi and *Carmen* with the wrong text because I don't know the text of *Carmen*. It was big fun.

You won the Mozart competition in Salzburg in 1999. What did you sing?

Queen of the Night, among other things.

Did you enjoy the competition experience?

Actually I wanted to cancel because I had a cold. I went to my teacher, Hanna Ludwig, and said, "Let's just work. I have to learn this and this." And then she said, "No, no, you're here; you will feel better; come on, try the first round." Well, I sang the first round and went on. Then I had to learn this modern piece of music—I was not prepared at all. So step by step, and finally I was in the finale. The great thing was that the opera director of Salzburger Festspiele was there and she heard the final round when I had to sing "Der Hölle Rache" with orchestra. She said, "I will organize an audition for Salzburger Festspiele," and that's how it started in Salzburg.

You had a big vocal crisis when you were really young. Tell me about that.

That was during my studies. I had an operation. They did complete anesthetics and they put this tube for breathing down my throat. It injured my vocal cords. Then I thought, "Okay, you're twenty-one years old, the body recovers very quickly." I went to thirteen different doctors over the years. One wanted to do an operation, and I said, "No, no, no, no operation. Nobody is going to touch my vocal cords again." I knew my body [would] recover but it really took long. That was a hard time.

And right at the beginning of your path as a singer. What amazing strength to come through something like that so young!

Yeah. I had faith. But then people around me lost their faith. In the end I said, "Okay, I will do it. Let's give this a chance. I will be okay again." And I found this doctor who discovered that my body was still intoxicated by the anesthetic—I'd had a problem waking up afterward. Nobody had been that interested in this part of the story, but I think that was it. So my body kept the poison. And then I cleaned my body through homeopathics and changing nutrition, and I got an acne I've never had in my life before or after. So everything was coming out. When a leg is hurting you, for instance, you move differently to compensate; it's the same with the voice. So the whole balance of the normal muscle tension was gone. I had to relearn breathing, relearn how to speak and how to use these muscles so that they'd work properly again. It was a lot of work. I learned a lot about the voice, about recovery and about what it is like if the voice is only tired or if it has a physical problem. You have to learn how to be a doctor to yourself.

About how long did it take for you to recover?

One and a half years. My teacher—Carmen Hanganu—gave lots of support but I couldn't sing; for three weeks, there was no speaking at all. And then I started too quickly, and it became bad again. So there were steps forward and backward.

Besides horseback riding, do you do any other sports?

Yes, dancing. Sometimes I take flamenco classes when I'm in New York or in Madrid. I dance with my dancer colleagues: a little bit modern dance. But not constantly and not very often. Or when I'm working out at home . . . I need nature and music for my sport. I'd love to learn tennis. I play a little bit.

Do you have to watch what you eat or you can eat whatever?

I eat whatever. Not too heavy, not later than two hours before a performance. But I also eat chocolate and drink coffee; no alcohol because it takes away the concentration.

So you don't drink alcohol at all?

Not before a performance. And not during a performance! Afterward, yes! I'm a little bit allergic to nuts, so I'm not eating any kind of nuts on the days I sing. But I like them.

I heard you can do Michael Jackson's Moonwalk . . .

I did it as Fiakermilli [from Strauss's *Arabella*] in Covent Garden.

Any hobbies?

I love taking photographs, and playing around with photos. I want to buy Photoshop now. I'm completely inspired. I had a photo shoot last week. Yesterday I was with the photographer. We chose the photos and did a little bit of Photoshop, and I thought, "This is amazing!" Once I took a photo out of a taxi in New York; it was at sunset so all the windows were bright and red and violet colors, and I just captured it with my camera, and it's fantastic! It was luck. I love this picture and I have it in my house.

One of your greatest inspirations as you were studying was Kathleen Battle.

Yes. I loved the sweet sound of her voice, and her artistry. And also, she sang the repertoire I was aiming for when I was a student. I listened to lots of her recordings.

Sometimes her Italian diction was not ideal.

Well, I was not aware of that. I had to learn myself, too!

What about any singers from the past?

There are lots. For every style. I love Edith Mathis for songs, for Bach; I love her Zdenka. The ideal Queen of the Night for me is Eda Moser; there is no other. My voice has a different sound and her sound was actually right for Queen of the Night. I can't say that I admire one singer only. Like [in] painting, you always have to use all the colors—and every color is beautiful.

Unfortunately Kathleen Battle earned a reputation for being difficult to work with.

Well, that's one thing I didn't want to copy!

I hear you are a pleasure to work with! Have you ever acted like a diva?

No. If I feel something is unjust, then I speak up. I need to understand what I have to do. It doesn't help being in your room stubborn like a child. You have to talk with people and then find a solution for the problem or ask, "Why do you do this?" It's all communication. The aim is the art, the evening, the story we are telling, and we all have to work together. I am not Diana Damrau onstage. I am Gretel, and I try to be Pamina and Queen of the Night and all of the characters. It's not self-indulgent.

Have you ever walked out of a rehearsal?

No. *Toi, toi, toi!*

What would you do if you did not sing?

Maybe I would organize guided tours on horseback or do something with nature. I'm interested in earthquakes and storms.

What would you hate doing as a profession?

I need movement in my life. I could never work in a sitting position the whole day at a desk. I need people, I need communication, I need different languages. So actually, yeah, I have the perfect profession for me.

Do you have any time for romance?

When time for romance comes, I have it!

Do you see yourself singing the Verdi roles like the Leonoras, Amelia, and Elisabetta?

I can't tell. Maybe.

What about Russian repertoire, like Tatyana, Lisa?

Beautiful! Tatyana, yeah, I love it. I love Onegin! I'd love to sing Onegin, as I'd love to sing Scarpia! The baritone roles, these are the best roles! I never want to be a tenor. I want to be a baritone! Renato, oh God!

What role do you identify yourself with?

I never thought of that. I don't know. Oh God, no, I really can't tell! I'm a Norina and I'm not, I'm a Fiordiligi and I'm not, I'm a Pamina and I'm not. I'm Diana. I can find colors of myself in every character but these characters have their own story and I have my own story. I can be funny but I can be serious, too!

What is a dream role? I mean, besides the baritone roles.

Well, then we have Grande Inquisitore.

I love that duet between King Philip and the Grand Inquisitor in *Don Carlo!*

I love it, too! This is the best part of the opera! Oh God! I mean . . . a dream role is Violetta—everything started with it! Another dream role with be Elisabeth in *Tannhäuser*, but that's a real dream!

You have a profile on Facebook. Do you know about that?

No. I don't use it. I have no idea. Funny!

I was going to ask you about using this popular social networking site. The Metropolitan Opera has a page, too. It's a way to be more accessible. And somebody did put your profile there!

Oh my God!

Are you interested in fashion?

I love beautiful dresses and shoes, and the whole thing! I need it for my concerts.

But in everyday life, what is your style?

Just normal. Casual. I'm not a brand person. Well, yeah, I look at what is "in," but I wouldn't buy it if it doesn't match my personality. There are people who'll wear everything with a brand name, whether it fits or not. I have to feel comfortable.

Do you have a philosophy of life?

Attacke! [Attack!] And you can use that in a soft way, in an encouraging way, you can use it in every way. Just forget about all your fears. If you don't dare to do something, you'll never succeed. Or if you don't succeed [at one thing]; it doesn't matter, you've learned something. Just go for it!

Any advice for students of singing? What would you tell someone who's at the beginning?

Patience. And get to know yourself and your body.

Natalie Dessay

Recorded October 2008 in Chicago, USA. Published here for the first time.

At first, you wanted to become a dancer.

My first choice was to become a dancer, and then at thirteen, I realized that first, I was not trained the right way, and second, I was not gifted enough. If you are gifted, it's already a nightmare, and if you're not, it's hell . . . trying to be a dancer. So I was very disappointed.

What made you think that you were not gifted?

It's very simple: I have no *en dehors* [turnout] or flexibility. Some people have that naturally and they work on it. But if you already don't have that from the beginning, it's hard.

Would you say it's the same with the voice?

Yes, it is.

So if an aspiring singer does not have the gift from the beginning, should he or she stop?

No, they shouldn't stop. But it's harder.

It was when you acted in a Molière play that you discovered you had a voice.

Yeah, because after the dancing dream was over, when I was eighteen, I started to study acting. I really wanted to become an actress. I still want to become an actress, by the way. But I was not the only one who had this dream, and I was not Sarah Bernhardt. So when I discovered that I had a voice, and that I was gifted for singing, I thought the shortest way to go onstage would be this, even if it was not my first choice but the third choice.

It chose you.

Yes, it chose me. Clearly.

Did you grow up in a musical family?

No.

Was there music in your house?

More or less. I studied piano, against my will, like many people, but that's it. We had some classical records. My mother, for example, had a record of Maria Callas, one of Montserrat Caballé. My father was very fond of Beethoven's symphonies. So it was kind of a musical environment, but not more than that.

You started voice lessons at twenty.

Yes. Quite late.

Would you think so?

Yes. For a high voice, and for a girl, it's quite late, but it's still possible. I'm living proof . . .

By that time, as you started the lessons, had you already decided this is the profession you want to follow?

No. Maybe after one or two years, I thought it may be possible to enter in a chorus, or something like that, but I never thought I would have a big career, or even an international career. I thought, "Oh, maybe, I'm going to do some operettas in France." That's it.

Was your coloratura ability natural?

Yes. I mean, the high notes were quite natural but the voice was very tiny, and I had no musical education. I knew nothing about opera, nothing about languages. I was speaking German, because that was my first foreign language in school, but I had no idea of how to pronounce Italian, for example. Actually, for ten years, I only sang in German and French, which is very unusual for an opera singer.

When you began studying voice, what was the most challenging part of the voice to master?

It was to try to make a beautiful sound. And to go up there without screaming, for example. I didn't want to go higher than a high C, because beyond that, it was horrible, and my first teacher told me, "Yes, but you have to give it to me and I will work on it." That was very difficult, and also to train the muscles, the cords, to make them flexible. Learning how to sing is really difficult.

And you had the natural ability anyway, so imagine for someone who doesn't.

I had the high notes, and the long extension, but that was all. I had to train for all the rest.

What were those first lessons like?

Training, very boring training on vocalises in order to stretch the voice. That was hard because the body does not want to go that way. It's very unnatural, this way of singing.

What were the basic principles you learned?

The goal is to be as round as possible from the low notes to the top, to try to leave your larynx as low as possible, because when you go up, the larynx goes up with you and that makes this strange, horrible noise. You have to train to leave your larynx as low as possible without pushing it down, so that you have all the space in your mouth and your throat to produce a round sound. But that's basically the same principle for everybody. My second teacher was a tenor—I had lessons with him for ten years—and he used a lot of images, like beginning of yawning in order to open the throat. Also, the way you take a breath is very important, because when you take a breath properly, by a sort of synergy, everything opens, your throat opens, and everything starts to be in the right position to produce the right sound.

Do you still think about any of these images and principles?

By now they are second nature. I don't think like that when I'm singing. I'm most focused on internal feelings and sensations. It's very difficult to speak about technique because when you don't do it, you can't understand it. It's like a painter speaking about painting; you can't put words in it, you have to do it.

But I think it could interesting for the fans to read your thoughts about technique.

They probably will think it's interesting, but actually it's not. It's not, because it's like sculpting: you have to put your hands in it to understand.

You have to "get dirty."

Get dirty! Otherwise you can speak forever, it doesn't mean anything.

You said that you wouldn't have the patience to teach.

Sometimes I give advice to young people. But I don't consider myself a teacher. If I can open a new way for them to think about it, it's already something, but I don't think I could teach them, for example, from the beginning until the end. I couldn't teach beginners because it's just too much work. But for people who already know how to sing and who need a little advice, why not? Again, it's such a personal way that I'm not sure I can help.

What would you say to someone who is beginning on this career path; something you wish someone would have told you when you started—advice, something to watch out for?

No, it's not in those terms that I would think. I would insist on languages, especially German, Italian, and French—more, if possible—but already it's very difficult only to learn these three languages. And I would insist mostly on acting, because I think young people don't realize that it's 70 percent of the job. Thirty percent is the voice and it is very important, but it's not the goal. For me the goal is not to sing—I mean, of course it is a goal, but it's only the first step. If you don't have this 30 percent, forget it!

You have to have this 30 percent completely, but that's only the beginning of the work. It's difficult for a young person to have confidence. It's already so hard to be able to sing correctly. It takes you maybe ten years at least. But then you have to search what makes you so special, and it's not a question of voice anymore. It's a question of personality. And nobody can teach you that. Nobody can tell you, "You're like that, and you have to express that." If you don't feel it for yourself, nobody will feel it for you. That's why I think in terms of acting, because acting makes you different. No actor is like another one. But it's also very difficult not to focus only on the voice, because the voice has to be as perfect as possible, and your technique has to be as perfect as possible, so that you can forget it, and start another work—what I call the real work—from there. That means that you have to invent something. But it's really something that you have to work out for yourself during the rehearsals. That's why I think to rehearse a long time is so important, because you find yourself through this period of time. If you arrive one week before, you can't find anything. You just do things, but you *are* not. You can't *be*. Because you don't have time.

And today that's pretty much the case.

Not always. For example, for this production we had four weeks. But even that was not enough.

How long of a rehearsal period would you be happy with?

Oh, six, seven, eight weeks. I mean, as long as you're with an interesting director. If not, three days are enough! But I don't want to work with people who have nothing to say.

You said the director is very important for you.

Yeah, because I have to enter in his universe.

Do you collaborate and share your ideas with the director?

Yes, of course. He gives me the way—the box. But in the box, I have my own world, my own personality, and I have my own ideas, my own suggestions, and everything I experienced in my life; it's really like acting.

What if you disagree with the box? Or if you don't like it?

It doesn't work like that. That is the point: He gives me the box; that's his job. I go into this box, and no other box. I don't have to choose the box; that's not my job! And that's what is interesting. For example, when I start with a role, I have no idea about it. I don't know who [Violetta] is, for example; I have no idea. I don't know even who is Manon. And I don't care. I don't care if I don't understand her, because that's not the point. The director knows better than me—in principle—he knows what he wants. In the frame he gives me, I can find my own freedom.

If the future of opera—the direction in which the art form is evolving—was in your hands right now, and you had to come up with a plan for it, what would you do?

I would insist on long rehearsals! But also, you can't force people to think like me. I think acting is more important than everything else. When people don't want to act or don't do the job properly according to me, what can I do? Acting is not doing the same thing, every time in every role, even if you did well. It's really diving into different characters. That means that you don't walk the same way, you don't move the same way, you don't look the same way—it's really a huge and hard work to transform yourself at that point. Some people don't realize that, and don't want to realize that's what matters. The audience also is responsible. The audience goes to the opera to hear this one or that one. I don't want that!

Going to the opera for the big names, you mean.

Yeah. I just want them to go to the opera to see a whole work, the work of a team, and a whole story.

Well, sometimes the name is a guarantee that the audience will get an amazing performance and rewarding artistic experience, don't you think?

No. For me, it's not. Because the voice can be interesting, but then the rest . . . What is the rest?

What I mean is that—for example, you—when the public sees your name listed in a production, they know they will be offered the whole experience: singing and acting, because it's you!

Yeah, but if the production is not a good one; it's not worth it. It's just not worth it! So I'm not a guarantee—only me. And even if it's already good on paper, sometimes it doesn't work in reality. But the thing is, if already on the paper it's not good, for sure, it won't work in reality.

Do you think you'd be a good director?

No. Because it's another job, another background, another preparation. As I used to say, I already have many difficulties to organize my own life, so how would I organize the lives of other people onstage? Because it's a question of organization. Being a director, it's just organizing the relationships between the people onstage, and it's a huge job. I don't think I'm prepared for that. For me that's probably the most interesting work in the world, because you're God. You're like God. You decide everything happening onstage. You need a lot of culture, a lot of reading, a lot of ideas also. I don't feel confident doing that. What I could do is help with acting direction, but I think a good director is anyway an acting director so he wouldn't need me.

In 1992 you worked with Roman Polanski for Olympia in
The Tales of Hoffmann. **How was that experience?**

Very strange, because although I liked very much working with him—he's a very nice, intelligent, refined man—I don't think opera was his world. So he was feeling very uncomfortable with that, and was consulting all the time with his set designer. It wasn't his universe. But for what we achieved together, it was great, I think, and I really liked it.

You're a master of physical expression onstage. Your physicality is incredible. When you study a role, do you consciously bring it into your body, or does that just come?

It comes with the rehearsals and that's why I need so much time to rehearse because it takes a long time. It already takes a long time for me to learn a role because I'm very slow and I have no memory, and it's really hard work. But then, as long as you have it in your mind, you're not even at the half of the work. The work is beginning really at that point and you already have six months of work behind you. But that means that the four or five weeks that you have to embody the role are very important because you never know how it's going to be before working with a director. It depends on him, on what he wants, on how he sees it.

But you feel it in your body. It makes the role complete.

Yeah, and for me that's as important as being able to sing it. In this production, for example, I worked a lot on trying to do nothing. Most of the time, a singer can think that because of the hugeness of the hall, they have to do more than what is necessary, to overact in a way. And actually I tried to reduce as much as possible. In this case, not in *La fille du régiment,* for example, because it's another kind of acting. That was more burlesque and more physical as if choreographed. Comedy is more rhythmic. Drama, real drama, here in this production was like being in a movie. So the challenge was to be able to do nothing but at the same time to feel so deeply the situations and the feelings that, it goes through and touches people way far. Because we are not at the movies! But I still think that if you dive in your character deeply enough, even if you don't move at all, people will feel it.

Sometimes stillness can be even more powerful, more captivating than movement.

Yes, that's what I think. But for me it's very difficult because I'm that kind of actor who shows a lot and who is really physical and who loves to move all the time. So for me, reducing more and more is a real challenge.

Do you have a role that you identify with?

No, I don't identify with any. But I like Manon very much because it's a real travel. I like travels, big travels. I think I will like *Traviata* also because of that. I like Lucia also because she goes very far in despair.

You're referring to psychological travel.

Yes.

What are you studying at this time?

I'm studying *Pelléas et Mélisande* and I'm totally in love with this opera. I will sing it for the first time in Vienna this January.

Do you still do Oriental dancing?

No. I did it after the birth of my daughter to recover. But I am not in Paris, I am not anywhere in the world for more than two months, so it's very difficult to have a regular activity.

How do you stay in this great shape?

Diet, and that's it. But I will do something. I really want to do yoga, and a bit of running, because I think I need that now.

Do you still work with someone vocally?

Yes, I have a teacher whom I see from time to time. It's like a control, a checkup, but we also work on technique all the time. Because the voice is changing all the time, so you have to readjust. It's like repairing a car. Your car is getting older and older so you have to fix things from time to time.

You are an intellectual . . .

Yeah, that's what they say, but actually I'm not. But I would like that. I have a huge complex of not being an intellectual.

Oh, come on! Really?

It's because I didn't study anything. I was one year at the university in German and I quite liked it, but then I decided to go to the theater, and I stopped. And it's one of my biggest regrets in life: not having done proper studies.

It's the way you approach the roles; the depth you bring to them that makes people think that . . .

But that's great. I'm very honored.

You achieve that great balance between the intellect and the instinct. Some singers get stuck in the intellect.

That's the danger. I used to say that to be a singer you certainly don't need to be too intelligent. It's an obstacle. I still think I think too much but I can't help myself. That's my dilemma. It's hard to live with it.

Do you take vacations from singing?

Sure, I had almost two months' vacation this summer, for example. That was too much, actually. I don't sing that much. I don't sing more than forty-five performances a year, which is nothing compared to other people.

Any hobbies?

When? In another life, maybe. I read a lot.

You had two surgeries on your vocal cords several years ago. How was the recovery process?

It was horrible. Just horrible! Because it took me a long time each time, practically eight months every time, but in mind, it took me three years. Because the problem is that you lose your confidence. Technically you could sing after one week, but psychologically, it takes forever to recover. I'm just starting to be okay. The last surgery was in 2004, so it took me four years.

I imagine the recovery period gave you time to think. What did you reflect on?

I had time to reorganize my life. And to think differently about this job.

In what way?

For example, I used to go onstage like you go to war, as a warrior. I probably needed that, but that was too hard. And I don't want to fight against myself anymore, so I try to enjoy it much more now. I like to go onstage like you would on a playground, when you were five years old. Then it was just the joy of it, and the feeling of freedom, and of expressing yourself.

You were born as Nathalie, but you dropped the h in your name because of Natalie Wood.

Yes, a long time ago. I was a teenager. I loved her because she was very beautiful and because of her fragility as an actress. It's something that I love about actors—precisely this fragility. It's one of the things I prefer in the whole world: the fragility of the actors onstage.

You said Maria Callas was an inspiration for you.

Yes, and she still is. She was a combination of everything: technician, musician, and actress. She's remarkable for losing weight to be more believable. And for her musicality—she is really incredible. When I heard her, for example, in a recording of *La bohème*, I heard things that I never heard before. And I was, like, "What is she doing?" And I ran to the score, and everything was in the score, every detail. That was really, really unbelievable: this thirst for details, more and more and more details. I think art is all about details.

You focus on details . . .

Yes. I'm very happy about this run, for example, because it's the third time that I'm doing Manon, and I discover so many new things, again and again and again. I think every time you do such a role, you can discover a thousand things that you didn't see the first time.

You're married to another singer . . . [Laurent Naouri]

Another intellectual.

How many years have you been married?

We married in 1994, but we know each other since 1989.

It must be challenging with both of your schedules to also raise a family. What's your secret in managing something like that?

The first secret is that we share the same passion and I think that's very, very important. The second is that we complement each other. He's very organized, I'm not. He can see in advance, I can't. He's a great father; I'm not a great mother.

What?

In terms of what should be a conventional mother. I think I'm a good mother, but I'm not conventional.

But why should you be?

Because kids need convention and routine. They love to have their mother right there all the time, with them, at their disposal, and they like their routine. They like to have an organized life because it's a frame for them; it's reassuring. If they don't have that, they are very anxious.

How old are they?

Ten and thirteen. But I think my husband gives that to them. And I give them the fun. They call me the crazy one, anyway: "Oh, but, Mommy, you're crazy! Thank God that we have Daddy, to count on him."

Are they musical?

Against their will. My daughter is very talented in drawing and painting. She wanted to be a painter since she was five years old. So she will probably do something like that; she's really, really gifted. My son is really gifted in saxophone; he has a beautiful sound, a great swing. We are fond of jazz, my husband and I. My husband, much more, because he always wanted to become a jazz singer. He knows everything. He has a repertoire of three hundred songs: Brazilian, English, French.

You're fascinated by roles like Lucia—women who are in between the two worlds of sanity and madness—and who fall.

Victims. But most of the time, women in opera are victims, so I don't have a choice.

You said once that these women are so opposite from you in real life. What do you think gives you your sanity? Obviously you are very sensitive and perceptive, but what keeps you anchored?

You know, I was thinking the other day that I would probably be very sick if I wouldn't do this [profession]. If I wouldn't have the occasion of being someone else from time to time, I would be very miserable.

How does it feel when you look at a DVD of yourself in performance?

It's horrible. I'm not interested.

You don't watch them?

No, because I see only what I don't like.

Do you recognize yourself in these DVDs?

No. And that's a good point, because sometimes I'm pleasantly surprised; most of the time I'm badly surprised. Also I don't like all this business around HD. It's so unforgiving. I don't understand why they do that. It's not beautiful; we look horrible. I don't see the point.

Do you use the Internet a lot?

No. E-mail, yes. It's so convenient to communicate.

Can you give me five adjectives to describe Natalie, the woman?

Hard-working, paradoxical, pessimistic, energetic, burning.

What about recitals?

I don't do them. It's too difficult; it takes too much time, and I'm not confident enough to do that. It's a big regret also, because of course it's a great way of expressing yourself, but again, I like to hide behind a character. I don't like to present myself as myself.

You mentioned that Martin Luther King had an influence on your thinking.

Oh, yeah. I mean, he has an influence on my life, because for me he is an example of integrity, which is probably the most important thing for me: Not to lose your integrity. Try not to lose your integrity in any situation. And he never lost his, till his death. For me that's the most impressive.

You dedicated a CD of Bach cantatas to his memory.

Yes, in honor of the fortieth anniversary of his death, last April.

What is the connection you see between Bach and Martin Luther King?

Same religion. And Bach is my favorite composer, so I thought it was beautiful to unite my favorite man with my favorite composer, and it happens that they had the same religion.

What's your biggest sensual pleasure?

It's very difficult to choose one. But I like to be on a boat, for example. On the sea. I remember once in Santa Fe we went in an air balloon, and for me that was a dream. I remember exactly the moment we just took off, and it was marvelous. I like to be in the air, on roofs. I could be a window washer.

What about your biggest intellectual pleasure?

Reading.

Greatest fear?

That something bad happens to my children.

Greatest pride?

To have managed till now to have a private life and an artistic life at the same time.

What profession would you never want to do?

Everything but what I am doing! Probably, prostitute.

Meryl Streep is your favorite actress . . .

She's my favorite living actress. She can do everything: drama, comedy, and also she's very original. I mean, no actor is like another, but she's very special.

What about an actor from the past that you really admire?

We have an actress in France called Delphine Seyrig; what I loved about her was her voice. I would kill to get this speaking voice.

Why are you so attracted to Santa Fe?

Because of the immensity of the landscape; such a landscape opens your mind and your soul. I never thought I could love the desert like that. But it has to do also with the spirit of the area; it's probably the Indian spirit, and the strength of the nature. I can understand that many painters—like Georgia O'Keefe—like to move there. Everything is different: the light, the earth, the rain, the air. Also the altitude must bring you something different, because you can't really breathe, so it acts on your mind, too.

You're doing your first Violetta there in the summer of 2009. Is that a dream role for you?

Yes. I think for a soprano it's the role of the roles. Also, for me it's like a tribute to Maria Callas, even more than Lucia, because Violetta was really her role. She achieved something really special with Luchino Visconti.

Is there one thing you could tell me that your fans would be surprised to know about you?

It's not very positive, but probably they would never know how insecure I feel all the time. That's it.

Plácido Domingo

Recorded May 2004 in New York City, USA. Published in Classical Singer, *September 2004.*

You are a phenomenon in the opera world, one man embodying three different careers: the singer, the conductor, and the administrator. You began your remarkable journey as the singer. At what point did the conductor emerge?

Since I was a child, I had a great love for the theater. My parents had their own zarzuela [Spanish operetta] company. The conductor in me was born very early, out of those times in my parents' company. We didn't have a very big orchestra. I would play the piano, and gradually, I got the feel for all the instruments. I was also preparing the chorus and started to conduct some of the zarzuelas.

Then, during my years at the conservatory in Mexico, studying piano, harmony, and all the required classes, I started to love conducting more and more. I was able to take some classes with Igor Markevitch, the great Russian conductor. I was only auditing because it was quite expensive, and the classes were only for conducting students, while I was studying piano. But I sat in, listening and learning along with a very dear friend: Eduardo Mata, who died a few years ago in a plane accident. He was the conductor of the Dallas Symphony, a great musician. He was studying conducting. We were very good friends and we even composed together.

I was enchanted by those lessons with Markevitch. I still remember what he was working on, and in my first concert in 1987, I actually conducted those same pieces. I particularly remember Tchaikovsky's Fourth Symphony; it was ingrained in me in those early days at the conservatory.

Throughout the years, my conducting has grown with experience. I conducted my first operas in the seventies at the New York City Opera: *La traviata*, and *Tosca*. In the beginning, I didn't have many occasions to conduct; it was about two performances in a year. Now, on a good average, I do about three or four productions a year. That's about thirty to thirty-five performances. I would like to do more, but I cannot, until I will stop singing.

Recently, I've done three operas for the first time: *Don Giovanni* in Washington [DC], *[La] Damnation de Faust* in Los Angeles, and *Manon Lescaut* in Washington [DC]. It's a pleasure to see that everyday I am getting better, and I feel the tremendous difference when I have an orchestra in my hands for a longer time.

Would you say that singers have a friend in you when you are in the orchestra pit?

I think so. I automatically understood the needs of the singers, but it was just as important for me to learn the needs of the orchestra. Now it's just a question of balancing the two.

SHEILA ROCK

In 1992, you were music director of the Seville world's fair. Is that where your third career—in arts administration—was born?

In a way, you could say I gained more experience there. I had been kind of involved with Los Angeles since 1986, when the L.A. Opera got started. I was singing and conducting there, but I was also adviser to Peter Hemmings, the general manager. I had been on the board when Peter Hemmings was selected. I advised him on repertoire and singers.

Then, in 1996, I started as artistic director in Washington. Now, I'm about to finish my eighth season there, and in L.A., I'm concluding my fourth season. I'm thrilled that this third career has developed this way. It's a lot of work, but it makes me happy.

How do you handle it all?

I have so much passion for what I am doing, that it hardly feels like work. If you have passion, if you love something, you can easily dedicate all your time and energy to it, and you have no doubt that it's exactly what you should do.

As a general director of both companies, I know now that you are not really a general director, if you are sitting at your desk all day. It's so important to stay on top of what is happening, to travel, to find out what other companies have to offer, to maintain all the connections to the other opera houses. I need to see for myself what is the best artistically in the world today.

Yes, my main specialty is artistic, but I also had to learn to handle the issue of raising money. I have to say, I am very lucky to have great teams in both theaters. The staff is really dedicated and we work closely together. Fortunately, we also think in the same way and agree on our ideas.

Do you have any guiding principles as artistic director?

Yes. [The] first one is to maintain harmony in the company. It's important that the staff believe in you and work in collaboration with you. Psychologically, that is the key. Second is to be able to listen and establish a good communication with the heads of all departments. It's easier to solve the problems together, if the communication is good. Third, and this is perhaps crucial, is to maintain a balance of repertoire, of the artists, combining big names and not-so-famous names with young unknown singers.

I have been very fortunate in that respect to have my competition, Operalia, as a source of new talent. It has created so many careers, because I've been able to hire many of those young artists in both theaters. The public likes to have the opportunity to discover these young artists at the start of their careers.

Perhaps a more difficult aspect is thinking about productions—what should be a new production or a coproduction. Because of the economy today, it's wiser if you try to spend the least money possible. You have certain productions [that] come out artistically very beautifully—but you have to be careful that you don't go out of the budget. It's tough. Sometimes, it's almost impossible, because you might have an artist and a creative team in the middle of rehearsals, and all of a sudden, they might need more things, so what do you do? You cannot drop a production in the middle; you cannot betray the high quality you want to present to the public.

Then, of course, you have to be on very good terms with the board of directors and to understand their worries. You have to be aware of the fact that they have many important things to do, but they dedicate a lot of their time to the opera world. Some of them spend as much time on the opera company as they do on their own businesses! So, as a director, you need to present the board with things that really make sense to them [as to] what you are going to bring as a new production and why.

And last, but not least, comes the issue of raising the money that the company needs. So, there are very different aspects to an artistic director's job. Every aspect offers its share of enjoyment and problems. Between the two companies now, I am practically responsible for eighteen operas, that means between 175 and 180 performances a year, and growing.

So, you just learned the ropes of being an artistic director by doing it. Did you have any training?

No. I was just interested in all aspects of my profession. Every day, I learned more about marketing, about everything. You know, it's unbelievable: opera is a world where people give you money and they trust you, but they are giving money for something that is not a sure investment. Okay, it's a cultural investment—one of the most important ones—because you are giving to your city a valuable cultural gift. But if you ask people to invest their money in a film or a Broadway musical, they are more willing to give, because they have a bigger possibility to make money, since those two artistic venues are so popular. But in opera, those who donate money have my deepest respect. They give it because they love opera and not to make money.

Speaking of Broadway, making money depends on how big the appeal is to the audience. Many opera companies have instituted various campaigns for expanding audiences. What are your plans?

Well, we have actually started our campaign from the inside of the company, by preparing a new generation of successful people in their midthirties as future board members. They are something like our junior board members. We are familiarizing them with the needs and workings of the companies, so that they make it their responsibility as the next generation [of] board members to really take care of those needs. I think that by doing that, we don't allow any gap to form between the generations; we maintain a continuity of people willing to devote their time to an opera company. To me, that is an important step in ensuring that the future of opera is in good hands.

As for expanding the audience, that is not something that can happen instantly. Obviously, like other companies, we do special performances for students and children, in both theaters. In Washington, we also have something called "Look-In," a one-hour program presenting the highlights of an opera to children and their educators. It's not just about the music; the children see everything, because the stage hands show them how to move scenery or how to create special effects, like in the storm scenes from *The Barber of Seville* and *Rigoletto*. The children learn how that is done through lighting and sounds of percussion or other instruments. It's a great learning experience for them . . .

The answer to this audience expansion problem—and I never tire to say this—is that it's a matter of education. If musical education would be mandatory in schools, if children would learn about opera from an early age, many of them will be open to it and want to know more. They will grow up appreciating opera.

How can you develop a love of opera if all you hear around you with your school friends is pop music, or rap, or hard rock? Many parents are probably playing pop or rock at home. Children go to school with their Walkman or Discman playing pop and rap all the time. They download this music off the Internet. In short, all the possibilities they have to develop their love for music involve only these types of music. If they have a school concert, you rarely hear anybody singing opera. Even if some children would want that, they are afraid others would make fun of them for liking classical music.

I'm working very much on getting the idea through to teach children in schools the best melodies of opera or of the symphonic repertoire. They could learn them easily without thinking that it's classical music, and without being intimidated. Then they would just know these melodies. You know, everyone learns the *Barney* song from an early age: "I love you, you love me . . . " so then why can't they learn some of the most beautiful melodies of great musical geniuses, like Mozart, or Brahms, or Puccini, or Verdi, or Wagner? Some of these melodies are really simple, too. If children are able to hum the *Barney* song, how hard can it be to hum the melody of "La donna è mobile"?

It's so sad, and you can't really blame the parents for not taking their children to the opera, if they grew up with rock and roll, themselves. It's just a matter of education. It's a matter of breaking this chain and beginning to develop familiarity with opera in the next generations as early as possible. I think the day when that will be accomplished will be the day when the opera world doesn't have to worry about its future.

Globalization and high-speed access to people and information have made the world smaller and more manageable. At the same time, people's perception of time has changed: things are expected to happen instantly. Sometimes that trend reflects in the opera world. The audience demands new stars. Spectacular careers begin overnight, only to flop because of starting too fast,

too soon. How do you think that today's fast pace affects the arts, especially such a time-hungry art like opera singing?

That's a tough matter. The speed today is precisely what makes the world better, and what can also create problems. But, you know, some singers of my age and older always thought, "We know better!" That's not true. Every generation is different. You just have to grow with the generations and the changes they bring.

I grow with my sons, to be contemporary to them. I mean, I try to understand everything they are dealing with. Now I am trying also to be contemporary to my grandchildren and understand their generation. Nevertheless, things change and you have to be smart to adapt without hurting yourself.

In the past, you used to have a bad performance in a theater, and maybe people knew it in that city. Today, everything is known. If it's not live, then it's known five or ten hours later; it spreads all around through the Internet. So, this news amplifies the effect it has on your career.

Yes, everybody has a faster life and we have to get used to it. However, I agree with you: everything needs its own time to mature. So, for singers, it would be good if they could avoid going along with this speed. They should not be in a hurry. Of course, they should make the best out of the Internet to spread information about themselves, and find out information, but their mentality should remain on a slower speed until the voice is ready. There are many more theaters, so the possibilities are bigger, and there are a lot of temptations. But you almost have to become two people: a modern person in your use of the Internet and business aspects, and a more old-fashioned person in your vocal development as an opera singer.

Obviously, everyone knows this is a very difficult career, because you go and you study, they give you your diploma—but is that a guarantee that you are going to make it? No. In all the other careers, if you study, and get a diploma, the percentage of getting a job is very big. But for singers, it is a mystery. It has to do with personality, the life and personal conditions they have. All the aspects have to come together—the musicality, circumstances, fate, everything!

So, you can have your house full of diplomas but it doesn't mean that you are going to have a career. It's a certain group that makes it, and that's just a fact of nature. It's as if we were athletes, and we think we can all run the hundred meters in the Olympics. It's a very select group of people that really get there. So, it can be disappointing, if those are your expectations. But that's the reason why you have to be very truthful. When I hear singers, I'm always truthful.

What do you look for in a singer during auditions?

I'm not looking for anything. I just want to be surprised. It just comes like a snap of the fingers. You hear a voice, and all of a sudden, you say, "Wow! I didn't expect this!" For instance, tomorrow we are having the auditions for the new group of young singers in Washington. There might be great surprises there. The important thing is to select a group of people that you will be responsible for. Their responsibility is to really dedicate their time.

Singers don't have it easy in the U.S. Many are working hard jobs as waiters; some have other extra jobs on the side. Maybe they have to take a train and travel two and a half hours for a voice lesson. So, we make it a special point to pamper these young artists in our program. They will have all the possibilities to study, to sing, to cover parts in the opera, and not to worry financially. They have the chance to attend every rehearsal and take part in everything that is going on. We are prepared to take care of them, so of course we have to be very demanding in our selection.

What makes a bad impression on you in an audition?

I usually don't like to judge by the very first visual impression, because otherwise you would be already discriminating. Instrumentalists audition behind a curtain so they don't have to worry about looks or visual presentation. I don't like to be influenced by that.

Of course, you find all kinds of people in these auditions: people who are very concentrated, people who already seem vain, shy people . . . You just have to hear the basics, which is the voice. Then you listen for the technique, the musicality, and after that, you start to see the whole person.

There are those unique moments when you see a person walk onstage and from the second they open their mouth, you say, "This is going to be a star." You know it. Sometimes, the opposite is true: you realize from the start that the person has no potential. Then there are other voices which you doubt, and you say, "This one would work, if the singer has enough perseverance." You have to take into account everything. But, I have to say that in the United States, singers are very well prepared. Good voices may come from all around in the world, but I think the level of preparation is highest here.

As director of the Washington Young Artist Program, do you work with singers one-on-one?

Yes. And when you are working with a singer, you really have to work. It's not enough just to say, "Okay, sing, and I hear you." If you go for a lesson, either privately or with a whole group, you cannot leave things on a superficial level. Sometimes, I will work on one phrase for a long time: on technique, interpretation, language, everything. If I let somebody sing the whole aria without saying anything, then why am I working with them? I prefer that at least, at the end of that session, they really have learned something, even if it is just five lines, but then I feel I have made an impact.

I like to work one-on-one when I don't know the voices well yet and I want to see their reactions, their feelings. Some people are more sensitive than others; it is important to find the right way to say things to them, so that they remain open to learn. When I know the voices, then I work with all of them together.

Other than that, do you teach?

No.

Do you think you will?

No. I will always advise. But, you know, if you are actively singing, you cannot perform every three or four days and give lessons. It takes a lot of your energy and vocal strength. Of course, for me, discovering new talent is one of the greatest satisfactions, especially when that person is able to grow after you have helped them.

Does experience count in selecting singers for the Washington Young Artist Program?

My idea is that we should have two different kinds of young artists in the program: those who are almost ready for a career, and those who are just beginning but have superb material. So, logically, the ones who are almost ready are going to stay a shorter time than the others. Basically, we are talking about two years. But you already know from the start that some of them are going to be there for three years. Others might be ready after one year.

What about a possible Los Angeles Young Artist Program?

We are discussing it now. We are very close to establishing one, but I cannot yet say when.

Tell me about your competition, Operalia. How did it start?

A group of friends said they would like to organize a competition with my name. So, we started in Paris and decided that instead of being in the same place every year, we would go to different places in the world. It's been like that for eleven years now. The next one, in August 2004, will take place in Los Angeles.

We try to select the city based on the interest they have, and also on my possibilities for being there. The competition is a great opportunity for singers to be noticed, and for me it is a resource of talent and a possibility to help talented singers.

You know there is much discussion about the higher tuning of orchestras, and its effect on singers. Can you, as artistic director, prevent the tuning of the orchestra in your company from going too high?

Well, if a singer's health depends on it, we can try, but there really is not much we can do. Of course, we have it harder today. Compared to the times when the orchestras were tuned at 432 [Hertz or cycles per second] or even 426, to go about the usual 440 today, it's a big contrast. I don't think that is right. It has to do with the way the instruments are built today. You know, there are many specialists who do a lot of operas—especially Mozart—with the original instruments, and the sounds are obviously different. I heard a performance of *Idomeneo* in Glyndebourne, conducted by Simon Rattle, and the quality of the sound was so different! I love it! It's so warm; it's beautiful!

I don't know what the solution is. I think the tuning is sometimes going to an extreme, especially in places like Vienna, or Berlin; it's quite a difference between where you start a performance and where you finish, and they already start quite high. Conductors look for a brilliant sound and new instruments are built, but human beings are not built differently or tuned higher! We have remained the same, with only these two vocal cords, throughout history!

As you know, the recording industry is in pretty bad shape; record label executives fear the classical department is heading toward extinction. How important was recording for your career? What would this extinction mean to the world of opera in general?

It was very important for me. I was very lucky. I really feel for some of the coming generations of singers, that they cannot record as much as I did. It's really a big danger, and I'm surprised that the recording companies didn't see the danger coming as soon as the Internet started. Everybody has access to it; so all my music is on the Internet—and everybody can hear it without any profit for the companies or any profit for me. That's true for all singers. It is a big tragedy.

I really hope that the circle will close at some point, and there will be a new era for the best young singers coming out; that they will be able to be

known through their recordings, as well. Perhaps the new generations will have to learn how to manipulate the Internet to their own advantage. But I don't see how you could stop piracy. Maybe piracy is the price you pay for being more popular and accessible through the Internet.

Where do you see yourself in the next five years?

I could still see myself singing, but that might be about the limit, at least for opera. I will devote myself more than ever to conducting, and to my work as director of an opera house, or two, like now. I don't know how things will develop, but I would really love to continue doing what I am doing.

As an idol and mentor to so many, what do you tell singers who come to you for advice?

The only thing is to try to be humble. This is a privilege for us. We do what we do in order to make people happy. We do it so that when people come to the theater, they can forget about their problems, and concentrate on this magic moment, which is singing live on the stage. Singers should remember that not only is this a privilege, but also we have great geniuses to serve: the composers. So, try to give very much every time you sing!

Of course, this is a career and a business like any other; some people rise higher and have better careers, others don't. But your happiness depends on your perspective. If singing is making you unhappy because you are not at the top, and you cannot be satisfied with a smaller career or simply with just singing, then you have to think of doing something else.

There is a place for everyone in the opera world, and if you truly love opera, you can do something for it, even if you are not onstage. You can be just as important behind the scenes. In fact, all the people that work in opera houses—the staff—have my great admiration because, in most cases, they are not making great salaries, but their love for opera is tremendous. On many occasions, they don't work from nine to five. They work late into the evening with total dedication.

In any case, whatever profession you decide to do, I think it is simply a matter of truth and passion. First of all, be truthful with yourself about your qualities and your limits. And second, follow your passion, because no matter how difficult it is, your passion will help you, and it will not even seem like work. I have been following my passion all my life. If I were born once more, I would do it again, from the very beginning.

Simon Estes

Recorded June 2004 via telephone. Published in Classical Singer, *February 2005.*

How important was music for you when you were growing up?

Music was an integral part of our family as well as our religious life. We were very poor, economically speaking, but very rich in spirituality and family values. My mother used to play the piano. I had three older sisters, and we would sing around the piano in the evenings. We would also sing in church. Music helped us in many areas of our lives. That is one of the main characteristics of Negro spiritual music: it gives you the chance to express emotion, whether it be joy, or sorrow, or hope.

Your grandfather was a slave who was sold for five hundred dollars at an auction. What did this story instill in you?

What it instilled in me came from my father. I never met my grandfather. I heard that story from my father, who couldn't read or write. He was born in 1891, and was taken out of school at about the third grade level. The African-American schools way back then were very inferior, I regret to say. Nonetheless, because of his father's story and his own, my father knew the value of education, so he always told me and my sisters, "Whatever you do in life, make sure you get an education. They cannot take that away from you."

Your mother played a very important role in your spiritual development.

Oh, absolutely. I grew up in Centerville, Iowa. At that time, Centerville was no different than any other small city in the Midwest. Kids picked on you and called you derogatory names, and so on. I would tell my mother about this and she'd say, "Well, son, you get down on your knees and you pray for them; and don't you be angry and don't hate!"

When I started singing opera, too, there were some times I would encounter discrimination, so I would call my mother and talk to her about it. Even then, when I was an adult, she would tell me, "Well now, son, make sure you don't hold any hatred in your heart. You pray for those people, so that their hearts may be touched, and that they will get rid of discrimination." That's been an essential part of my life and my faith: not to hate, regardless of what happens, and to "pray for your enemy." I would definitely say that my spiritual background has always been the way in which I get my strength to carry on in life. Even today I still read my Bible and pray basically every day.

When you started singing, you were actually a boy soprano. How did you get to the opposite extreme of bass-baritone?

COURTESY OF WARTBURG COLLEGE

I was singing first soprano in the high school chorus, and after the summer holiday before my senior year, I realized I didn't have my high voice anymore. So I went from first soprano down to bass-baritone! Well, not directly! First, I went to the University of Iowa. There I sang as a tenor in a group called the "Old Gold Singers." But later, my voice teacher, Mr. Charles Kellis, said, "Simon, you are a bass-baritone!" Mr. Kellis is the one who really discovered me at the University of Iowa and told me I had a voice to sing opera. I had never seen or heard an opera in my life. He brought me some recordings of great opera singers, like Cesare Siepi, Leontyne Price, Maria Callas, Eileen Farrell, and Jerome Hines. I listened to those, I went back to him the next day, and I said, "You know, I really like that stuff!" And he said, "I think you need to go to an all-music school, Simon." So he arranged an audition for me at Juilliard in 1963. I went to Juilliard and was there for a year. Then, in 1965, I started singing professionally: *Aida* at the Deutsche Oper in what was West Berlin at that time.

Then you didn't really study that long?

No, I did not. I was very gifted, and I thank God for this gift of singing and learning music. I was very blessed, so once I started singing opera, it just kind of took off, in 1966. I was one of the prize winners of the first vocal competition in Moscow: the Tchaikovsky competition. Once I started, I realized I had a gift to memorize very quickly, so that helped my career in the beginning, too, because whenever they needed someone to learn something fast, I was able to do it. I'm grateful for that.

So you didn't have any technical challenges to overcome when you were studying?

No. I really didn't. My teacher taught me a very natural way of singing and didn't use a lot of technical terms. I'm teaching now at Boston University, Iowa State University, and also at Wartburg College, a private college out here in Iowa. I'm very happy that my teacher didn't tell me so many things technically, because what happens with singers is that sometimes we "learn" problems. Teachers will tell you, "This is your passaggio, that is where your voice breaks," and they tend to generalize that for all singers. So we start thinking, "Oh, when I go to a particular note, this or that is going to happen!" And maybe that's true with some singers, but it's not always the case with every singer. My teacher also never forced me to sing beyond my chronological years, and he never wanted me to sound much more mature or older. So I credit Mr. Kellis with the longevity I've had in my career, because he was a very careful, wise voice teacher.

You know, I was doing King Philip in *Don Carlo* in Florence, Italy, in the late seventies, with Mirella Freni and Piero Cappuccilli. Both told me they had never studied with any voice teachers at all! That's not to say that all singers shouldn't study, but voice teachers should be very careful not to create problems sometimes by telling young singers too much. I think we need to let them sing, and apply technique very carefully with each individual singer, because we are all individuals of our own DNA.

It's simple: one must be able to sing and have good breath support, and one needs to sing without any tension in the body. But it's very important that we teach singers to sing with happiness and joy, and not with fear. Fear can come about sometimes, if one is told too much of, "Oh, if I don't do that, this might happen." So you might anticipate something that would not happen if you didn't think that much. And we need to listen to the students, also! When I teach, I always say to them, "Tell me, if I ever ask you to do something and it doesn't feel right." I'm not a dictator.

When you teach, you don't get very specific technically?

No. Absolutely not! I'm very grateful that the students with whom I've worked in Europe, as well as in the U.S., have been extremely appreciative, and that I get along with them so well, because I have respect for them as individuals.

If I can teach singers to teach themselves, so they do not have to be dependent on me, it's good. And it's like with an automobile: once in a while, it needs a checkup. I think that if you have a good teacher, then yes, [you] should go back to that teacher for a checkup. I often tell my students: I teach with my eyes, my ears, my heart, and very little of my brain. The brain is the part that makes things a little complicated, when you think too much.

So what do you do if someone comes to you with vocal problems?

First of all, I like to ask them why they feel they may be having these "problems." I want to get their input—not just a technical description of what is wrong, a description [that] someone else may have planted in their minds. Once I get their personal input, we start working, very peacefully and carefully. I tell them never to be nervous when working with me; that's very important. As I work with them, I ask them, "How do you feel about this?" We have to establish an incredible rapport and trust in one another. I'm not teaching them so that Simon will be glorified. I'm teaching them so that they will be able to enjoy singing and bring a lot of joy and happiness to people, wherever they sing.

I also don't believe in forcing singers to sing something they don't like. Many times, a teacher will impose certain repertoire on a singer. Singing is very personal. It comes from our hearts, our minds and our souls, so it's very important that people sing something they really enjoy. When we sing, we should bring peace and joy to people, so that their hearts and souls are touched.

I sang a lot in my career—101 roles! I've been very fortunate to sing opera for about forty years, and I'm still able to sing. I think that's because God gave me a very special gift, and I was very blessed that my first and only teacher gave me a great foundation. Now I want to share with young singers what I have learned from the great conductors and stage directors I worked with, [and] from colleagues like Birgit Nilsson, Joan Sutherland, Leontyne Price, Marilyn Horne, Leonie Rysanek, Plácido Domingo, Pavarotti, and [José] Carreras. I want to pass on this knowledge. I tell them, "Whatever I share with you, if it's something that helps you, you take it and use it; if it doesn't help you, you discard it, and I will not be offended."

What do you advise your students to do in competitions?

I always tell them, "See it as an opportunity to perform! Don't go always thinking that you have to win." Obviously, everybody wants to win any prize, but many times, there are other things that are involved to prevent one person from winning the competition. It could be sociological problems; it can be that that particular competition that year is looking for a particular vocal category, and a person can sing magnificently and still not win first prize. So you go there, and sing with gratitude that you're able to be there and you're getting the experience of walking out onstage to sing for people as well as for a jury.

Go out there and enjoy yourself as much as possible! Even if you make a mistake, don't let that bother you. We're not computers, we're human beings, we're fallible. If a mistake is made, we hope that people will be understanding, and if they are not, I say, "Perhaps it's their problem."

In 1978, you were the first African-American male to sing at Bayreuth.

Yes. I sang the title role of *The Flying Dutchman* in a new production conducted by Dennis Russell Davies, opening the season that year. That was a great honor and a great experience. I will never forget it. It really helped to catapult my career, and I really enjoyed being there. I felt deeply honored because of the way the audience responded to me. There were reports in some newspapers predicting I would be booed because of my skin color. That did not happen. I not only sang *The Flying Dutchman* for six years in a row there, but I also sang Amfortas in *Parsifal*. I think it's because of the Bayreuth experience that I ended up singing the Dutchman hundreds of times all over the world.

Is the Dutchman one of your favorite roles?

Yes. It's a very challenging role, not only dramatically, but musically and vocally. It's exciting because of the way it's written. Wagner was very young when he wrote this.

I happen to like Wagner's music very much. I sang all of his operas, except *Die Meistersinger* and *Rienzi*. One of my favorite roles is Wotan in the Ring.

Your approach to Wagner has a touch of bel canto.

It should be bel canto! Wagner wrote so phonically, as though the voice was one of the instruments of the orchestra, and he wants that music to be sung. I believe he wanted it to be sung with beauty and musicianship, and that is what bel canto is all about.

You believe in the importance of balancing opera performances with recitals.

I do, because it helps one maintain flexibility in the voice, generally speaking. In a way, recitals are even more difficult to sing than an opera, because in an opera there are many other—and I don't mean this in a negative sense—distractions people can concentrate on, either someone else singing or dancing, the scenery, the costumes. But when you sing a recital it's just you and the pianist. You're very exposed and it requires a certain type of different vocalism. I've done a lot of Schubert, Brahms, Mahler, Hugo Wolf, and Negro spirituals. Recitals are very important for singers to develop their musicianship and intellectual interpretative skills, and to be able to transmit a message through each song. I'm grateful that I've done so many recitals in my career, as well as oratorio.

In 1985 you sang Amonasro in Leontyne Price's farewell performance. She had been one of the singers you listened to when you discovered opera. What did it mean for you to be able to go onstage with her?

It was one of the greatest honors to sing with Leontyne Price at her farewell at the Met. I had sung with Leontyne before that, in San Francisco. Leontyne stepped in for the other Price—Margaret—who was ill. I remember at the rehearsal, during the duet, she started crying a little bit, and that was amazing, because Leontyne is a very controlled, very private, very strong lady. She said, "Simon, I'm so honored to be singing with you." I said, "No, Leontyne, it is an honor for me to be singing with you!" And then, when we sang again at the Met, I cannot tell you—it is one of my most memorable experiences, to have sung with this great artist and great human being in a role that was so meaningful to her and to me. I will always treasure that performance.

What did she mean to African-American singers?

She represented our first real groundbreaker. We'd had some before, but Leontyne was the one that put us on the map. We owe a lot of gratitude to Leontyne for what she has done for all of us.

You once said, "Many people never treated this as an opera but as a musical, a kind of musical ghetto." What were you referring to?

Porgy and Bess. And I didn't say "musical ghetto"; that was a misquote then. To me, *Porgy and Bess* is one of the greatest operas ever written. I don't think it's always been given the respect that it deserves. In my opinion, it is truly an opera, not a musical. But because of sociological problems years ago, the Met didn't do it until 1985, I think. I sang Porgy and Grace Bumbry sang Bess. Then it finally got some of the true respect and dignity that it deserves.

You also sang a lot for world leaders—kings, queens—connecting through music with the authorities who have power over people. What did that mean to you?

I consider it an honor, and it makes me feel more humble. My mother always taught me, "Simon, remain humble in all that you do in life." And

I really do feel blessed to think that I've sung for four U.S. presidents, for Nelson Mandela, for kings and queens of Spain and Norway, for the leaders of Germany and France. Actually, I'm the only person in the world to have sung for the twenty-fifth anniversary of the United Nations as well as the fiftieth. The twenty-fifth was in San Francisco—Beethoven's Ninth—and in New York City we did the fiftieth with Kurt Masur. They wanted people of different colors, and for some reason I was asked to sing at the twenty-fifth and the fiftieth. So that's another unique experience I've had. I also sang for the present pope twice at the Vatican, and for Desmond Tutu. I thank God for having allowed me to be in proximity to some of these great people of the world.

In the past you have declared that African-American singers, especially males, don't get many opportunities to affirm themselves in the opera world. Do you think that has changed for the better today?

I say, with a tremendous amount of sadness, no. I think there are still problems. I know that because I spoke out about these issues, it did cause me problems; some people were not engaging me or were unhappy with the statements I made. I am not bitter at all, because my mother taught me never to be bitter. Yes, as a human being, I was sad and it did hurt, but I think that we have to address problems with looking for a way to find solutions to correct them. It doesn't mean that we have to be combative, that we have to fight or anything. But we need to sit down and talk. We should realize that we are all God's children. God gives all groups of people talents and these talents should not be denied because of their ethnic background and their skin color.

It is all about the voice, after all.

It is about the voice! A voice is a gift that should be able to be shared with people of the world. Many people don't get to hear a great singer, regardless of their skin color, if a particular conductor doesn't like that singer—for whatever reason that may be—so that city, or that opera house, or that country is being denied the privilege of hearing a great artist.

Do you think conductors have too much power in these decisions?

Well, that's something we could debate for a long time! But take a lot of my students now, who happen to be non–African American. I'm working with them on Negro spirituals. And I explained it to them; I even gave lectures about it. You know, all of us have a spirit. The spirit has no color, and the spirit knows no color. Therefore, to call a song a "Negro spiritual," with this adjective modifying the word *spiritual*, simply means that it was a song composed or written by a person who in those days was called a "Negro." But isn't it the same with German lieder or Italian songs or French songs? Those words are just adjectives modifying the words *lieder* and *songs*, and they refer to the composers' nationality. But everybody can sing them! All you have to do is work with someone who understands that style of music.

A few years ago, I was working with a non-African-American student at Iowa State University. I worked with her on a Negro spiritual. She sang it for a master class—and she had people in tears. You see, music does not know barriers. These are man-made barriers and I hope they will continue to be broken down, so that no one will be denied the opportunity to share a great gift just because of their skin color. I hope those who do the hiring can understand that.

I read about a production of *Aida* in Italy in which you were required to wear white makeup. Is that true?

When I first made my debut in Berlin at the Deutsche Oper in 1965, I sang Ramfis. I had never been on the stage in my life; it was my first opera. They made me up white, not white like a Caucasian person, but white as snow! I remember I was shocked when I saw myself. Now, I must say, that doesn't happen, unless it's some production in which they want everybody made up like snow.

How did they propose that to you back then? What reasons did they give you?

They never even told me why and I did not ask them, because, look, I was a neophyte. I was just making my debut. I went in to be made up, that's the way they made me up, so I wasn't going to question it. I just remember I felt very strange, but I went ahead and I sang.

Are you still singing?

Yes. But I'm reducing it, because I've been doing it for forty years. It's time to let other people step in. But I'm grateful that I am still able to sing and to share this gift. Before I sing, I always pray and ask God to take me and use me as an instrument of peace, and faith, and hope, that people in the audience will be moved toward love and faith, through the gift that God has given me. That has always been my purpose in singing.

You have established several foundations to help students.

Yes. There are four scholarship foundations: an International Foundation for Children in Zurich, and the Simon Estes Educational Foundation in Tulsa, Oklahoma—through which we've given about three hundred scholarships to deserving students out there who have gone on to colleges like Harvard and Yale. Then there's the Simon Estes Iowa Educational Foundation, and another foundation in my hometown of Centerville. I worked my way through the University of Iowa because I was very poor, so I shined shoes, scrubbed floors—you name it, I've done it! Now that I'm blessed, I want to finally help students get to college and not have such a financial burden. There is also a school named after me in South Africa, in the Cape Town area: the Simon Estes Music High School. I founded that school about seven or eight years ago. We have about four hundred students. They have my choir, which sang for Nelson Mandela and Desmond Tutu. So, I'm constantly in contact with all these foundations.

Tell me a few words about your favorite roles.

Well, one that I've sung since 1965 is King Philip in *Don Carlo*. What I love about King Philip is that this is a true story, this man existed. It is a great role to sing, with its famous "Ella giammai m'amò," and the great duet with the Grand Inquisitor. It's not nearly as complicated as some of the other roles I sang. I also love Wotan, especially in *Die Walküre*, because it's such a diversified character to act and to sing. That is very challenging vocally and musically, but on the other hand, it's tremendously rewarding.

I love Jokanaan in *Salome*. The character of John the Baptist is this great spiritual leader. In my humility, I can identify with him because I am a very spiritual person. And the music of that role is just absolutely fantastic. I also identify with the role of Amfortas in *Parsifal*. Then, Boris Godunov is a great singing and dramatic role. First time I sang it was in Lübeck, Germany, in 1971. Opening night we had fifty-four curtain calls!

Another favorite is Porgy in *Porgy and Bess*. I could just go on and on, but these are some of my favorites. Of course, among the most challenging were the four villains in *The Tales of Hoffmann*.

Do you have any words of advice for singers?

Have patience and learn to say a diplomatic no. If someone asks you to sing something that's really not right for you, try to be diplomatic and explain to that person, "I'm not ready for that role now. Please understand." Let's say it's a great conductor or a famous stage director, tell them, "It's not easy to say no to you, but I want to be able to sing a long time, and [want you to] respect me for saying no." Many times people ask me what the secret to a career is. I say it over and over again: "Patience and a diplomatic no; that's the secret! What do we usually say? 'Patience is a virtue.' You want to be a virtuous singer? You must be patient!"

Renée Fleming

Recorded February 2005 in New York City, USA. Published in Classical Singer, *September 2005.*

In the spring of 2003, you received an honorary doctorate at Juilliard and delivered an inspiring commencement address in which you encouraged the graduating students to continue being "students" as they go out into the world. Is the idea of being a constant "student" a driving force in your life?

Absolutely. I think the most important characteristic of a student is openness: being open to criticism, to learning, to growing, to other people's ideas. A student of singing is also a student of life, in a sense. We are always learning and evolving, particularly in music. We make our living reinterpreting the creativity of others, especially in classical music. We may often repeat works, but if our interpretations don't evolve, it wouldn't be very interesting for the public. It has definitely been a crucial aspect for me, because without these qualities of being a student, I would have never come this far. I didn't have a natural voice as a singer.

So you believe there are natural singers?

Yes. I think more great singers than not are born with their voice. Their gifts are tremendous—and not just the vocal gifts and the facility, but their interpretative gifts as well. Bryn Terfel and Cecilia Bartoli are two singers from my own generation who represent that. Already, in their early twenties, they were very mature, well-rounded artists. The rest of us have to really struggle to gain technical facility or range, or to develop interpretation. For me, only a few things came naturally. I think my breath control was natural. But I needed to be able to develop all those other qualities.

On the other hand, someone who has worked as hard as you have knows their own voice inside out, whereas sometimes a natural singer may find it difficult to fix problems, if they appear.

Right. That's why it's so important to really know every aspect of your singing. There are many singers who've told me they don't have a clue how they do what they do. The really fortunate ones do it for thirty or forty years, and they never have to question too much, because they never get into trouble. For them, singing is very intuitive, not an intellectual process.

KEN HOWARD

But when you are trying to understand your mechanism, especially if you are not a "natural," the process tends to become cerebral. How do you balance that with the instinct?

That's why instinct is so important, because there's a part of you that will say, "This is getting too intellectual, and it's tying me up in knots! I need to find someone who works in a more intuitive way." So that's where the individual has to know which direction to go. It's not easy, because there is another voice in your head: "Well, if I just stick with this long enough, and try to understand it, it will make sense."

In a sense, that can be the motivator for every singer, that can lead them to find their own path—which is why in my book [*The Inner Voice*], I tried to say specifically, "This is not a general 'how-to' for singers. It is only the illustration of my own path."

If one sentence or one concept makes sense to a young singer and can help them, that's wonderful. But the book's intended production is to illustrate my path, and, in a sense, to help singers understand that a career does not happen overnight and it's not necessarily easy.

Another trap for some singers: They take a teacher's method as the definitive method, trying to adopt it completely, erasing their own individuality.

For that reason it's very important not to give up responsibility in singing. It's not about going into a practice room and trying to relive every sentence and idea from the lesson. Bring your own creativity and imagination to the process, and explore, really explore! Use the mirror, the piano, the floor; use whatever tools you need. Be creative about it, because singing is in a sense so ephemeral.

I always say it's a miracle that humans learn how to sing. It is not a good idea to abandon yourself entirely into the hands of someone else. If you do that, you are giving that teacher a little too much responsibility. It's not fair to them, because they are not inside your body and they don't know exactly how it feels for you. They are guessing, and trying to feed ideas to you to help you.

The connection between teacher and student is very personal, which is why I always recommend that you consult with a number of people until you find the right one. Also, be cautious following the "buzz" about the best teacher of the moment. Sometimes that can work against you, because the best teachers are not necessarily going to have the time and energy to invest, particularly in someone with a lot of problems. You need to find [the teacher] who speaks to you best.

It was obvious from your book that you actually love to practice.

The process has always been fascinating to me, which is why I wanted to write this book and enjoyed writing it. If I had been asked for an autobiography, I would have said no, because my story isn't particularly interesting, and I wouldn't enjoy that. But when I was told, "We want a book about your process," I said, "Ah! That is interesting." I really liked trying to articulate ideas about music and singing. It wasn't always easy to find the right words, but it was a fascinating pursuit.

Do you teach or do master classes?

I love teaching and I used to teach a lot. I grew up in a family of teachers, so it is certainly in my genes. Now I don't teach, because my career is too demanding and I have two young children. I enjoy doing master classes, so if they fit between engagements and I am already away from home, then I am happy to do them—but I wouldn't stay an extra day for that. I just won't take time away from my children.

Do your children sing?

They have a variety of pursuits. I think that's appropriate at their ages. They should just be exploring everything.

How do you find the state of music education in America today?

I think that orchestras and opera companies are better about developing their different outreach programs; they're very focused on it. I also think that children should be exposed to classical music at an early age, when they have no preconceived ideas and are completely open. The conservatories and universities are producing great musicians. The problem, however, is that while we're producing musicians at a very high rate, we are not producing audience members. The goal to get everyone to appreciate music and be exposed to it is important and worthy to pursue, but we're not doing enough.

I believe one of the most unfortunate things to happen is that classical music has been slowly disappearing from the media. The beginning of the Met telecasts, with *La bohème*, had started a real interest in bringing quality art to television. Recently, that has been waning dramatically. Vast amounts of the public who don't have access to a company or orchestra, or who might be too intimidated to go if they did have access, are now being deprived of the television exposure, too. That saddens me.

How have today's technological developments and fast pace—the Internet, for example—affected you as an artist?

The Internet might be very useful to us in the future because of its potential for streaming live performances—so we can find an audience that way. As for other technology, I am an avid iTunes and iPod user now. I mean, to be able to go to iTunes and plug in a song makes my research quicker and easier. Of course, not nearly enough music is offered on the service yet, but eventually it will be. To have ten versions of a song come up is a fantastic tool for me!

The unfortunate part of everything being fast paced is that our attention spans have been shrinking and shrinking, and there is so much competition for attention. We're being bombarded by information in very short sound bites. It wasn't that long ago that people would go to an opera, and in the afternoon, they'd actually take the time to read the libretto. Who would do that now? Nobody has the time!

Ironically, the life span has gotten longer, but people seem to have less time.

Yeah! But I do think that as we live longer, that extra time will be special. I almost look forward to retiring, because I'm hoping I'll then have another twenty years to go back to things I want to learn about: art history, literature. I imagine myself auditing classes at the local university. That's when I'll pick up my education again and pursue other things. It has also been proven that we stay healthier the more we use our minds that way, so that's also an incentive!

As a singer however, you need time to develop.

Absolutely. It was at least ten years for me, ten years before I could just get through a performance. I had so many technical obstacles to overcome.

What was the biggest obstacle for you?

The most important element was that I was a soprano with no top. I had a very unreliable top. When I sang anything above the staff, I'd break out in hives and get very nervous. That was the crucial obstacle! Everything else was icing on the cake.

An amazing strength that shines through in your book is that you face whatever you fear.

That, and resilience, are very important to develop—and I am still using them every day! The obstacles are still there. No level of achievement protects anyone from the day-to-day disappointments and ups and downs that we all face; it just happens at a different level. My life is no different than anyone else's in that respect.

It's tempting to imagine that when you are at the top, life must be easier.

Not true! Whatever challenges you face personally, they stay the same, but they're just on a different level. I used to think that, too. I used to imagine that when I "made it," everything would be easy. I remember the first time I said that to someone, and they told me, "Oh, dear! You are in for a surprise!"

You really have to love this profession.

Yes. It can take a long time. However, if over a period of years, people are still saying no, then maybe it's time to regroup, rethink the goal, and do something else. I know some actors are told that the only mistake they can ever make is to quit. I think that's actually not correct.

I am not one to suggest that someone should never give up. Maybe someone's talents are better used serving music in a different way, whether it's in administration or education. This is why I love that the conservatories are getting more creative about training musicians and telling them, "Okay, we're not all going to be stars, so just in case, start thinking now about what else you'd like to do. Here are the different levels of training in the opera: administration, marketing, publicity." It's getting the students to at least think about other options.

On the other hand, for some people, it's music or die! They really just have to be performing. That's their raison d'être. It was never that way for me. For me, it was more about the process of growing and achieving. I could have continued loving music at an amateur level. It wasn't about performing. In fact, I never really enjoyed performing. I had to learn how to do that, because I am not a natural performer. So it's always been easy for me to imagine doing something else—but I would want to be successful at it.

We all have to discover within us what the driving forces really are. Is it music? Is it singing? Is it performing? Or is it more a need to be loved? Is it a need to be validated publicly? Could any of those things be achieved some other way?

How do you keep in shape?

I've become a Pilates fanatic. Pilates is especially beneficial for performers, because it's strength and flexibility training. I enjoy it. That was my gift to myself when I moved back to New York. I decided to do something for my body. I also like to ski and I walk, but I've never been very athletic. In terms of food, I lead a low-carb lifestyle—that's been crucial in maintaining a reasonable weight. Those two things together have really done a lot for my health.

What is your philosophy of life?

Well, I can say that what I'm trying to do now is find balance in my life, which is not easy, because I've always been somewhat of a workaholic, and I finally recently acknowledged it. I just enjoy work. I am fortunate because I am very passionate about my work. However, it should never be everything.

I try to always imagine that it could all be over tomorrow. The voice can fall apart for many different reasons. I try to keep in touch with the fact that that could occur and I would still be okay. So, if I have a philosophy, it's in a sense staying connected to that idea. It's keeping my feet on the ground.

What is the experience like for you to learn a piece of music especially written for you, such as Brad Mehldau's songs, which you will premiere at Carnegie Hall?

I enjoy it. I love new music. I love the idea that I am potentially making a contribution to the real creative work—which is the music itself, because we are re-creative artists. Brad's songs are so beautiful; I've always been a huge fan of his and his jazz playing. He's managed to maintain and keep this unique voice I like so much, while, in a sense, allowing it to morph into a more classical genre. The lines are very fine, and one can sense them a bit more as classical music rather than jazz.

Does the composer give you a lot of artistic freedom in collaborating?

He has actually never done this before. He's been very serious about it, and has taken a year and a half to write these pieces—a forty-minute song cycle; it's a substantial piece. He came to me early on with the first examples, and I was able to guide him a little bit, so I did have some input. In the end, he's managed to put on paper, very specifically, exactly what he wants. I have a big job ahead of me to learn them, because the rhythms are very complex. He means every little rhythm and every little syncopation. I am proud to be part of this.

Any words of advice for singers?

I would say that young singers tend to get so caught up in the minutia of what it is that they're trying to do vocally, artistically, musically, interpretatively, and in terms of their image. I would just connect them to the big picture. The big picture when they go into an audition is presenting, in a sense, their personality. That's so much a part of the presentation. It's so important that they feel confident about who they are, and if they're not confident, that they at least pretend to feel confident from the moment they walk in the door.

They also have to put themselves in the place of the judges, who want everyone to do well but have heard two hundred singers already, or maybe more. How are you going to stand out? It's not by singing the most difficult, longest piece, and making the jury suffer through a whole scene. It's by doing what you do best and being as artistic as you can be in that moment.

The goal should be to make the judges forget that they are in a small room, so treat it more like a performance. Sing what suits you best!

Peter Gelb

Recorded August 2006 in New York City, USA. Published in Classical Singer, *October 2006.*

Tell me about your childhood.

I grew up in Manhattan. When I was growing up, my father was not only working as the second drama critic at the *New York Times* but he was also moonlighting with my mother—who is a writer—preparing a highly regarded biography of Eugene O'Neill, the playwright. As a child, I was very jealous of O'Neill, because I felt that he was robbing my parents from me. I didn't get to see enough of them because of him, although I did have a perfectly happy childhood.

As a result of my father's position, I was introduced at a young age to theater and music. I would go to performances. I remember seeing *Hamlet* when I was five, and *The Taming of the Shrew* in Central Park when I was seven. My mother's uncle was the great violinist Jascha Heifetz, so I had a strong connection to the music world. I also remember, as a kid, I used to go to bed at night listening to WQXR radio under my pillow.

Since your parents were involved with words and the ability to write, how do you think that influenced your development?

I think that because they wrote about music and theater, it opened up that world, which struck me as being very glamorous, appealing, and exciting.

You started working at the Met as an usher at the age of sixteen. Can you recall any memorable performances you experienced during that time?

Yes. I particularly remember Leontyne Price singing Aida. That was amazing! Two other great singers I heard then were Renata Tebaldi—in what must have been a very old production of *La fanciulla del West*—and Franco Corelli in *La bohème*.

Was the house packed?

It was always packed! My assignment was to be in charge of the stand-ees in Family Circle. They were a group of boisterous and "fanatical" fans who would often get into arguments with each other, and I would find myself in the position of trying to keep the peace. In those days, there were claques that demonstrated on behalf of the singers; there would be confetti demonstrations at times. There was a lot of excitement!

Do you think opera is still capable of generating that kind of excitement today?

Yes, but I wish there were more of it. That kind of excitement was present last season at the opening of *Don Pasquale* for Anna Netreb-ko—a very thrilling moment in the theater. My hope is that it will happen more and more by dramatically increasing the number of new productions and getting more top directors here. With that, my plan is certainly in no way to diminish the importance of the singers. In fact, if anything, I hope the opposite will happen: By having more new productions and opportunities available to the top stars, they will sing here more often and in greater concentrations.

You are bringing back the glamour of the opera star and the tradition of creating a production for a star singer. For example: *Tosca* **for Karita Mattila, and** *Carmen* **for Angela Gheorghiu.**

That's what the Met has always been about, and it's not that it isn't that way now. It's just not as consistently planned as I think it can be. For me, the dream production is one where you have the great stars, director, and conductor, and the right repertoire in a harmonious combination. The future *Tales of Hoffmann* is a perfect example, with the dream cast of [Anna] Netrebko, [Rolando] Villazón, Elina Garanča—a wonderful mezzo who hasn't made her debut here yet—and René Pape, who will be making his Met role debut as the four villains, with Luc Bondy directing and Jimmy Levine conducting.

Of course, one hopes everything will come to pass the way one plans.

But if you don't have great plans, you can't possibly have great results, so you have to start with great plans.

Who were your favorite singers of the past?

There were so many great singers—but when I was eighteen, working as an office boy for Sol Hurok, I heard Maria Callas in her farewell concert tour. Later, in 1983, I produced the first satellite television production that involved multiple locations connected live to each other. I believe this was the first one in history, long before any international rock satellite concert! It was a tribute to Callas, in honor of the sixtieth anniversary of her birth. It involved live performances in the four theaters she had had the closest association with in the later part of her career: the Lyric Opera of Chicago, the Royal Opera House, the Paris Opera, and La Scala.

In each opera house, I arranged a live performance tribute to her with an amazing collection of stars. Each house had a giant screen so that when there was nothing onstage, the audience could enjoy what was happening in another opera house, shown on the screen—so the performances weren't overlapping. The whole production was televised all over the world at the same time.

Another wonderful singer I heard on recording is Björling. And then, of course, Pavarotti. I remember hearing him and Sutherland in *La fille du régiment*.

In your opinion, what makes a singer a star?

I don't think you can define the qualities. Even if there was a formula, it wouldn't be one that human beings can necessarily precalculate or know how to apply. It's that magical chemistry that involves artistry: great vocal ability and theatrical charisma. Either you have it or you don't.

Of course, some stars may have such an abundance of qualities in one area that the other aspects are less important. Look at Pavarotti. He is not a great actor and yet his voice contains all the elements of theatricality, musicality, vocal beauty, and incomparable artistry—more than enough to make him one of the greatest singers in history.

It's not definable, and yet when you hear a star, you know you've heard one! I wish there were more, because we need them all! Anna Netrebko, Karita Mattila, Renée Fleming, Angela Gheorghiu, Natalie Dessay, Deborah Voigt . . . these are just examples of the sopranos, and I don't want to leave anyone out. But these singers can transport the public. They have the ability to appeal to an audience beyond just aficionados. This is what we need if we're going to increase and replenish the opera-going audience, which is an aging audience.

That's why the challenge the Met and I have together is so great! We're dealing with an aging art form. The only hope we have to keep this thirty-eight-hundred-seat theater filled with people and excitement is to be more energetic and creative than ever in trying to galvanize the art form, with new productions, [and] exciting combinations of artists and directors—to be tireless in creating opportunities without in any way diminishing what has been and is already great about the Met.

Many singers regard the Met as the greatest house in the world—and it may be the most challenging, too. But the foundation is there. The Met is a magical name throughout the world, and I need to be able to take advantage of that to create these opportunities!

Do you have any plans for the Lindemann Young Artist Program?

To be honest with you, at this point, I have not delved into that yet. We have wonderful artists in the program, like Mariusz Kwiecien, who is a truly spectacular talent, a real star.

The program is a very important part of this institution, very close to Maestro Levine's heart, and I support its activities. I am not an expert in how it runs yet—but it is critical that we continue developing young artists. At the same time, I think it is interesting to note that Italy is producing fewer great new talents than other countries.

Why would you say that is happening?

I think it has to do with the fact that opera is declining in Italy. This is a country that has an opera house in every city, and most of those houses have significantly declining audiences and operatic programs.

When I was president of Sony Classical, it was very obvious that Italy had become one of the least important markets for the sale of new recordings of classical music and opera. I think there is a direct correlation to the fact that Italy is not producing the same proportion of great new singers as it was before. Other art forms are draining the pool of operatic talent. A hundred years ago, a serious composer would write classical music. Today a serious composer can write pop music, or movie soundtracks, or music for video games; there are so many different opportunities.

I believe it's more than coincidence that many of the top singers now are coming from Latin America or Spain. Perhaps that has to do with the fact that opera in those parts of the world has a more important place in society and culture than in most countries. This is something worth examining more.

The outreach programs are another important aspect of the

Met's work in developing new audiences. Will you be involved with that?

Most of these educational programs at the Met are done through the Metropolitan Opera Guild, but this is certainly an area that needs to be supported and expanded. My ideas for the Met in building bridges to a broader public include reaching out educationally, and they will help the Guild's efforts to amplify its work in this area.

My project to create a much broader and more active media program has an educational component. All my plans for the Met include not just changing or expanding the artistic activities, but also finding ways to make the Met a more transparent institution in terms of its relationship with the public.

You are also instituting the "family opera," beginning with an abridged version of *The Magic Flute* in English.

Yes, although this will not be the beginning of a trend of abridged versions. In the case of *The Magic Flute*, an abridged version is appropriate. The following season—2007–2008—we're adding another new family opera production of *Hansel and Gretel*, in English but not abridged, directed by Richard Jones, the English theater and opera director. For the next four or five seasons, my plan is to rotate *The Magic Flute* and *Hansel and Gretel* as our family entertainment operas in English during the holiday season. It's our operatic response to the *Nutcracker*.

What did you learn from Sol Hurok that continues to influence you today?

There are several things I learned from him. One is actually being put into place at the Met: our ticket pricing. Hurok believed that the most and least expensive tickets always sold first, and what we are doing now is a variation of that. A handful of the very best seats in the house are being dramatically increased in price, with the understanding that a subscriber who doesn't wish to pay for this additional increase can move a seat or two to the left or right and remain almost in the same location without having any price increase. In fact, 90 percent of ticket prices are unchanged. It's only the superexclusive locations.

So would the thinking behind this be: If somebody can afford those high prices anyway, another fifty or seventy-five dollars would not be such a dramatic increase?

Well, you said it, not me! But I agree with you. I don't want to be cavalier about it, and some subscribers are not so happy about it. On the other hand, we have taken the lowest-price tickets in Family Circle, which were twenty-six dollars, and reduced them to fifteen. So there will be ninety thousand seats through the course of the season available at fifteen dollars apiece, and that—as somebody pointed out to me—is lower than any Broadway ticket!

You have to be very mindful of your audience—Hurok was a master of that. One of his favorite sayings was, "If the people don't want to come, you can't make them," which means you have to know what you are doing.

I think one of the reasons the Met board turned to me, as opposed to someone who had been the Intendant of an opera company, is because of my experience as a producer who thinks about art and commerce and who has worked in both the for-profit and nonprofit worlds of the performing arts. My experience began with Hurok, and it's that kind of approach of being a producer and entrepreneur that I will bring to my work at the Met.

You are developing the visual aspect of opera to attract more audiences. Is there any concern that sometimes the staging might inconvenience singers who are not so physically able, and how would you negotiate that with the director?

First of all, I would advise singers that if they want to be successful in the twenty-first century, they have to think about opera in terms of musical theater, meaning: It is to their advantage to be mobile. They should realize that they're putting themselves at a terrible disadvantage not to be physically able to manipulate the stage and [not] to be theatrically savvy. Sure, if the next Pavarotti comes around, there will always be room for a singer whose vocal abilities are so great that they transcend any physical challenges. But it's to any singer's advantage that they have the voice and physicality to be the complete package. However, that's not going to replace a great voice.

This theater demands great singing, there's no way of getting around it. We're not looking to replace great singing with great bodies. We want both. That's what singers need to train themselves for, if they want to be successful—and that's what we need if we want to keep this art form alive, because we have to convince the public that opera is a satisfying experience at all levels, musically and theatrically.

So would the director have complete autonomy?

No. It's a collaboration. The way the Met has functioned in the past was that sometimes directors were not consulted about singers, resulting in many of the world's greatest directors not wanting to work here. So, my job as head of the theater is to find partnerships between directors, conductors, and singers that work. If they don't work, then people won't play together. My job is to combine these different forces. Certainly, any great director is not going to work here unless they approve the cast, whether the cast is appointed before the director is hired or afterward, and the same thing is true of a conductor.

It takes great skill to bring all of these factors together.

That's what I've been doing all my life; it doesn't always work but the attempt must be made. What the Met cannot do is have the attitude that, "We are the Metropolitan Opera and we will operate in a vacuum and make imperious decisions!" I said this at the press conference, and I repeat it to you: The heart and soul of this institution are Maestro Levine and this orchestra that he's molded over almost forty years into the greatest opera orchestra in the world. All of the decisions I am making are in collaboration with him, and he is very eager, for the sake of stimulating the orchestra and for the art form, to have other great conductors come here. The same way he would never allow a cast onstage without approving it, no great guest conductor or director would do that either. It's a question of being mindful; it's all about communication.

And about being a great diplomat.

I'm not saying I'm a great diplomat. Great diplomacy is not so difficult; it's a question of timing and making sure decisions are not made peremptorily, in a way that artists are affected. If all the artists involved are consulted, chances are things will work well.

How will you select movie theaters to show the live transmission from the Met on Saturdays? Are you focusing on particular areas of the United States?

It's based on a number of factors. We have a very strong and devoted radio public so we're trying to identify movie theaters in sections of the country where there is a concentration of Metropolitan Opera audiences in existence. The other very important factor is that, even though many movie theaters across the country already have high-definition projection systems, only a few hundred are equipped with satellite dishes at this point. So we are limited to those theaters because I want this to be a live experience. Whatever arrangement we make is not going to be on an individual theater-by-theater basis; it will be with a distributor who deals directly with movie theaters. It's the same way a movie is released.

What is your advice to conservatories and universities in developing the stars of tomorrow?

I think that conservatories and teachers should understand what the needs of the twenty-first century are for opera. That includes the whole package, the physical and theatrical aspect. They should know what opera companies require and be very careful to nurture talent within the right technical foundation. And I also think they should strongly encourage each student's unique individuality, which is an important factor in becoming a star.

Angela Gheorghiu
and Roberto Alagna

Recorded August 2002 in Salzburg, Austria. Published in Classical Singer,
January 2003.

How did the *Tosca* film come into being?

AG: I was singing in a new production of *La traviata* in Paris and the film's producer, Daniel Toscan du Plantier, came to me after the performance and told me, "You are Tosca!" This was in 1997. It was understood that Roberto would be Mario. As for the director, Daniel wanted a true film director, without preconceived ideas about opera. Benoît Jacquot, who was friends with Daniel, was completely "fresh" in this respect, his ideas were new and innovative, and he didn't care about others' opinions about how an opera film should be done.

Mr. Jacquot mentioned that you came on the set with clear ideas about your character, and it was easy for him to work with you, since he didn't have to give you too many directions.

AG: Yes, that's true. I admired him because he also came completely prepared. Every move of the camera, the lights, every angle . . . he knew it beforehand.

The film is extremely innovative as it approaches the subject from three perspectives . . .

AG: Benoît had a vision of the score, as these white sheets covered with notes dating back one hundred years . . . He wanted to show how the characters, the story, and the different settings are born from the score, but to show it as a painter's palette, better said, a work palette that audiences are not acquainted with. Not the just the story, but other aspects of creating an opera film that he wanted to present to the public, and he had the courage to do that!

The duet scenes give the impression that you are dancing with one another. Whose idea was this?

AG: It was an idea that was created between Roberto and the director.

RA: Benoît just came to me and whispered, "Make her dance!" I liked the thought and tried it out during the duet scenes.

AG: We understood immediately what he was trying to say. He didn't have to show us what to do in terms of gestures, expressions, movements . . .

RA: Yes, through this very simple idea, we knew what he wanted to see, and we knew he wanted it to be natural and simple, nothing extra was needed, just a dance.

How was the lip-synching experience? Did you have to sing out on the set during filming?

AG: We sang sometimes. In close-up moments, it had to be very believable. If, for a second, your mind went in another direction, the character escaped you. You always have to be very present to be believable.

RA: That applies to every time you sing but especially when you're filming; it takes so much concentration because the camera will expose the slightest nuance.

AG: You know, you were right when you said before that it was easier with the two of us, because many scenes came naturally. However, Benoît had this idea that he wanted the whole film to be a whole, and didn't want a clear-cut separation between the principal scenes or the arias and the moments in between. He just didn't want to interrupt the characters and break our flow. It was so hard to be so concentrated because one camera was moving, there were so many lights, and a huge crowd of people . . . I remember for "Vissi d'arte," there were fifteen people in front of me.

RA: And not only do you have to maintain the character but also to synchronize yourself with the lip-synching. We rehearsed [lip-synching] every day for one and a half hours before makeup.

Making an opera-film is no doubt a very different experience for an opera singer used to the grandeur of the stage. How would you sum up this difference between acting on camera and acting on the stage?

AG: Even though I was singing Tosca for the first time in the recording for this film, it wasn't the first time that I was on camera, because I had filmed a lot of opera scenes in Bucharest, Romania. The difficulty is to construct an entire role during several weeks. However, there is nothing more difficult than being onstage and singing. To make a movie is

easier work. The hard part for me was just to wait, and wait, and be prepared for a few moments of filming. It's completely another type of work. But I love the camera.

RA: Well, on the stage you also have to become immersed in the character, you have to feel it and breathe it. Even in a concert version like this *Roméo et Juliette* we're doing here [in Salzburg], we act our parts. It's very natural. Just like we are at home!

Where does vocal technique come in? Do you ever help each other in that respect?

RA: We seldom speak of our profession, technically!

AG: We don't really talk about technique at all.

RA: Technique is something very personal. Everyone is different.

AG: We each have our own technical "kitchen." I leave it at home, and on the stage, I think of the text in each phrase, of the character, how to make it as credible as possible. If I can believe in the character myself, then I can make you and everyone else believe in her, too.

RA: Of course, it's not just the character onstage. You have to concentrate and pay attention in certain moments when it's more difficult vocally. If you have a high C, you can't just sing it without preparing. It has to be thought before, so in that sense, you are aware of your technique. Besides, every day your voice is different. It depends on everything, on your emotions . . .

AG: Yes, on emotional and spiritual states of mind, on your health, on how you slept . . . Our instrument is our body.

RA: The acoustics can affect it, the public as well . . .

AG: Your nerves, too . . . it depends on whether you have good colleagues or not, good productions, conductors, everything. It's an ensemble of factors.

Do you ever allow yourselves a break, time off from singing?

AG: I do, a little more . . .

RA: And I, a little less . . .

AG: And that is because he is not just passionate about music; he is an opera maniac, addicted to singing! But, of course, we are so busy that a small break can be good for us. Every artist is different. To tell you the truth, ever since I can remember, I have always been able to stop singing for more than a month, and without much vocalizing, I am all set to perform. That doesn't mean it's good or bad. Every vocal instrument responds differently, because we are all built a certain way.

RA: We all have a different technique and everyone needs to follow whatever works for him or her. In any case, a complete singing break does not exist for us. We always have something to learn.

AG: Oh, no, a total break, no. Partially . . .

RA: In this profession you have to study everyday if you want to maintain your level and to continue expanding.

What would you tell a beginning singer as well as the singer in midcareer, if they came to you for advice?

AG: Not to lose the pleasure . . .

RA: The pleasure in singing is the most important thing. And to have a good soul. If you are negative, you will not go far in this profession.

AG: In Romanian, there is this special expression, hard to translate . . . it's not to be [fierce] in singing. Never lose the patience to study, to listen, and to listen to everyone! There are many young singers out there, even some of our colleagues who don't want to listen to anyone or hear anything ever. Wrong! You can always learn. When you attend a performance, when you listen to a CD or see a video, it gets you to think . . .

RA: You analyze: "I should do it like this, and I didn't like that particular expression . . . " and so on. You can learn from anyone because we all have a variety of ideas. Everyone should be respected and at least listened to once.

AG: Yes, because we all work very hard in this profession, and you can't always judge how good someone is by one performance! But those who "arrive"—I'm not talking about a level—to perform on the stage, that in itself is enormously hard: existing on the stage. So, the fact that you are even there, hired to perform, already means a great deal.

RA: Of course. No one in the world wants to perform on the stage and give their worst. They are there because they want to give the best of themselves . . .

AG: In every artist—not just singers—there is a human being who is exposed to many thousands of eyes, and what is extremely important is to have the self-confidence to endure that exposure, and not be influenced by hundreds of "well-meaning" advices and opinions, because the singer will be completely lost, it's all so relative!

RA: And subjective! Obviously, self-confidence and innate talent are crucial but still not enough. You have to gather knowledge, to pick it up from everyone else, from all that surrounds you, because everyone and everything can teach you something.

AG: A lot of colleagues and conductors think that no one else is good, just that they are the best. Everyone says the same about themselves. But there will never be a "best." And that is a good thing, because then we have reached the top, the limit, and it will be over. They will say, "Look what Angela and Roberto are doing or what others did and are doing, that's it: everything else is finished; there's nothing new to be discovered!" You can never express everything in classical music.

RA: Oh, it's never-ending!

AG: The same score has been sung so many times over and over in the whole world. But each of us comes with another idea, another personality and another voice. That's why it's so interesting and never boring.

Unfortunately, we don't have any time left . . .

AG: The line of reporters is getting impatient!

I would like to thank both of you for taking the time out of the series of interviews you have ahead of you, to answer my questions. I have seen you perform separately, and you have such distinct artistic personalities. However, I have also seen you perform together on several occasions and something happens between you. You manage to maintain your unique- ness but you become a whole. Now that I had the opportunity to speak to you together, I can say I am a direct witness to the artistic power that you two, as a couple, generate in real life as well as onstage. Life imitates art, and in your case, your art imitates your life together . . .

RA: You're right!

AG: Yes, like I said before, we each have our own personal way of dealing with our voices, separately. That is a subject we leave at home and we don't interfere in each other's "kitchen." But then when we rehearse, when we are in the opera house, or we are recording, then we are in agreement.

RA: We know each other very well, too, but we also share the same tastes in the method of interpretation. It's very real to us, our life on the stage, just like our life together.

AG: And you're right that something happens when we perform together, there is always a natural and perfect osmosis between us.

David Gockley

Recorded October 2004 in Houston, USA. Published in Classical Singer, *May 2005.*

You studied voice and sang as a baritone.

I studied voice and sang as a baritone without a top!

When did you decide you didn't want to be a singer anymore?

It was about 1969. My singing teacher at that time was Margaret Harshaw. She said, "David, I think you need a break! A long break!"

Were you working too hard?

Yeah! I was trying to earn a living, so I was teaching and talking all day, while studying voice and coaching, and taking acting lessons. I lived in New York, and in the summers, I was fortunate enough to go to Santa Fe Opera, where I was an apprentice for three years. But I never jumped from apprentice to anything more, so I said, "I better get the hell out!"

What do you think it was that held you back from making progress as a singer?

I was too analytical and tried to understand each technical detail intellectually. And I could never get the whole idea of support. I just worked too hard at it!

What oriented you toward getting a business degree at Columbia?

I wanted to get a job to support myself, and then I decided to work in the arts.

Once you got your degree, you came directly to Houston.

About thirty-four years ago, I rented a U-Haul truck, put all my belongings in it, and drove from Manhattan to Houston.

Why Houston?

It was fate! Well, fate in the form of a job! It was the number two job here in what was then a very small opera company, and I thought, "Well, maybe there's upward mobility." It also seemed like the people here were very nice and supportive. I liked it from the very beginning. Of course, the thing I liked most was that I had a paycheck.

Only two years after your arrival, you took over as general director in 1972, and you began a trend that would in time establish Houston Grand Opera as a groundbreaking company. You presented a world premiere: *The Seagull* by Thomas Pasatieri. Was the introduction of new works, and especially new American composers, a high priority for you from the start?

Yes. It was a high priority to do works by Americans. Actually, the first opera I did after I became general director was Carlisle Floyd's *Susannah*, at the Miller Outdoor Theater. Trying to bring new opera to a wider audience is one of my passions.

Was the Houston audience always a fertile ground for planting new "seeds" in the form of new works?

It was always a less traditional audience.

Why?

Well, they did not have traditional opera for generation after generation, and there weren't very strong European communities here—like there were in Chicago or San Francisco, which would encourage mostly old-world repertoire and values—so they were very open to everything here.

Do you approach composers with your own ideas for a work, or do they approach you?

Most of the time, the composer comes to me with an idea. But there have been situations where I liked a certain idea and found the composer to do it. Sometimes I put a composer together with a libretto. Other times they have someone they want to work with. So they submit the idea to me—what I call a "prose scenario," which breaks it all down into acts and scenes, and talks about the role the music will play. On that basis, we decide whether we're going to go on with the commission.

Some directors don't understand the physicality of a singer's vocal production. With your previous singer's experience, do you watch out for these things when you take on a new production?

Oh, yes! In terms of stage directors, we've had Bob Wilson here, David Alden, Christopher Alden—they're all Americans, and probably the extreme to which we've gone in terms of stage direction. But that is nothing compared to the way direction is done in Stuttgart, or sometimes Munich and Hamburg—the so-called *Regietheater*. The *Regietheater* is not to my taste and I do not support that. I support the music being very important, and that means the singers, while the staging and concept should come out of the music, and not be overlaid upon it.

How do you govern this institution?

Management by consensus. I talk to all my people, to get their thoughts

and ideas. Obviously, I've got to make the final decision, but that is not in any way authoritarian. I try to get good people in the various departments. We all meet together, and I also meet with them individually to set goals. Then I pretty much leave them to make the goals. If they have major changes or need feedback along the way, they can come back and seek it.

You know, I'm a very boring general director. I'm not a demagogical dictator or anything like that.

How do you handle behind-the-scenes politics or power struggles, if there are any?

There have been very few. If I figure somebody is really not making their goals—not necessarily over one year, but over two or three years—or if they're being a negative influence to the unity of the operation, then I will get rid of them.

How do you deal with divas and divos?

That hasn't been much of a problem over the years. We had some challenging moments with Renata Scotto at times. If a diva is really important artistically, if she sells tickets and creates great excitement in the community, then it's worth taking care of that person and understanding their needs. If the diva has a production or a tenor that she feels comfortable with, I will cooperate. I will not try to get somebody like Renée Fleming here for *La traviata* and throw her in a new, progressive production. We talk about it, and we understand each other. So, if the diva is really worth it, we try to cooperate—but not to the extent that the work we do is all about her or him. The divas or divos have to fit into the direction and the rest of the cast, and be good colleagues.

What is the key in attracting donors and maintaining such lasting ties with them? What is your secret?

Since I've been here so long, I found that donors kind of come in, have their time, and then go out. I've had very few who have been supporting us my whole time here.

My secret is that I am enthusiastic about what we are doing. Either they give to us because I can enthuse them about a particular project or about the organization as a whole, or because I can convince them that a good opera company is good for the whole city. A city has a baseball team; it should have a good medical center, great universities, and great cultural centers. Houston is a major city—it's the fourth largest city, population-wise, in the country. It should have a great opera house!

In the HGO magazine, *Opera Cues*, you write "The Gockley Chronicles," a day-by-day account of your latest trips. Tell me about that.

I only write this when I have a ten- to fifteen-day trip. I think it gives opera fans a chance to understand what their opera director is doing, how he's spending his time, who he's meeting with, what singers he's planning on bringing here in the future, and his thoughts on particular productions. It keeps people informed.

I imagine you have to be constantly on top of what is going on in opera houses around the world as well as at home.

I like to be constantly aware of that, whether it's going there in person or not. There's a lot of traffic in videotapes these days for the purpose of viewing an artist's work or a production. My job is also about keeping up with certain artists that we like to have relationships with: taking them to dinner, seeing them backstage, deciding on their next two or three productions in Houston.

Do you miss singing?

No. I struggled with it at the end so badly that . . .

You don't even sing for yourself anymore?

Maybe after the fifth mojito.

If a singer keeps struggling as you did, would you tell them to give it up?

I would. It's hard—it's so courageous to try it, but I go back to what Margaret Harshaw said. In a fairly nice way, she told me, "Listen, you're trying too hard and getting less good." So, if I thought that were true of somebody, I would tell them. I'd do it in a very nice way. I would say, just as she told me, "Take some time off, do some other things, and then if you do come back to it, you'll come back fresher and with a new perspective."

What do you look for when a singer auditions for you?
A gorgeous voice that is technically healthy and shows personality.
What about experience, acting ability, looks, all of that?
All of it.
Does age matter?
I find that younger singers are more capable of growing and changing, and for our studio, it would be very unusual for us to take someone over thirty, because the older someone gets, the more resistant they are to somebody telling them how to improve, and their bad habits are more ingrained.
How much does European experience count when someone auditions?
Not that much.
What makes a bad impression on you?
Not having a beautiful voice, not having high or low notes, being boring, not being musical, not knowing how to use the voice in an expressive way—you know, all of that.
If someone has a bad audition, would you ever hear that singer again?
Yeah, if there was enough to give me the idea that they were having a bad day, or if they had a beautiful voice but their top was not yet worked out.
Where else do you discover talent, besides going around the country?
I discover talent in Europe—I try to hear singers in the major cities I go to, like Vienna or Munich.
Do chorus members ever become soloists?
Yeah. I would say that during my time here, maybe ten singers who were in the chorus as younger singers went on to have solo careers. They can use our chorus for as long as they want, to get experience [and] earn money while they're studying—but then it's their choice.
How many new singers do you hear a year?
Me personally, maybe 150, but the company as a whole probably hears a thousand. I don't hear them all.
Through the Opera to Go initiative, you introduce children to opera by having children's stories and fairy tales set to music and performed?
Yeah, like *The Princess and the Pea* and *Velveteen Rabbit*. Our idea is: before kids get into their difficult adolescent years—when they don't like things

that their parents like—to give them three good experiences with something called opera. We also appeal to teenagers, it seems. Last night we had a high school night. It was amazing! A fabulous performance—and there was not a sound during the performance. The high school students received it at the end like an audience at [La] Scala. And they were dressed up!

HGO has won awards for marketing and advertising. You are constantly looking for new and innovative ways to advertise in order to sell your "products." How would that apply to a singer's career? What would you advise singers in regard to the marketing aspect of their careers?

I think [marketing is] very important in creating stars that have some sense of recognition in the world beyond the tiny world of opera. Over the last six or seven years, singers have tried harder and harder to get publicity—there are the Rolex ads, and for a while, opera singers had a mink ad. They try to get an article in *Vanity Fair* or some wider publication, or guest on *60 Minutes*. I know that Renée Fleming, for example, has a Hollywood publicist to break into the world of popular culture. She may be our most famous singer these days, and her Hollywood publicist can't get her booked on *The Tonight Show*.

Why not?

They're not interested; they think their public will just not care for an opera singer, or opera singing in general. Twenty-five years ago, Beverly Sills hosted *The Tonight Show* when Johnny Carson went on vacation. Pavarotti and Domingo have also been guests. Then, of course, there was *The Bell Telephone Hour* and every Sunday night you heard famous opera singers on network television. Now even PBS doesn't have that anymore. Pop culture is crowding us out.

What was the Texas Opera Theater?

It was a touring company that went around Texas, Oklahoma, Louisiana, and New Mexico. It presented small productions, just like San Francisco's Western Opera Theater. It started in 1974—but when the economy got terrible here in the mideighties, we lost our support from the Texas state government, and just like in San Francisco, the main company had to subsidize it . . . So I said, "Well, if the communities don't value it enough to support it themselves, then it has to go out of business."

How does a ten-company production work?

We create a budget to build the show: sets, costumes, props, rehearsal, et cetera. Let's say it costs one million dollars; each of us puts in a hundred thousand. We administer it, and it goes from one city to the next, almost like a tour. This season's first world premiere, *Salsipuedes*, was a coproduction between three companies—Arizona, Opera Pacific and Houston—but that was different than our ten-production *Porgy and Bess*, which was a tour. In the case of *Salsipuedes*, Opera Pacific does it in two years, and Arizona in two or three years, so they just take the sets, costumes, and direction, and they can cast it differently. We hire the director or his assistant to re-create the production, but usually with a new cast.

How do you see the future of opera in general?

If the trends continue this way—with the triumph of pop culture, the high ticket prices, difficulty with funding, especially from corporations—I would think that the opera companies would get smaller and smaller; it's like a circle of decline.

So you think it's headed toward extinction?

Well, I think we have to do things that combat that tendency: much better education programs, and lots of outreach programs that reach new people, including nontraditional kinds of people. I think we have to do more over the electronic media. We have to learn to market much better, and use the Internet as a way of communicating with people . . . making arias available on the Internet, and getting people to come to our Web site; create traffic.

You've been heading HGO for thirty-three years; you're a perfect example of devotion and constancy. How does one stay constant to an institution for so long?

By continuing to think of new ways to do things, implementing new ideas and new operas, and bringing in new artists. There are interesting things happening all the time that continue to fire the imagination and the interest.

In 1975, the company's budget was almost $2 million dollars. Thirty years later, it's $21.5 million! What do you say to yourself when you look at these figures?

That's a lot of growth! And most of it has gone into quality.

How do people in Houston regard the opera?

I think we're much better known to the general public than we used to be, but I continue to be dismayed that more people don't know about it, and that they are preoccupied with other things: sports, and their work, and other activities. I mean, this is not an environment that has had generation after generation of culture—they didn't have it in this city—and many people who live here come from surrounding states that are more rural than urban.

You have just been announced as the new general director of the San Francisco Opera, and your tenure begins in January 2006. Did this come as a surprise to you?

It came as a surprise to me when I realized that the position was open, because positions like that are open very seldom, and there it was!

Was I surprised to be chosen? Gosh—I don't know that I was surprised. I was delighted and flattered to be chosen. After so many years in Houston, one could ask the question, "Why do you start out and do something brand new at this stage of your career?" This is a challenge for me; it's a really stimulating step to take at this stage.

Do you have any general plans for San Francisco right now, or is it too early to tell?

Well, right now it's about just trying to figure out how soon my own planning can be feathered into their operation. It seems that the 2007–2008 season is mostly unprogrammed, so we are hurriedly checking out the availability of artists and thinking of overall repertoire. Am I going to continue to program new operas? Yes. Am I going to try to get the world's great singers to San Francisco? Yes. Am I am going to pursue a policy of diverse production style and diverse repertory? Yes!

So you would basically follow the same ideals you had for Houston?

Yeah. Of course, there are more productions in San Francisco and more opportunities to do some of the things that have not been possible here, including a Ring cycle, which Donald Runnicles, the music director, and I have discussed. We want to do this as soon as practicable.

Any words of advice for singers?

The most important thing is to sing well, and to think in terms of having a technique that allows you to sing for thirty to thirty-five years and be healthy. I think looks, acting ability, and intensity and interpretation mean more today than they did thirty years ago, and that people should think in terms of the entire package that they need to develop to be a total performer.

Sheri Greenawald

Recorded January 2007 via phone. Published in Classical Singer, *April 2007.*

How did you decide to become an opera singer?

I grew up in Iowa, in a community of about a hundred people, so the only contact I had with opera was through *The Firestone Hour* and the *Ed Sullivan Show*. But I remember that when I was in third grade and kids were asked what they wanted to be when they grew up, I drew a lady with a large bosom and declared that I wanted to be an opera singer. However, since I was always good at science and math, I was planning to be a doctor as I grew up. But, at sixteen, someone heard me sing at a music camp and that changed my world.

I ended up going to the University of Northern Iowa as a music major, and studied with Charles Matheson. Then Virginia Hutchins came to Iowa as a guest teacher, and after she heard me sing, she took me to New York to sing for Maria de Varady. I met composer Thomas Pasatieri at the same time. After graduation, I moved to New York and lived out of the YWCA studio club for women.

When you were studying, did you face any particular challenges [in] mastering your voice?

I was lucky. I was very precocious musically and had a vibrato when I was five, so I didn't have many vocal challenges. I was also a cheerleader in high school. When you lead the cheers, you learn how to use the breath in similar ways to singing (which is controlled screaming). I credit cheerleading with having given me a sense of how to use my breath. This has been one of my strengths.

As you age, menopause does most female singers in, because the support mechanism weakens; but if you are a master of your breath, it can help prolong your years of singing.

How did you start singing professionally?

I did some things at Hunter and Brooklyn colleges, and at the Manhattan Theatre Club. Then I met Matthew Epstein, who introduced me to the Alden twins, Christopher and David, with whom I played together a lot, and by *playing*, I don't mean just performing. There was also a sense of play in our collaboration, and that is so important for singers—to be playful because this fuels spontaneity and frees up the voice. Then I landed a job with Texas Opera Theater.

So your transition to the professional world went smoothly.

Yes, but there were also challenging moments. At twenty-six, I was ready to go back to med school, but fortunately, I got the job in Texas. Then at twenty-nine, I found a British teacher, Audrey Langford, who saved my life, because she spoke to me about anatomy and physics. It's amazing how other teachers don't go into these important details. So there were always serendipitous moments that kept me going in the beginning, as well as hard work. I remember Matthew Epstein's saying, "I can get you the first job, but you need to get the second one yourself." And then I had success, which kept me going.

Success feeds success, but the beginning is hard. As a singer, you end up putting all your eggs in one basket, and you can't go at it hedging your bets.

As a teacher, when would you advise a singer to stop trying for a professional career?

Well, large voices take longer to develop. If you have a large voice, and if you're still rejected at thirty, you might want to hang in there for a while. But if you're a lyric coloratura and you're still getting rejection in your early thirties, you might want to think about it. The reality is, not many people are going to make it in this profession. Luck does play a part in a certain way. In my case, I met people who introduced me to other people who were helpful to me at the right time. But nothing would have happened if I didn't have something to offer or if I wasn't prepared.

When did you stop singing?

I sang on a professional level until the age of fifty-six. We lyric sopranos have a problem around that age because we can't really go into character roles like mezzos. In my fifties, I also started teaching and doing master classes, and I discovered I enjoy working with young singers.

My parents, who are both science teachers, taught me good deductive skills. I don't flatter singers at all; I work with what they have. One of my favorite sayings is, "You can't make a silk purse out of a sow's ear, but you can make a purse." I believe you can improve anyone's vocalism, but that doesn't mean they'll be a star. There are basic tenets to what makes vocal

cords function. I can make you function vocally.

What characteristics do you look for right away when someone auditions for you?

I look not only for a unique instrument but also whether the singer is a communicative performer. Sometimes the voice is so spectacular that even if the singer is not such a great performer, we'll try to work with him or her to improve that aspect.

It doesn't take a genius to recognize talent. When the Merola board members attend the general director's audition, they instantly recognize the singers who will be stars.

What disturbs you most during an audition?

Very little. It bothers me if I hear an interesting voice that's not being produced correctly, or if [the singers] make musical mistakes but this usually doesn't happen at the level of our auditions. Mostly, I am looking for the positive.

Have you initiated any major changes since you started as director of the San Francisco Opera Center in 2002?

It was fairly easy to come in here when things were set up so well in the first place. One of the things that, unfortunately, I've had to do was cancel the Western Opera Theater tour, which caused a lot of chagrin, including my own. We did the 2002 tour, and I had to cancel the 2003 tour. Nobody is doing touring anymore because it's so expensive!

I completely understand everyone's sorrow over that. I did crazy tours when I was growing up in the business. You learn a lot when you're on tour; it's a real test of your professionalism. I don't think I reinvented any wheels. I try to keep the wheels rolling, but everybody comes with their own subjective opinions about what is important. For instance, now I always bring in a breath specialist, Deborah Birnbaum, because for me, one of the most crucial issues is breath.

How does the Adler Fellowship program work in conjunction with Merola?

We select the Adler recipients from the Merola program.

When do you hold auditions for the Merola?

We start in October and we have about a four-week period of audi-

tions in San Francisco, Chicago, Houston, and New York—four sections
of the country.

How many people get accepted usually?

Every year the formula for Merola has been twenty-three singers.
Starting this year, it will also include five pianists and one stage director.

How long can someone stay in the Merola program?

You can come for two summers. It's an eleven-week training program
in the summertime.

After that, do singers need to audition for the Adler?

No. Being in Merola is like one long audition process for an Adler
Fellowship. That's very advantageous for me, because by the end of
eleven weeks of having seen their work in coachings, master classes, and
onstage, and just being able to socialize with them slightly, I really know
my candidates.

**I understand that the Merola participants also perform in
two full-length operas.**

Yes, I produce two full-length operas, and a semistaged concert for
those I call the wild-card singers: unusual voices that didn't fit in any
particular production but whose talent we still want to explore. Often
that's where the dramatic voices will end up. Then, we have the Merola
Grand Finale, a big semistaged concert at the end of the summer.

What are the Schwabacher Debut Recitals?

James Schwabacher was one of the founding members of Merola and
chairman of the board for many years. He endowed this program. We
do four recitals in the spring. Usually, one of those recitals is by a recent
Merola graduate. There's also one by a Merola graduate who's out in the
world performing. A current Adler will also get one, and recently, we've
presented Steven Blier with the New York Festival of Song in one of his
recitals, and the Adlers are his singers.

**What is a typical day like for you with so many
responsibilities?**

I do a lot of work online everyday. Then I work with the Adlers on a
given day. I have to be coordinating productions, hiring conductors and
stage directors, looking for designers—my producing responsibilities are
very much a part of my day. I attend Merola board meetings.

Do you work with the Adlers vocally, too?

If they choose to. I offer feedback when they coach, for example, asking,
"Are you coming across the way you think you're coming across? Here's
what I see; is that what you meant?" We're a pretty tight-knit group. My

job is to tell them if something needs improvement.

How do you find working with David Gockley?

I've known David since I was twenty-five. I was in his troupe in the second year of what was then known as the Texas Opera Theater. I like to think David was a champion of mine. He hired me a lot at Houston Grand Opera. I knew his family and his children. So he is not a mystery to me, nor am I to him, I'm sure! I love Pamela Rosenberg as well and I have tremendous respect for her.

You've lived in Europe for eleven years. What would you say distinguishes American singers from European singers in how they present themselves professionally as a result of their training?

The argument I always heard in Europe was that Americans always came extremely well prepared and were technically proficient. The biggest complaint about Americans was that they didn't have an individual sound. I think the reason we're technically prepared is that Americans are into efficiency as a rule, sometimes to the detriment of life experiences. Efficiency is drummed into us from college on: you have to be a good musician. It's literally part of an American contract that states you must arrive at your job knowing your role. It's how we approach our work, which I think is very admirable.

Having worked in Europe, there were times when I was thinking [of European singers], "Why don't you know your part already?"

The idea of efficiency also fuels my whole theory about vocal technique. A voice teacher needs to make the voice function efficiently, meaning healthily. Then whatever sound comes out is that person's individual sound. I don't believe in *making* a sound; I believe in helping singers produce their sound as efficiently and effortlessly as possible. Of course, singers end up making a sound, but hopefully, it's *their* sound.

Everyone comes with their own baggage so I don't have a particular formula when I teach voice.

With your intensely busy schedule, do you have any time to teach privately?

Oh, yes, I do! I really enjoy it. One of the great things about my position here in Merola, and particularly in the Adler program, is that I've been able to watch a lot of other people teach voice, like Robert Lloyd, Jane Eaglen, Dolora Zajick, Tracy Dahl, Tom Allen, and Håkan Hagegård. I have friends who teach, and we talk about technique constantly.

Some teachers start to guard what they think are their secrets. Well, it's not about the teacher. It can't be about *your* secrets; it has to be about what's going to work for the singer. Certain words and imagery work for some and not for others. You just have to keep trying. It's scientific in that way, you have to keep applying yourself until you find the solution in unlocking the concepts for each singer.

What I first say to any private student that comes to me is, "I want you to tape this, and when you listen to it, if you like what you hear, then call, and we'll see each other again. If you don't like what you hear, you don't have to come back." The singer is the client; it's not about me. That also applies to singers who start to think that it's about the teacher. It has to be about empowering the singers to deal with their own demons in singing, and giving them the tools to understand what they're doing. That's why I think talking anatomy is so important.

One of the most fascinating things I did was when I invited a physicist/horn player from the University of California at San Jose to explain resonance to my kids. We worked with spectrographs, and the way he talked about sound demystified so much! For instance, he said that *pitch* is a subjective word, not a scientific word. *Frequency* is the word that physicists use. His semantics really pulled back a lot of curtains! It enlightened me so much that it even changed the way I talk about sound, because I understand it in a much more objective way.

What are your thoughts on today's emphasis on the visual and the importance of looks onstage?

Let's face it, it seems that people in America are just completely obsessed with the visual! There is no way to say to a singer that it doesn't matter. If you're a lyric soprano—which is the biggest pool of singers in the world—you can't be overweight anymore. When you're a lyric soprano, which I was, there's always someone with another beautiful voice standing next to you. Some people [have on their] album covers, "The most beautiful voice in the world!" Yeah, yeah, yeah. I can't stand it. It's like, come on! Who are you kidding? By whose standards, yours or mine? That's just hype!

You have to have a particular package if you're in that voice type. Now the truly dramatic voices are few and far between. With those voices, you can just barely get away with being heavy now. Even within that voice category, I constantly encourage girls to keep the weight down; if for no other reason but health. You can be severely heavy up until you're about forty, after that it will become increasingly difficult to support.

Since you're so aware of the scientific and functional aspects

of singing, when you were performing, how did you maintain a balance between that and the emotional aspect? When you were onstage, did you let go of the technical side completely?

No, you never can. You have to work out the technical issues for yourself before the first rehearsal. During rehearsals, you've got the time to make the role yours, but you never let go of technique. One thing that made me different from other people was that I never marked in rehearsals. The one time I did, I had bad performances because I didn't "sing the role in." It's important to sing the role in, particularly when you get busy and you're jumping from job to job. If I was singing *Traviata*, I'd mark the high notes once in a while, but mostly I tried to sing them in rehearsal. When I did Violetta for the first time in Opera Theatre Saint Louis, every time I was in a staging for the aria, I sang it.

Some singers mark because they want to save their voices.

But I don't know what you're saving if you have a basically sound technique, and as long as you give the cords time to rest, and you drink a lot of water. If your technique is poor, then you'll be in trouble. I mean, would you expect a runner to half-run his practice races? Would you expect a sprinter not to sprint, and then suddenly on the day of the race, sprint and win?

How did you approach a complex role like Violetta, from an acting point of view?

I read the novel and the novel-based play that Dumas *fils*, himself, had written and which Verdi actually saw. If you compare the play to the libretto, it's almost a direct translation. I watched Garbo playing the role and then I just went to the score. I would coach the role and I would always want to shy away from those crazy accents, so my coach would constantly say, "Go to them, because they're indicating her illness." Those accents can be her suppressing a cough. The little details that you can find in a score are so important! If you do what's in the score, kids, you've got your characterization; you don't even have to think!

Any words of advice for singers?

Objectify, objectify, objectify! The more you can learn to be objective in this business, the easier it will be for you. If you aren't having luck in auditions but you're really convinced that you have something special, then objectify: What is going wrong in that audition? Is it that my technique is not good? Am I with the right teacher?

I had five different teachers in my career. Leaving one's teacher is very emotional and complicated, but it's your vocal cords and it's your life!

Thomas Hampson

Recorded June 2003 in Vienna, Austria. Published in Classical Singer,
October 2003.

What did you want to be when you were a kid?

Well fed! . . . Well, I don't remember those childhood ambitions. I was
raised in the tricities in Washington State, in a very fundamentalist Protestant religion, the Seventh Day Adventists, which, like most Protestant
denominations, have a fantastic commitment to music. I always sang but
had absolutely no idea about being a professional musician. Thinking of
what I wanted to do, humanities played a large role in my decision.

**What drew you to study government and politics, and how does
the knowledge you acquired serve you in your artistic career?**

I chose political science mainly because it was a way to coalesce all
the various interests I had, such as: literature, history, politics. I met my
voice teacher during this program at Washington University, in Spokane:
Sister Marietta Cole. She was a nun with a wonderful singing voice. She
opened a whole new world of poetry and music to me, when she gave
me a stack of records with Fischer-Dieskau, Hermann Prey, and Tom
Krause. From that moment on, my political science studies started to take
a more humanistic direction. I shifted my focus from prelaw to government, with the emphasis on public administration, and started a BFA at
Fort Wright College. I was still not thinking of a musical career, but I said
to myself, "Well, if music is going to be important, I could remain in the
musical world, running an orchestra or a festival." . . . Of course, everything I learned has helped me. I feel that, as a singer, you need to know
as many things as possible. If you haven't read history, you'll have a hard
time with psychology, and perspective, so what are you going to bring to a
role? How does Onegin think or walk? What about Don Giovanni? What
is a Byronic character, and why do we use that as a euphemism of the
nineteenth century troubled characters? What is the difference between

Classical and Romantic? If we don't know that as a singing community, as a musical community, then we will be the victims of outside influences. People come to the operatic world with no musical culture whatsoever, but yet with a great theatrical dramatic background, and therefore, opera becomes this sort of theater inside a musical frame; that's just nonsense! Most importantly, I think singers must incorporate and re-create human beings. That means: their psyche, their religion, their spirituality, their thoughts, their emotions, and their intellect. That was how my educational background, steeped in literature and history, has amalgamated into a bigger picture for me.

When did you finally decide to devote yourself to singing?

Well, in 1978 I went to the Music Academy of the West. There, among other singers my age, I realized that what distinguished me was my innate commitment to poetry and songs. I considered that a fundamental part of singing . . . I think it is important for everyone to find their intrinsic distinguishing characteristic or perspective. It's not about talent . . . To me, talent is something that has been galvanized. There are a lot of gifted people who are never awakened to their own talent. If I can come out of these various middle-America experiences, out of a world completely divorced from opera, and go through the discipline and metallurgy of this work, then anybody can . . . Anyway, then it became clear to me that I needed to move out of Washington State. So, I worked different jobs: did landscape work, sold advertising for the Spokane Symphony, waited tables as a singing waiter in a German restaurant! You know, whatever you have to do, you do! It was a great tough time! I was already married and we moved to California. I am very grateful to USC for their policy: if you had any degree, you could enroll and pay fees for graduate classes. I did not want to be in the music program because I couldn't afford it, and I just wanted to study song with Gwendolyn Kodolfsky and opera theater with Franz Burlage.

Then in 1980, you were taken into the San Francisco Merola program.

Yes. Back then, if you won their regional and state competitions, you were selected to come up for the summer for a ten-week semiprofessional program. At the end, your work was measured, prizes were given and some participants were invited to go into what was the touring Western Opera Theater group. I got a nice mention but was not invited to stay. In 1980 I also won a bunch of competitions. I had met Elisabeth Schwarzkopf and she asked me if I would come to Europe. The main judge from the

Zachary competition—where I had placed second—was an agent who offered to help me, if I [went] to Germany. So, I decided to leave the U.S. The decision had somehow been made for me, and this is something I tell all singers: for talented and dedicated people, things get put together, especially if you are awakened to your possibilities. Never put all your eggs in one basket, neither emotionally nor career-wise. And one more thing: no disaster is ever the last disaster! The good side of that is: they can only

DARIO ACOSTA

be disasters if you put something really terrific together. What I mean by *disasters* is, when things fall apart. That can only happen if you work on a project or a goal. That's why I don't think you should be terribly preoccupied with the negative things that happen, because it's not how often you fall, it's how often you get up. Not being invited to stay in the Merola program was a mini-disaster. I have always been very suspect to my own abilities. I didn't have the kind of voice that when I sang, everybody went, "Oh, my God!" I was a good singer, able to do things at an early age, but I was not a vocal wonder. I'm still not a vocal wonder, I was never vocally driven; it was more about the completeness of singing. In the early days of my career, I felt frustrated to get up the ladder and get things going. The big moments in my life came because I was prepared, but they also just kind of came.

Tell me about going to Germany.

Well, I sang two auditions there, got a job in Düsseldorf, and that's where I started. Actually, I had always wanted to go to Europe, to the tradition, to the country that had this huge system for singers, and find out whether this was really a life I wanted to lead. The idea of getting on staff as a young opera singer made a lot of sense to me. I always had a particular affinity for the German language, and the poetry. Everything kept sending me in that direction. The Düsseldorf experience was very important, and those who supported me agreed.

Speaking of supporters and advisors, how important is it to listen to others' advice and opinions as opposed to following

your own instincts, which are sometimes more accurate? How do you find that balance between listening outside of yourself and paying attention to your inner voice?

Well, that conundrum is part of one's life. My life has been dominated by concentrating on singing as well as I could, and that included my brain, my health, my languages, my experiences, my teachers and coaches. Yes, I walked away from some very famous coaches because I didn't feel what they said was right for me. Now that I am older, I get respected for it, but it is pretty tough to be instinctually stubborn at the age of twenty-eight or thirty-one. In fact, it can have some very bad consequences. Sometimes things went terribly wrong because I didn't follow opinions or advice. On the other hand, when they went well, it was because people admired that quality. Lenny [Bernstein], Jean-Pierre Ponnelle, Jimmy Levine, Nikolaus Harnoncourt, as well as others appreciated this seriousness and commitment. I think that as a young singer, you have to be very protective of a very personal communication with yourself. It is very easy to get distracted by outside influences, by all the things that need to get done, and you can forget the meditative center of your life, which is not some sort of bamboo-waving obsolete place divorced from life. I see it more like the inside of a volcano, the hot burning core in all of us, out of which this or that can happen. Instincts are terrific, but on the other hand, instincts that are enlightened become talent! I do not believe that there is a path or a set of answers that guarantee even a shot at it. I do know a few things that are nonnegotiable: if you are going to have a career, you must sing well and have this built-in notion, "Don't do this now, because it will shorten your career." What I find is very tricky for young singers today, is that most of the world is driven by usefulness and speed. Quick learn, pretty voice, good figure for both, men and women . . .

So, you are saying career building today can be superficially motivated . . .

Exactly. This is probably the most dangerous cancer coming to the business of music, and eating away at the substance of singing. The substance of singing is not driven by our sense of career. It is driven by our sense of beauty. I love to work with my younger colleagues, especially over a few days, and create this wonderful warm, cozy, but disciplined atmosphere where singers can step back from those career pressures and just concentrate on, "Is that really what you meant to sing?" I don't care if it's a Goethe poem or an opera libretto. It can be Rosina or Mignon's Lieder. Why were they written? That has got nothing to do with me, the singer.

We are vessels in which our talent is to recreate; we are the doorway for everybody's imagination.

In master classes, sometimes you ask singers, "How many ribs do you have?"

Which is a very silly question; everyone thinks it's funny . . . I find it absurd that pianists, and even those who can't play the piano very well, know that there are eighty-eight keys on it. So, why wouldn't you know your own body, especially as a singer? It is important. To sing well, you must know how your body works.

Let's talk about your teachers and mentors and how they influenced you, most significantly: Horst Günther, Elisabeth Schwarzkopf, and Leonard Bernstein . . .

I met Horst Günther in 1980 when I came to California. He was the visiting professor of voice at USC, a lyric baritone, so it was a good idea to study with him. I had never studied with a man before, other than Martial Singher. Singher was a brilliant performer, a wonderful pedagogue. He had controversial ideas and was a difficult personality, but the older I get, the more devoted I am to him. I think his ideas would get more credit today. He lived in a time when the big, open-throated singing was in. His was a much more vibrating, centered tone that did not concentrate on huge amplitude, but on the idea and emotion. I only worked with him in the summers, not privately, and he was a very important influence in my life. At the same time, I started working with Horst Günther. He helped me synthesize all this theoretical knowledge, all of those wonderful things, and, yes, how many ribs? . . .

Twelve on each side!

Very good! There goes my million-dollar question! . . . When you are onstage, you don't have time to think about the lifting of that and the separating of that. Probably the most fundamental thing that Horst taught me is: when we are singing, and making those decisions to deal with whatever status or ability we are in that night, we base those decisions more on a world of feeling than a world of sound. Singers listen to themselves too much. I think we sing infinitely more by radar than by sonar. That is fundamentally linked to your perspective of resonance, and therefore, your perspective of breath control. One of the valid and important paradigms of the old school, that we have wandered away from a little bit, is that legato is a function of resonance and not of breath control. If you don't hear what you are going to sing, before you sing it, it won't be what you want. What you hear and what you know you need to do to re-create that sound, has to become automatic. It's your professional key, which is also your sense of beauty, your sense of thought, of recreation; it is the reason why you are singing in that particular moment. If you are preoccupied with the state of singing because *you* are singing, I think you are on the wrong track. So, Günther, gave me my professional feet. I was not singing the Barber's aria when I auditioned for him, but once we cracked that nut, the Barber became a big deal for me. The first time I ever sang Figaro's aria publicly, I was sweating bullets, absolutely scared out of my mind. I was not thinking about any internal reasons for the Barber of Seville! I was thinking about one thing and one thing only: "Do not crack, do not splat, do not die! Get through it!" This aria then got me through the regional finals of the Merola program, and I won . . . I also had this wonderful coach in California: Jack Metz. He was a natural force to be reckoned with; Leona Mitchell's vocal guru. I worked with him for two years, at the same time I was working with Horst, and the two approaches were not always compatible. But Jack was a fantastic coach who understood sound and the release of voice. Jackie [Marilyn] Horne had worked with him, so did Anna Moffo, and Maria Chiara . . . he was one of the great old coaches! He handed me the aria "Mein Sehnen, mein Wähnen" from *Die tote Stadt*. I loved it immediately because it allowed me to show the kind of singer I was. I was the first to sing this aria in auditions, and now it has become a staple of the lyric baritone repertoire. It was as much the singing of this aria that won me the Metropolitan position later on as anything else.

When you started singing, was it evident that you were a baritone?

Well . . . Even though my voice was never terribly powerful, there has always been this sort of burnished, inner darker quality to it. People couldn't decide if I was a dramatic tenor or a bass-baritone. Horst settled those issues for me, you know, are you a tenor or a baritone? The upper baritone, the lyric baritone that they all so loved in the nineteenth century, is very much more the first cousin of the tenor than an extension of the bass-baritone. A lot of people try to push lower voices up, and it never really works, because the point is not to be loud or dramatic. The point is, in the upper middle range of the baritone voice, to have the elasticity that can manifest itself into expression that is either angry or loving, doleful or euphoric. The building of that voice was essentially bringing the tenor down and saying, "Okay, you don't have to worry about the As and B-flats, but you better give me one hell of an F-sharp, and every palette of human emotion in that upper baritone range, from B-flat to F-sharp or

G. What I got from Horst was the use of the voice, getting rid of the baggage, and understanding that when you sing a high note, you don't need to prove to everybody that you've got all the low notes below it. He gave me the confidence to trust that feeling. He is now the resident professor of voice for the Zurich Opera Theater. He's still got very good ears. The world of opera has become something that isn't part of his tradition and it's very hard for him sometimes to see and hear the kind of misuse of the voice that happens today, but he remains deeply committed to good singing. What is wonderful is to see these kids, when they are twenty or twenty-one, working with a ninety-year-old guy who had a forty-five-year career, and saying, "He's right, it's easy, it's terrific!" These young singers are having their own awakening, even a bit of a revolution in their minds. They realize, "We work too much at it, we need to sing more!" . . . I also had Elisabeth Schwarzkopf's advice. She was one of the most charming, innovative, and alive partners you could possibly find, to help you discover the truth of what you are trying to sing.

So, what happened after Düsseldorf?

I went to Zurich, and became part of the ensemble, singing twenty-five nights of a specific repertoire. I was paid on a thirteen-month basis, which gave me a certain financial flexibility and a lot more time to guest. Zurich was a monumental change in my life. Düsseldorf had been a great starting point but I knew I couldn't stay there. Nevertheless, I had a great time in Düsseldorf; it was a wonderful learning experience.

How did your Met debut come about?

In the summer of 1985, I sang for Jimmy Levine in Salzburg. My debut at the Met was then planned for 1988 as Schaunard. In 1986, as Ponnelle was to revise *Le nozze di Figaro*, the Met was suddenly left without a Count. I had just worked with Ponnelle, I knew the role, Levine liked me, so, all of a sudden, in the middle of a cast that was: José Van Dam, Kathleen Battle at the top of her form, Elisabeth Söderstrom, making her last appearances at the Met, they hire this young unknown lyric baritone! It was a huge moment of trust that Jimmy Levine gave me, and which did define my career at the Metropolitan, as well as my American presence. Just like there are very few violinists who didn't have Isaac Stern's help, very few great American singers have not been guided and helped by Jimmy Levine in the last thirty years.

How did you then come into contact with Leonard Bernstein?

Well, at the time of my surprise Met debut, Leonard Bernstein was doing auditions and Matthew Epstein was helping him put together an

American cast of *La bohème* to take to Santa Cecilia in Rome. Bernstein had heard about me through his manager, Harry Kraut . . . You know, my motto has always been, "Fortune favors the prepared mind!" Everything spins from something else. There is always some connection. What is the constant? Sing as well as you can. Get close to who it is you need to go to the next level. Most of it is somebody showing you what the next level inside of you is. There is nobody you can hire to tell you how to sing. There are people you can get coaching and information from, and all of this releases and unlocks the secrets of you to yourself. But how you put that together for yourself as a singer is your own personal map. You must sing well . . . because somewhere, someone hears something you do and then says something to someone else! That is part of the artist's life, part of public life, and it needs to be held in deep respect. I don't mean a paranoia—[an] oh, what-do-they-say-about-me kind of thing—no, rather the permanent awareness of your responsibility to singing. But anyway . . . so I sang for Lenny, and my fifteen-minute audition turned into an hour and twenty minutes! Then I worked with him, and for two years, I was part of his inner singing circle. He solved a lot of issues about intellectual activity, which is very necessary. The discipline is iron-clad, and the thought process as clear as can be. Do not leave any stone unturned, do not leave any thought process out, but when you're going to make music, make music! Do it! Give yourself up!

I think it is always difficult to find the balance between the intellect and the instinctual, emotional side. Sometimes too much analysis and intellectual activity hinders the freedom of the voice, of the artistic act. How do you maintain this equilibrium?

√ That was what Lenny did for me! He was exactly that perfect equilibrium between the intellect and instinct. I mean, to see Leonard Bernstein come out and start a piece of music with that phenomenal intellect, and knowledge, and yet make it all about soul and guts and heart, about the human being, was unbelievable! But Lenny would not have been the kind of soul-and-guts-and-heart person that he was, had he not had his intense intellectual life. I don't think some people are only about soul and guts and heart, and other people are heads and brains! We are all the same, and one side of us informs the other. I believe that my soul and guts and heart have been taught by my brain and my ears and my head, and, more importantly, vice versa. That amazing amalgamation of heart and mind was Lenny! The other person who is like that for me is Nikolaus Harnoncourt. Bernstein and Harnoncourt both had phenomenal respect for one another. Bernstein told me I could learn a lot from Harnoncourt. He said, "Be sure and ask [Harnoncourt] the right way to get from the recitative into the musical part. This is a huge problem with Mozart." I can't think of a more substantially differing approach among conductors, than when it comes to performing Mozart operas. It is tied to the dramaturgical context of tempo markings. Andante is not some decision to be made on the evening, it belongs to a decision that takes into consideration: "Well, if this is andante, then what is allegro?" There is a structure to that, and I think it is one of the most phenomenal truths to Mozart's dramaturgy, especially in the later operas.

You've referred to Mozart's music as very theatrical.

Hugely theatrical! It's there for us to understand, it's not for us to create! It's fantastic! It's about people. I have now taught so many soprano arias from *Idomeneo* to *Così*. Fiordiligi is a wonderfully complex young woman. It's not about the aria, or about a Mozart style. It's interesting that composers, even today, don't really talk about styles, they talk about recreating people and personalities. You cannot show me a letter—from the greatest opera composers—that mentions timbres of voices. Rather, they talk about singers understanding the recreation of psychologies. If it is not about why you are singing, then I don't care how you sing. I am not interested in voice production. It only really makes me excited, when it's emotionally connected! One of the most phenomenal things I've ever heard in my life is this pirate recording of Leonard Warren at the age of twenty-nine in Town Hall, singing "Cortigiani" for the first time with all that young enthusiasm.

Speaking of pirate recordings, what do you think about them?

I think it's wrong. I don't believe in stealing music, but I believe there are two sides to it. Records are just too expensive. The monopolizing control of the big record companies has created this problem, and in some ways, alternative methods, such as piracy, are a revolt to that. There are many Web sites from which you can legally download music. Right now, there is a huge development happening on my Web site: www.hamp-song.com. I am also making a foundation for song, and hope to offer a lot of information on new technology as well as singing in general, especially in the world of song.

You enjoy teaching very much, and call it a "sharing of knowledge." You don't refer to those who participate in your master classes as your students, but rather as your "younger colleagues." How has teaching enriched you?

You know, I sing like a bird for the first ten days after a class. There is something so purely positive about trying to articulate what you think about. You also remember the fundamentals. So much with young singers is getting them to settle down, stand up straight, let their body be their body, hear what they're going to sing, think—that's always an issue! Think it, hear it, breathe into it, and then sing. But so much of singing today is concentrating on the idea of air becoming some sort of power source to vibrate the cords to make sound for somebody else's purpose. I think that's a negative way to look at it. It's sad that my activities as a human being focus on propelling something into a public forum for which I will then be measured and approved or rejected. That will destroy your nerves. It has to be an internal process about you becoming the singing entity. People come to hear you be what it is that you're going to be, you do not go out onstage to convince them of what you know. *Projection* is probably the most vulgar word I know in singing! To project a personality is obscene. To project a voice is acoustically and physically impossible! It is also wrong to try. You can project a broomstick, a bullet or a paper airplane, but a voice resonates. Take the word for what it means: *re-sonate*. It re-sounds. So what is sounding in the first place? If we are concentrating on resounding, what is it that is sounding?

Well, you can imagine it is already there . . . the sound, the music . . .

It is already there! Exactly. And we are the ones who call it into being. Our voices however are much more about how we are built. I love to work technically, especially with singers who are having crises: young, old, whatever.

But you don't teach privately.

No, because I think there should be consistency, and I can't offer that. I'm here today, in Zurich tomorrow . . . I like to have four-, five-day symposiums where I can get about ten singers. Everyone sings every day. We develop our own language in the first couple of days, I talk a lot, and then we let the pony run. Unfortunately, I see that fundamentally good singing, and technically based singing is becoming less and less a priority. I am dead set against this idea of concert singer versus opera singer; it is bullshit! It would be such an abrogation for the opera singer not to sing lieder in concert! The same goes for a concert singer who doesn't even look at opera roles. The problem is that concert singers have a hard time getting into the opera world. But on the other hand, people who are active operatically seldom bother to sing recitals. There are plenty of places to sing concerts, if you are willing to go out there. In the year I made my Met debut, I did a recital tour, and if I got from zero to zero between the costs and the income, I was happy, I considered it a success. We need to support the whole recital experience. What Marilyn Horne is doing with her foundation is fantastic. The arts and the humanities are the blueprint of our existence, the diary of how we have been as human beings from time eternal to time eternal. If we don't know what has been before us, how can we possibly know the fantastic possibilities of the future? I think it is also important to know who your God is, whatever that may become for you. The spiritual goal is a very personal decision. It is where you live, it's the "om" of you. The path to enrich that inner core, however, is a wonderful dialogue of various influences. That human recognition of being a human, and believing, searching for a spiritual "why am I here?" answer is enlightened through the arts and humanities. That is why they are not divorced from religion. That is why I sing Don Giovanni. Giovanni is a nasty piece of work, but there are few greater places to confront the dark side of your soul than this character. It's about power and sex, society, nature, and God. The problem with a modern production can be that you walk around in your own clothes, and it takes the story out of its social context. To simply come in and drape something on top of it in order to make it something it isn't, works very little in operas that are so specific about social context, like the Mozart operas. That is what really fascinates me . . . concept-driven opera is very seldom successful . . . it is sometimes box-office successful, but only for one or two seasons, and then, who cares? That is why you can have some of these rather monolithic forty-year-old productions with dusty furniture, because it's not about that. What you want on that evening is: What is that person singing to me? What intellectual emotional experience as a human being am I being conveyed through the music? To me, that is the genius and the miracle of opera.

What was the hardest part of your voice to master, and why?

Well, there wasn't one part specifically . . . Certainly, keeping the upper "zing" in the middle part of my voice so that it carried, and doing that without pressing or grabbing in the throat, has always been a challenge. I have always preferred to err on the side of, "Don't grab, don't push, don't yell," and as a result be more lyrical than I perhaps wanted to be. I had to limit my repertoire at certain times, because I simply couldn't maintain the kind of resonance and constancy of sound, so I was patient. Whatever problems you have, you must be patient. There is no person, program, or étude that you can do today that will fix it tomorrow. Vocally, it is always linked to a more complex physical structure of you as a human being. You have to find out: what you can't do with one part of your body or your brain, has little to do with that particular part. Most troubles of the high voice come because you don't know how to sing the middle voice. Schwarzkopf told me very early on, "Take care of your middle voice, and it will take care of your high voice." You're not going to find high ringing notes by singing high ringing notes. You are not going to find low, relaxed, and vibrating notes by singing only them. Do you know what I mean?

Yes. You are not going to "find" anything by creating an inner idea of it and aiming for it specifically, separating low and high from one another, for example . . .

Exactly! Low and high are not separated from each other! It is always a cause-and-effect relationship. You must be patient, disciplined, and organized. My own little definition of discipline is not that sort of, "Oh, my God, I have to strap myself in and beat myself!" No. Discipline is the ordering of the random. In singing, there is absolutely nothing that is random! Only through this discipline can you actually be in a place where you could be spontaneous. Spontaneity is not randomness, and vice versa. A lot of people think that coming out with this emotional, big-heart, "Aaaah, here I am!" means some sort of spontaneous emotional experience. "Oh, my God, wasn't it moving? She started to cry, singing 'Vissi d'arte!'" No! That is masturbation! Nothing else but!

What is the first thing you do when you feel a cold coming on?

Well, first of all, make sure that you recognize the symptoms early! There is probably no product in the last years that has caught more people's attention, and rightfully so, like this Zicam. It is a gel you put in your nose very early on, it sinks right back through the nasal pharynx, and it has zinc and B_{12}, which will fight an infection on the spot. It's terrific. The chicken-soup-go-to-bed-shut-up rule is always a good idea. It is the hardest one, because it means pulling yourself off the conveyor belt for a while. Sleep is without question the singer's best friend. Most of us have problems with sleep. I have problems sleeping; I get my big energy in the evenings. My most important thing is to sleep after a performance. Don't get up too early. Sleeping long the day of a performance doesn't do me too much good. In fact, speaking and taking care of things are probably better to get me awake and energized. Sleep off the performance! The question of a career and of theatrical energy is not about how many volts you can get going. It's, how deep is the reaction after the volts you applied? Long-distance runners are not concerned about speed, they are concerned about the valleys and peaks of their energy—stamina, endurance—and that's the same with singing. It is more athletic than people think. That has as much to do with cold remedies as anything . . . Menthol of any type, in any form is dangerous. That means, any cough drop that has menthol or eucalyptus in it. Bad news! What does it do and why does it feel so good? It dries the membranes, so if you are horribly sick, menthol can give some relief to all those swollen tissues. For that purpose at that time, you're gonna be fine, because there is so much fluid involved that it's okay. But otherwise, avoid it. As a rule, you are much better off with liquid and sleep! These little black currant tablets of glycerin are great; so is honey, and horehound, which is one of the old herbs starting to make a comeback in alternative medicine. A singer should be well versed in alternative medicine: homeopathic remedies, vitamin therapy, aroma therapy, massages . . . you know, all these things that ignite and enrich that physical, alive feeling . . .

What about exercise?

It's number one! Movement, air, exercise plus a good diet. Thin[ness] is actually not the goal of losing weight! It is a question of fitness. A sumo wrestler is an obese person by physical visual standards, but you'd be hard put to be healthier than those guys! We could learn a lot from the fitness and diet gurus—the good ones, because there are so many out there in this billion-dollar diet business. But it's not whether you eat more protein than carbohydrates, or whether your fat levels are this or that. It is always a question of balance and sanity. It is also very personal, linked to your own metabolism. This means that the diet gurus who actually want to know about your blood are probably the most serious and helpful. As for exercise, there is probably no better physical discipline to know about today than Pilates and yoga. But a lot of people think yoga is about finding that calm, nonengaged center somewhere in there. The most interesting aspect about the calm center of a singer is that it is a volcano. It is a burning, engaged core, which ignites when you want it to ignite for the purpose you choose.

Some yoga teachers actually refer to stillness as not being still. It is similar to a wheel that spins so fast that it looks still, yet the energy there is incredibly intense.

Yes, that also involves vibration and resonance. It's like a gyroscope, exactly! Well, we are talking about natural laws of nature. It is all so incredibly connected, it's fantastic! So, exercise, jogging, anything that heats up the muscles to get them awake and the blood pressure going is important. I tend to low blood pressure, so I need to run. I will go out and run a little bit this afternoon, just to get going.

So, you do run before a performance?

Oh, sure. But not a lot. Just jogging.

Have you sung any roles that were hard to recover from psychologically and/or emotionally?

A lot of them. That's also a question of, "Do I know where home is, so that when I become Hamlet, I can go back home? Do I know where my sense of truth is, so that when I go to the very edge of that with Don Giovanni, I can recover it?" I am inevitably in a bad mood after Don Giovanni. I need time to blow it off. And I am not trying to give [an] oh-the-troubled-artist kind [of] image. We let a lot of big-time stuff inhabit us. After a big lieder concert of any repertoire, you are exhausted, you've emptied yourself. *Onegin* is a very tough evening. If I've done the role well, there is just an overriding sinking feeling in the pit of my stomach about *Onegin*, because it is such a phenomenal potential lost—as a human being, as a love story, as a society. The novel has as much to do with the bigger social paradigm, as it does with the specific story. The age of the nineteenth century was the waking of the feminine. The feminine was always the new life, a positive energy that could temper the mundane and the banal of the male leading to so much destruction. That was why Mozart was so unbelievably ahead of his time. All of the protagonists in his operas that carry the essence of humanity are women. Most of the men are fodder! In the *Don Giovanni* story, the women become the true protagonists . . . Some of the roles I do are ungrateful anyway—the baritone roles!—because people want to clap for the good guys and be indifferent to the bad ones or the idiots! But there are also roles that have a profound influence on me, like Simon Boccanegra. This is a very beautiful human being! Posa is a wonderful guy. But he is ambiguous. With Posa, you have to ask yourself, "What is the difference between zealous behavior and being a zealot?"

You mean, how much does he actually believe in his own behavior?

Right. Is he just a fundamentalist or is he a revolutionary?

As the audience, you are never really sure of what he is after.

Yeah. Though, I don't think he's duplicitous or dishonest or after an ulterior agenda. We know how far he'll go, and that's what so beautiful about his story. When he sacrifices, he knows what he has to do.

You referred to the French *Don Carlo* version as conveying more of Posa's ambiguity than the Italian . . .

Well, there is a difference between, "Don't forget me" and "Remember me." That is also one difference between the Italian and the French versions. In French, he says, "Remember me"—"Souviens-toi"; and in Italian, it's, "Non mi scordar." I prefer the idea of "Remember me." This goes back to the fantastic ambiguity of Schiller's novel. The theatrical tool is that every scene transforms itself into the next, and nobody ever leaves a scene in the drama the same person they were. It is actually a very modern technique. The popular writers today use that. People didn't write like that before Schiller; it was more dramatically episodic. Well, Shakespeare is perhaps the exception to that. So when I say *ambiguity*, I refer to something that also contains its opposite. That is crucial for singing, too. For every matter, there is antimatter; for every effort, there is noneffort . . . Schiller was a master at that; he illuminated the world of ambiguity and compromise, as well as the other natural rule that in the absence of activity, there is activity. Something is going to happen. The question is, are you determining it or not? Also, as wonderful as the Italian version is, Verdi set every word of *Don Carlo* to French, except for a little fragment in the middle . . . The musical structure of Posa is very interesting. He sings everybody else's music, and he sings the language that he could be understood in by every character. He is a great diplomat. Don Giovanni also has no music of his own. The only particular endemic music to Giovanni is an ascending fourth. This fourth comes in Mozart's music for baritone characters, especially when they are trying to be seducing, because the fourth is a perfect interval, isn't it? It is also interesting that when the Count seduces the Contessa wrongly, he sings this ascending fourth upside down . . . Isn't that great? I don't think these things are by accident. But, Giovanni speaks also in different languages to Elvira, to Zerlina, and especially to Donna Anna and Don Ottavio, since their language is also musically different. When they come back in the sextet, you have these thirds and sixths in the music . . . they are not by accident. Unless you take these kinds of quick examples seriously, then the characters won't find their center of musical gravity for you. You can set it in modern times, put them on motorcycles or on a bus, but you are still stuck with thirds and sixths. It is the essence that counts, not the so-called interpretation . . .

You referred to Gérard Souzay's statement that, "Interpretation is for people who don't get it in the first place." What do you think he meant by that?

Isn't that a wonderful quote? I think he is just warning people against overintellectualization, and thinking that the essence of a musical moment is to be found through bone-picking analysis. If we look at the word *style* as a very healthy representation of a body of experience after its composition, then that's okay. But to define what the composition is, because of a notion of style, is somehow incomplete. Style is a past-tense experience, a label. What is a Schumann style, what is a Schubert style, and where do they coalesce? We are trying to order things to understand them better. Okay, that's fine. But is that what "Im wunderschönen Monat Mai" is all about? No. Most of the question of style in music is: when we use the word *style*, we inevitably refer to the composer. This is, especially in the lieder repertoire, a fundamentally wrong perception of the use of word and tone. There are some wonderful people, such as Susan Youens, writing on this subject. She gives me the feeling that everything she is analyzing is only to understand better what the real message is. And that message will change in various performances. So, I think what Gérard Souzay was saying is, "If you can't, either as public or artist, allow yourself to dance the dance, to realize the moment, then probably reading about it or studying it isn't going to help you a lot." The musical artistic experience is in that moment in which it happens. As long as we know anything about humans—whether they were carving on rocks or flying around billions of light-years away in *Star Trek*—whatever we project into the future, whatever we read about the past, we know one thing: Humans communicate with one another. We tell stories and jokes, we sing to one another. We are always trying to ignite each other in an emotional, intellectual activity. I think Souzay was right. What he said is a wonderful idea and not a polemic. Quotes like that sometimes give the feeling that someone is wagging a finger. It's not about that. Besides, if you try to teach by wagging a finger, you won't get very far. Teaching is simply the sharing of knowledge and it should be taken as such. Afterward, what you do with this knowledge and information is your personal responsibility.

Catherine Heiser

Recorded January 2005 in New York City, USA. Published in Classical Singer, *April 2005.*

Tell me about your background. How did you get into fashion?

My first dream was to be a ballet dancer. I studied for years. Then I went to Texas Christian University and got a degree in liberal arts. I had also played piano since I was little, so I've always understood music as well as movement, because of my ballet training. I even danced with the San Antonio Opera. So it's interesting that many years later I design clothes for opera singers. The first singer who called me was Judith Blegen, and then Ashley Putnam who was singing at the City Opera and she was getting ready to do a recital. In the past, I was also an actress at the Cleveland Play House where I got my Equity card. I made a big hit there in *Who's Afraid of Virginia Woolf?* After two years at the Play House, I moved to New York with a college friend who was a model. She got me in touch with a beautiful boutique on East 54th Street owned by Kenneth, the famous hairdresser who did Jacqueline Kennedy's and Joanne Woodward's hair. So, gradually we started making one-of-a-kind dresses that were held in consignment for the shop, and a few of them sold.

Did you want to make clothes for performers because you had been part of that group?

Yes. I actually made this decision while watching the Bach B Minor Mass at Carnegie Hall. The soloist's dress was very inadequate. She was wearing a white dress made out of a not very fine silk. She also had on a jacket [that] seemed tight. The dress was too snow white and the seams were not absolutely flat; they just didn't look good. And I said to myself, "Oh my God, this beautiful singer, who is famous enough to be hired at Carnegie Hall, doesn't have a very good dress for the occasion!" I thought I could do something for singers. Then I made up a card—a mailer—with an extraordinarily beautiful picture of a gorgeous white chiffon gown.

It had been taken aboard a ship with the model twirling. I designed the cards and sent them to several singers at the Met. I found out when they were singing there and just did it. Now, I'm giving away my secrets of how I got in touch with my first clients! Of course, word of mouth is very powerful. Even though they are in a competitive field, performers do pass on information to each other. Now I don't design just for singers, but for instrumentalists and dancers as well.

ARTHUR COHEN

Do you design for large-size singers?

Yes, but I don't have a lot of large clients. One thing I keep in mind is: I would never put large singers into something bouffant; they shouldn't go out with big brocades or big bows; I try to minimize the look by creating vertical lines. Big people can also have a beautiful face with gorgeous skin, so the clothes shouldn't take the attention away from those assets. Usually if I can, I try to open up the neckline so you see some skin.

Also, women in general have to be very wise about their arms; for most women, biceps are not in such a great condition after thirty-five, unless you're Jane Fonda . . . But singers must understand that dressmakers have almost twice as much distance to cover with a fifty-two-inch bust, instead of a thirty-four. That's handwork. Then it's not four yards in the hem, but eight. I recently had a request from a big girl who wanted a black gabardine coat. I would make that coat with pleats down the back of her shoulders so that the pleats would flare out into a soft, full coat in order to cover her ample form.

What are the best colors for the stage?

There are a few good stage colors. Black is a frequent one. People don't always want to be in black; however for a first dress, frequently I suggest a beautiful black chiffon dress. Once a singer starts basic, she can build a wardrobe. It's not always practical for a singer to buy five different gowns. The other good stage colors are: red, white, and cobalt or royal blue. Brown is not that great; beige tends to look like the skin so it seems nude, and somewhat dead. Another beautiful color for the stage can be a jade green, an emerald green. Then you have to choose a fabric that doesn't eat the light.

How would you know that?

When I'm choosing the fabric for a client, I look in the mirror either in the fabric store or here in the studio, where I have very good light. I hold the swatches of fabric up to the light. Shimmer is great for stage because it picks up the light.

What fabrics are ideal?

Four-ply silk crepe is wonderful; it has a soft luster. Sometimes, a fabric could be shot with gold or silver, but you have to get the right balance of gold or silver. If it's too bright, it looks like a show girl. I had a girl come here with a dress from Filene's Basement. She was in the Liederkranz competition. The dress had a slash up the front and it was spattered in rhinestones, with a draped effect on this matte jersey white. I almost had a heart attack when I saw it! She was a young pretty woman. I told her, "My dear, you just cannot wear this. I don't even care if you order from me; I'll tell you where to go."

So you also act as a wardrobe adviser to singers?

Yes, of course! I couldn't let someone look like a Las Vegas show-girl going out on the stage for the Liederkranz! You sing classical music, you can't wear those things! I even tell people where to go for shoes or a haircut. Over time, I sent girls to Tip Top. They used to have all kinds of silk wedding shoes and bridesmaid's shoes, and they dyed them to match the gowns.

What colors look good or bad on TV?

The camera is a little tricky. Red never seems to work much on TV; it goes fuzzy. White can be okay. I did Judith Blegen's white silk dress for the 150th anniversary of the Met gala. I called Kirk Browning, who always directed the live telecast. I told him I have Judith Blegen in white silk, so was that an absolute no-no? He said, "I don't see why not, I can handle it!" He did and it looked great. I don't know why everyone is so afraid of white.

Would black be a good color for television?

Not necessarily, because you don't really see the design of the gown in detail. Some black gowns may work. Strong colors usually work. Baby pinks and powder blues are not power colors, not on TV and not on the stage. Most people should never wear prints; it's better to stick to solid colors. You do have to be careful with prints. Some people can pull them off, but the prints have to be just right. You can't get a large floral print that looks like a target, or you don't want a print that makes a "stripe-off"—the optical illusion where you see the flowers or the lines going across on the screen.

What are the ideal colors for blondes, brunettes?

To tell you the truth, you never know. Color is very tricky. I mean, you just have to hold it up against you, and just see . . .

Do you ever take off-the-shelf dresses and improve them for clients?

I have done some alterations for people that didn't order from me, as a courtesy. If a dress off the shelf needs alterations, it probably isn't going to work in the long run. However, I've transformed some vintage dresses for a few people. Most of the gowns I see in the stores now, for example, do not have sleeves. I have some very mature women coming to me who need sleeves. But it's better to start from scratch.

What exactly do you charge for—the design, the fabric?

I charge for a design fee, and singers must pay for the fabric immediately to marry themselves to the project. I can't pick and buy all this stuff without having a deposit. Do you know, there are places in town that require payment in full before doing anything?

Do you charge by the hour or by the intricacy of the work?

Not so much by the hour. You know, at least forty hours can go into a dress. I also spend almost a full day in and out of fabric stores, so if I would charge a hundred dollars an hour, I'd be rich! What's fascinating to me is that people pay two hundred and fifty dollars an hour to a lawyer, and I hold the visual aspect of their career in my hands with some beautiful dress that makes an impression, and some are reluctant to invest in that. The first impression is how we see you, even before you sing! I just did this tuxedo for the associate conductor of the New York Philharmonic—she's a woman and they wanted a tuxedo for her. This came to me through the Michal Schmidt agency. In this case, I worked with the management because this manager had the sensitivity and the thoughtfulness to have her client's appearance in mind. Managers should do that more often.

Do you only design for women?

Yes. However, I am doing restoration on a very fine Catholic priestly vestment right at the moment. From 1992 to 1997, I was the robe mistress for the St. Thomas Boys choir at the St. Thomas Episcopal Church. I took care of over two hundred vestments: mending, pressing, dressing the children for the many beautiful sacred services. That's how I came to know clergy and restore priestly vestments.

How do you save money using a designer?

Well, trust me on this one: you will save money with me! This sounds so self-aggrandizing. But you can get a gown here that fits; it looks fabulous for ten years, it's the best quality, made well, not too big or too small, it's cut correctly, the grain is right in the fabric, and it's not going to fall apart in the first dry cleaning. These clothes feel divine. When you get good haute couture clothes, they are not heavy or bulky; they don't grip your waist. They're like stepping into a vat of cotton candy. Four-ply silk crepe, for example. It's very basic but gorgeous.

So, if I sang at Carnegie Hall in September and in February I am singing at Merkin Hall, I wouldn't want to wear the same gown. Does it make sense to invest in a designer gown that I can only wear once, if I keep performing in New York? What would you suggest to get the haute couture glamour but be practical and budget-savvy?

I would get the basic gown underneath; a beautiful black slip gown. Then for your two concerts, I would do two different tops. One could be a beaded jacket and another, a lace robe or cape. I don't know if a singer wants to deal with a stole, but sometimes stoles are okay; you have to be pretty experienced with it to handle it while you sing. Then if you want to do an afternoon concert, maybe you can be in black silk pants and a little black jeweled camisole with a top over that, and change tops for different concerts.

Do singers ever join you to shop for fabrics?

Occasionally, they agree [to] or ask if they could shop with me. It's a pretty serious business because it's very fatiguing. I have to know what to show them and where to take them. I recently had one singer go with me, but after a while she said she couldn't stay in that store anymore. I always ask the client first, "How do you want to look? What impression do you want to give? Do you want to be imperial? Do you want to be soft and delicious? Do you want to be filmy and divine; are you singing Debussy or Fauré?" The music of a recital can affect what a singer wants to wear.

You know, this is a very serious matter: people have become so accustomed to stretch fabrics, stretchy wear [that] accommodates our growing bodies, that they have forgotten what it means to tailor and nip and tuck and cut perfectly a woven fabric. That means it can't always accommodate. It is what it is for that particular time, we can't stretch it out. People are used to going out in stretch stuff; there is Lycra now even in blue jeans. Of course, I would sometimes underline material with stretchy nude fabric, especially a material like a soufflé fabric; it's quite transparent, it offers maximum nudity, and it stretches, so I would use a stretch material for under it. Soufflé is hand walked into the U.S. from Switzerland; you cannot buy it here at any other store, except on West 57th Street. They actually ran out for a while and I said, "This is a nightmare, you have to get more!"

So when a singer comes in to order something, first you ask them what they want to look like . . .

And where do they sing, what music they're singing. Then they look at my samples and get ideas from them. I give them a price range and always remind them that fabric is additional. After that I decide on a design but that can morph slightly because fabric speaks to me. I also have to figure out if a figure accommodates itself to a center back zipper or a center front closure. That's going to affect the entire way I cut a dress. Then I start. Just to give you an example of how I work: In 2003, Susan Graham called me because she had to sing Ravel's *Shéhérazade*. The first thing I did that afternoon was to get out the CD, play it, and read the words. I wanted to know what she was singing and what the music was like. She wanted the gown to have a vague India flavor but it had to be very exotic and chiffon-y. She wanted the colors to be strong melon colors. She met me and we went to the store—to Weller. I also got a strapless bra and built the dress on the bra. The gown is total silk chiffon, hand draped with beaded silk at the top. I got the idea from the cover of one of my film scores called *Kama Sutra*. All the gowns of those Indian girls had these colors. So I took the cover of the CD to Weller and said I wanted those colors. It was quite an ordeal getting jewelry for Susan, too.

When you're working on a gown, how often does a singer have to come in for fittings?

As often as she can. For a good dress, you can count on at least three fittings, and I can usually always finish it in four.

What's the time frame?

That depends on how many projects I have at the time. I had good clients here that have called me two weeks before a major event. That puts me under a lot of pressure; it's enormously stressful, those deadlines at Carnegie Hall! I ask, "Where were you in the summer, when I didn't have much to do?" People have to think in advance.

What about big feet?

Can't do anything about them! Shoes are, by and large, the client's problem, but I have to mention this: I went to a concert the other night, the girl had on black pants, a black camisole, and creamy white shoes. That's just impossible! You cannot do that! You must have a pair of black shoes!

How does dressing for the concert stage differ from dressing for being a bridesmaid?

The bridesmaid would not be as showy or as dramatic because she shouldn't upstage the bride. A singer wants to have power when she walks on the stage.

What about going out or attending a formal event?

Anything goes! You have to go to an event and look fantastic. I am a little saddened by the way people are dressing these days; they're not dressing up for events or even for the opera. Forget sneakers and jeans; the women are so frumpy! What could they be thinking of?

Do you think singers should look elegant when they go to rehearsals?

Yes. I think singers should look extremely nice. If you have to get on the floor at rehearsals, you need a pair of durable beautiful trousers and maybe a silk blouse or a beautiful turtleneck sweater. Add some earrings. You should look good. I once saw the great diva, Leontyne Price, in a store here; she was mesmerizing. She looked great and so elegant, and just for going to the store. Would you ever see her in blue jeans or some hideous coat? I guess the word *diva* does have a sort of awkward connotation these days, but the public wants to see you look great. I always suggest to my clients: Don't be afraid to build your wardrobe as if you were in front of an audience all the time.

What if a singer is really tall and wants to appear shorter to fit in with her duet partner or the ensemble?

Why would someone want to appear shorter? Just so she could fit in? No. If you are tall, use your height and be imposing. I don't think you should hide your height to accommodate others. Just be what you are!

Is it better to wear something that may be a touch larger on you so it doesn't create any wrinkles in certain places?

Absolutely. Clothes should skim the body. Never wear clothes that are too tight. Let people think you're smaller underneath.

How do you stand out when you are thin and small in an ensemble and taking up less space than other singers?

Just by your presence, and your inner light. Someone said about the great dancer, Mikhail Baryshnikov: he was fantastic not just because of all he did on the stage but because you couldn't keep your eyes off him, even if he did nothing.

Should you coordinate bags and shoes perfectly?

No. As a matter of fact, you shouldn't. I think that looks a little too matched. No cheap plastic handbags, no three zipper compartments, and never advertise the name of the designer on your bag! Why would you get a bag with a name or letters all over? Get one good black handbag, one good beige one—crocheted or straw—or a caramel color.

What about white handbags?

Not that great. It's a little Sunday school–ish. Besides bags, I insist that good shoes are essential. I recently watched this girl perform and one of her shoes had the leather peeling back around one of the heels. In a small hall where people are sitting close enough to notice shabby shoes, you can't have that!

What about dry cleaning? How often should you do it?

I am opposed to over dry cleaning. It wears clothes out. After a performance, it's better to hang up your gown in front of a window and let the fresh air do the work. Do not rush to the dry cleaner's until really necessary, like if there's been too much perspiration. But if you don't have to, don't do it. I have some dry-cleaning fluid here and you can do a little touch-up under the arms. Another problem is static cling! I had a client—a famous singer—go onstage at a Rossini gala about five or six years ago, and she got static cling. And someone had the brilliant idea of shooting her with hair spray! Go figure! The fabric was imported from Florence; it was a lace top and a silk georgette skirt. I can tell you the gown didn't take too well to the hair spray! Whenever they perform, all singers should carry with them a can of No-Stat spray or Static Guard. They are a singer's best friend. If she is walking on carpets going from the green room to the stage—boom—the static will happen! Then there's another problem: not being careful with your gown. A client-singer leaned against the sink in her dressing room when she was doing her makeup. Imagine: she had on a satin gown with water stains on her lap, and no time to change! You have to be extra careful. These are very fine clothes.

So, what you're saying is, once you put that precious gown on, do nothing and don't touch anything before going onstage.

Yes! Just like at the hairdresser's. Wait and try to relax. You have to accommodate and take care of fine clothes. You can't look like a queen unless you give it your full attention.

What do you recommend as audition outfits?

A pair of good shoes would be very important, because those you audition for are sitting pretty close to you. A skirt, or if you're wearing pants, a pair of good silk trousers—and they must be pressed, no wrinkles! Don't wear a pair of wrinkled pants because that would make your possible employers think you just took these pants out of the closet and you didn't care enough to press them. It's all in the details. Wear something simple, solid colors, so the eye doesn't get distracted by prints; but something that moves and walks well, like a skirt that falls well over the hips with a turtleneck, or if that bothers you when you sing, a beautiful silk blouse. Occasionally, if a girl doesn't have a big budget, she can cheat by buying something that has a great look but . . . doesn't have to be a thousand-dollar blouse from Bergdorf or Armani. She might find something more convenient at Lord and Taylor. They have great sales there. So if she wears her silk blouse—pale gray, shell pink, creamy beige, or white—with a gorgeous flared skirt, believe me, she will look good.

I've seen some singers audition in a very corporate look, like a business suit, pants and jacket. What are your thoughts on that?

Don't do it. That's corporate life. And you don't want to start looking like a man. If you want a jacket that looks great, get a soft, feminine one—I call it a dress-maker jacket. This is an artistic profession after all.

What about a daytime, afternoon dress for an audition?

A dress would be fine, but a great daytime dress is hard to find in the stores.

Any tips for a travel wardrobe?

If you travel a lot, get your wardrobe started in black, white, and beige, with accents of red or maybe cobalt blue in a jacket or some scarves. Another thing, don't put too much emphasis on scarves; have two or three great scarves but you can have a very good travel wardrobe with one scarf. Everybody should have one black jacket when she is traveling. It goes with blue jeans; it works for a cocktail party, even a barbecue. There's nothing you can't use it for. The very fine fabrics, like the four-ply silk and some silk chiffons, travel quite nicely, too. Occasionally I find a beautiful synthetic that I can use, if it has a personality I like. Synthetics do travel well.

When singers are traveling, can they just go casual or should they have a certain "airplane look?" How important is it to dress up on the plane?

They should look absolutely great on the plane! I'll tell you a quick story to illustrate. I went to Mexico on October 30. I was dressed in a pair of good jeans with a fabulous silver belt and a white silk blouse with a black blazer and a black cowboy hat, and black sunglasses. The check-in line was huge at JFK, but when they saw me dressed like that, someone came and took me aside to a desk and I got checked in before the crowd. It was almost embarrassing. Then I got to the gate and when it got close to boarding time, one of the girls from the ticket desk came over and checked my ticket, after which she said, "We don't have many people in first class this time. We can put you in." So I traveled first class! And all that happened because I was very stylishly dressed and made an impression. The first impression! The look just did it for me. Hats are a great thing! Wear them, tip them over your eyes with great sunglasses, and you might get into first class! Also, I was wearing makeup on the plane.

Speaking of makeup, do you have any suggestions for auditions?

Be as natural as you can. No colored eye shadows, only maybe soft amber or sepia tones, but no blues, no greens. Ever. Emphasize a natural look.

What about hair?

Get a good haircut!

Huge hair or no huge hair?

Well, you have to be able to recognize if it's great hair or not. If someone's a good-looking gal with beautiful red hair and she wants to fluff it up and hit the stage with this cloud of red hair, I'm all for that. As a former dancer, I always looked at myself so ruthlessly in the mirror, so brutally. All dancers do that. Every finger, every step, every movement had to be perfect. You either get extremely critical or narcissistic looking at yourself, but it does makes you realize what looks good and what doesn't. You have to develop discernment. In the end, I ask myself, "What makes a singer look good on the stage?" Courtenay Budd, for example, is blond and beautiful but she also has this radiance that comes from the inside. I saw her in a recital; she came onstage to sing Rachmaninoff songs, which are very voluptuous and beautiful, and she sang with such sincerity. She was creating a Russian atmosphere and she wasn't trying to show off any technique. The inner light, the radiance of a personality is what people love to see. Fashion helps to enhance that and make you feel beautiful, confident, and desirable, but the presence has to start within.

Ioan Holender

Recorded September 2002 in Vienna, Austria. The first part was published in
Classical Singer *in October 2003. The continuation* dates from*
August 2008 and has not been published previously.

How does the fact that you were a singer yourself influence your decisions as director of the Vienna State Opera?

Well, foreseeing the development of singers, evaluating them, predicting the direction they are going in—whether good or bad—all of these qualities are vital to an opera house director. You hire someone now and plan to do a certain repertoire with them in several years.

You have to know intuitively where that voice is going to go. I think that having been a singer is a big advantage and it shows. A whole generation of singers began here in the past ten, eleven years, under my direction: Ramón Vargas, Angela Gheorghiu, Roberto Alagna, Vesselina Kasarova . . . Bryn Terfel and Michael Schade had fixed contracts here. So did Barbara Frittoli.

Like many European opera houses, the Vienna State Opera has its own ensemble, its "fixed" singers. Of course, we have the guest singers, usually the big stars who sell out the house, but the ensemble consists of singers who have signed a fixed contract with us for two or three years. These singers learn and perform the roles assigned to them, and there are several outcomes: they either develop further and grow into more important roles, they stay the same, they leave of their own accord, or their contracts are not renewed.

Hard work is encouraged, though sometimes I have to say it is not fairly rewarded. Some singers from our ensemble sing more, others less. It's based on their artistic quality, on their ability to sell tickets. So, let's say you have a singer who works very hard and gives respectable performances, and another singer who maybe doesn't make such an effort, but because of his or her natural outstanding artistry, this person gets to sing more.

Of course, it's not fair. As the manager of an artistic institution, you can't possibly be completely fair all the time and prosper. You choose what sells.

Does image count?

Yes. I believe it counts more here than in American opera houses.

How about age?

Not really. They say that I am against mature singers; that is not true. I just cannot hire singers who are honored for what they've accomplished in the past and who no longer can match their former glory.

I don't believe in hiring any tenor—or any voice, for that matter—who cannot handle even half of a role, and has to transpose, tacitly asking for the indulgence of the public because of the fact that his name used to be associated with magnificent performances. When you cannot sing what is written in the score anymore, why bother?

I prefer to make a mistake with a young singer than to continue with someone well known who cannot offer his or her best anymore. On the other hand, if a mature singer can sing, age doesn't matter.

From what I have noticed, you are a father figure to many of your ensemble singers. You "raise" singers here, guiding them from role to role, caring for the development of their voices. Is this appreciated?

Yes and no. Some do appreciate it and follow my advice. Others don't, because they are in a hurry. I believe that it is not important when you, the singer, will "arrive" somewhere, whether you'll get there today or tomorrow. What matters is how long you will stay there. Some singers tell me, "The Met called me. I cannot possibly say no." So I tell them, "Go if you want, but they might never call you again in the future."

This "now-or-never" mentality can do a lot of damage. When an opportunity like that comes, a lot of singers overestimate themselves and jump at the chance, only to make a poor impression and not be hired again.

So, can any singer audition here?

Yes. Of course we need to see their résumé first.

Do you listen to them personally?

No, not at first. But if I hear good things from their first audition, I'll listen to them.

Do you have a young artist program like the Met, for example?

No. If the young artists are exceptional, I hire them and they go directly on the stage in whatever roles suit them.

How are American singers viewed in Austria?

They are seen as very well prepared and easy to work with.

Do chorus singers ever become soloists?

Yes, in many cases, though a lot of singers prefer the security of their job as a chorister, because they make a good living. We recently had two tenor chorus members who are now soloists. It is a legitimate way to start. However, don't count on it. I would say it's good for experience in the beginning, as well as for the contacts, but don't stay in the chorus too long if you really want to become a soloist.

Any other advice for singers?

Stick to the repertoire that suits you for as long as it suits you. When a lyric-spinto tenor stops singing the Duke in *Rigoletto* and wants to sing [in] *Ballo*, that's when the danger sets in. This is extremely important for a singer: there is no turning back from a heavy repertory to a lighter one.

Unfortunately, a lot of singers fall into that trap. They move into heavier and more difficult repertoire, it doesn't work, then they want to go back to their former lighter repertoire, and suddenly they realize it's not the same.

A certain flexibility gets lost in the process. Once you've stepped over the boundary, you can't come back, for example, from Otello to Alfredo, and do it well. Maybe there is that rare singer who can, but in general the comeback doesn't work. Look at what happened to Ben Heppner who, in my opinion, never was what he sang, even though he was very successful and I consider him an exceptional artist.

But agents, recording companies, directors, conductors . . . these can be the greatest criminals in the destruction of voices. Let's say you sing Carmen and a certain director comes to you and says, "With your looks, you should try Dalila because that's what we're doing now and you'd be perfect." Now, you are aware that at the moment Dalila is too much for you. But then the conductor joins the director and says, "Listen, you can sing this part; I'll conduct it in such a way that it will be easy for you."

So, you have a famous director and a great conductor, and you do it. But you sing Dalila with your vocal capabilities, no matter who conducts or how big the hall is. Every singer gives their all onstage, whatever the circumstances.

What I am trying to say is that you must be capable of brutal honesty with yourself. If you can't use your judgment, be discerning, and resist certain temptations, you can get in trouble. It's so easy to say yes. You overestimate yourself or you fear that if you don't accept this now, it will never come again. That's not true. I truly believe that saying no will many times turn out to be much more important to your development as a singer than saying yes.

*Since we spoke last, have there been any fundamental changes in your vision and in the direction the Staatsoper has taken?

In the last four years, opera has received a much greater popularity, mainly through two singers. There have never been two singers like Anna Netrebko and Rolando Villazón to contribute in such a very large way to the popularity and mediatization of this art form. This is something completely new in the whole four-hundred-year-old history of opera! Without making any vocal, artistic, or musical comparisons, this girl, Netrebko, who came from the Urals to America and then to Europe, is revolutionizing opera. This popularization is fueled by a happy convergence of aspects—maybe not necessarily artistic—mediatization through her looks, her spontaneity, her sincerity in both singing and in what she says, and the world of advertising. I say that all of this helps the lyric art because she's one of us, not a singer from the pop, rock, or other fields. This is a novelty that developed within the past four years, together with Villazón, who has great appeal to the public; even to the nonopera public. The news about me is that I am unique in the Vienna State Opera history—a director who within one tenure has put on the tetralogy—Wagner's four operas—twice. We started the second tetralogy already: *Die Walküre* and *Siegfried* are out. *Rheingold* and *Götterdämmerung*—the crowning achievement . . . over sixteen hours long with great artistic, vocal, and staging demands—will follow in the 2008–2009 season. We've also had the premiere of [a new production of] *Capriccio* by Richard Strauss—an opera of a very high artistic level but also greatly demanding on the public, always very respected but not too well attended. These current performances were sold out—which is unique in the history of the Vienna State Opera, where *Capriccio* has a past, with Lisa Della Casa. This production, with Renée Fleming in the main role, became more sought-after by the public than *La traviata* or *Don Carlos*. In 2005 we celebrated fifty years from the reopening of the Vienna State Opera after the reconstruction in November 5, 1955, and on this occasion we opened the first Opera Museum for the Staatsoper. We also did a concert of parts from the first six operas that were the first six premieres in that week of the Staatsoper's reopening. I decided to do something different, not to gather all the famous singers in the world, but to do it with a few high-class conductors. So in one evening we had Thielemann, Zubin Mehta, Welser-Möst, Muti—conductors who have made a great contribution to the high standard of the Vienna State Opera.

The 2008/2009 season is an anniversary season for the Staatsoper . . .

Yes, 140 years from its construction. On May 25, 1869, the opera—the Imperial Opera, Hofoper at that time—opened its doors with *Don Giovanni* in German, as was the custom, and so we're doing *Don Giovanni*, too, on the day of the Staatsoper's 140th anniversary.

Benoît Jacquot

Recorded July 2002 via telephone. Published in Classical Singer, *January 2003.*

**Mr. Jacquot, for what audience is this film [*Tosca*] intended?
An opera-, a movie-going audience or both?**

I am a filmmaker before anything else, and I am not an opera expert. I wasn't asked to stage *Tosca* but to make a film, and it seemed interesting to try to do something different than what I usually do. So, I wanted, first of all, to address myself to the movie-going public. Obviously, since this film is about *Tosca*, among those who go to the movies, there will certainly be opera fans. But it is not intended mainly for them. True, it is an opera film . . . but my ideal spectator is someone who will go to see this film without knowing anything about the opera, and leave with *Tosca* in their heads and in their hearts.

What inspired you most, the music or the story?

The music! I was familiar with the music, because it's such a famous opera, but when the producer proposed to make a film out of it, I listened to the music very carefully. It was the music that gave me the desire to make the film, as well as a lot of my ideas. I let it guide me. The music was the screenplay.

**It must be challenging to make opera seem real on film.
However, with Puccini as with most verismo operas, this task
was easier perhaps, since the drama is more plausible . . .**

True. I knew that opera in general involved a great deal of convention, especially on the stage. Through the film, I tried to pull opera out of its conventional state. The singers were very willing to work with me, when I presented my ideas; all three of them were extremely interested and passionate about this perspective.

**Did you have to explain or choreograph each scene, or did you
leave the singers the freedom to express themselves within their
characters?**

Each of the three is very different, so I tried—just as I do with actors—to explain what I wanted in the beginning, but in different ways. For example, Ruggero Raimondi had already been in other films, so it was simple  with him. With Roberto Alagna, it wasn't the same, because he was just beginning to act in front of the camera and depended on me for some guidance. With Angela, it was again, completely different, because she has an inner power, enthusiasm, and a very strong will. She had very precise ideas about what she was going to do. It was impossible to direct her as I would direct someone else. Besides, I didn't really need to guide her gestures, her movements; I got her to do certain things by explaining to her she'd be more beautiful, more visible, better, in a certain angle or suite of movements. She understood me very well.

Did you find it different to work with opera singers as opposed to actors?

A priori, it is different, but actually, no, not too much. Since the music is the screenplay, they would interpret what the music required of them. It's just the same as speaking a dialogue, only that it is music, and thus interpreted in another fashion. But even if you ask actors to sing in a film, that also changes their acting, no?

Did the famous couple of Angela and Roberto inspire you in creating the scenes between them?

Yes, a lot! All I can say is, if they weren't such a couple in real life, the scenes between them would certainly not have the same power. I was interested in them from the start because I knew I wasn't filming a tenor and a soprano, but a man and a woman who are intimately connected in life. It is not the same thing as filming two singers that don't know each other and are just acting. With Angela and Roberto you can tell, that they sing together and live together . . .

Tell me about lip-synching. The singers hear the music while filming, and they have to synchronize themselves to their prerecorded voices . . .

Yes. Well, the black-and-white scenes were shot in the recording studio . . .
I wanted to show that aspect of making an opera film as well. The opera had
been recorded in London, a few months before. Then in the studio, in costume, while being filmed, the singers heard the soundtrack for the film, which
by the way, is not the same recording as the CD that came out.

**A lot of scenes are shot against a black background. What was
your intention?**

Well, I wanted the sets to be realistic, to reproduce more or less the real
setting in Rome, but at the same time, I wanted this reality surrounded by
night, so that the sets within this darkness created a kind of mental space,
you see?

Like a world within the characters' mind?

Right. A fictional world in which the drama could go very far, to its
limits . . . If you think about it, all three main characters die.

What about the reverse-action sequences?

It's almost as if, before ending, the film wants to remind the audience
of what they have seen, just as one's whole existence passing in front of
his eyes at the moment of death, but in reverse. To tell you the truth, the
idea came to me because I didn't really know what to do with the beginning of the third act.

**You made the idea of singing one's thoughts—another
operatic convention—more real by having the singers actually
not do any lip-synching when they "thought," their expression
tells everything, their lips don't move, and only their voices
are heard.**

Yes, and that was especially suitable for Scarpia, as he addresses himself to others but at the same time he speaks to himself a lot. In this case,
film is the only way to portray "singing one's thoughts" as you say, and
make it seem real. You can't do that onstage.

**In the life of an opera singer, there is always the dilemma of
voice versus image, physical appearance. A lot of singers have
glorious voices but they don't land certain roles in certain
companies because they don't present the image required by
those who audition them. In the film industry, it's even more
exclusive . . .**

Oh, yes. In the film industry, often someone is hired mainly because of
their physical appearance, and then you find out if they have the talent
to act.

Well, opera is above all an auditory art . . .

True, but in this case, the visual corresponded, too. Angela and Roberto are very good looking.

So, *Tosca* on film becomes a dialogue between the auditory and the visual.

Yes. But opera should not become too much of a visual art because one will forget the music.

Then, where do you think one can find the balance between the auditory and the visual?

Basically . . . at the movies!!! At least, it's interesting to try, through opera films.

In the past, there have been films in which famous actors played an operatic role, lip-synching to the voice of an opera singer, like Sophia Loren in *Aida* . . .

That was an interesting solution to making an opera film. The concept is a bit like Japanese theater, like Kabuki, but I find it more interesting to film actual singers.

So, should a singer study acting separately? If he or she would like to explore that aspect of their art, and even venture on to film as a singer, what would be most important?

If singers have the chance to be filmed while they sing, they should above all present their art, which is singing. They shouldn't all of a sudden think that because there is a camera in front of them, they have to do something different to become film actors rather than singers. This is exactly what I explained to Angela, Roberto, and Ruggero, and they understood very well that they will not be good actors unless they continue to be great singers. They should never above all sacrifice their art of singing in order to be good actors. If they stay true to their art, the rest will follow.

Vesselina Kasarova

Recorded January 2004 in New York City, USA. Published in Classical Singer, *July 2004.*

Did you always want to be a singer?

No. I wanted to be an actress. But I started studying piano when I was four. My parents noticed that I was musical, and encouraged me.

I was actually a very shy child, but I wanted to be on the stage, in the center of attention. That is the phenomenon of performers, isn't it? Many are shy in real life, but they love the stage. It's like they live in two worlds.

But I can say that having studied piano has been quite helpful. It's not just because I can learn the music alone; that is the smallest advantage. Rather, I think like an instrumentalist. As a piano player, you have to express music without words. When you sing, you have the text, of course, but I think you shouldn't count on that, because sometimes the words are repetitive or don't make sense. The voice alone should tell the story and arouse the emotion, just like an instrument.

How was your life in Bulgaria, as a student during the Iron Curtain years?

Difficult. But I believe two of the very few positive things in that regime were the disciplines of music and sports. We received a very good education in those two fields and had the best teachers to develop us. In our country, and in Eastern Europe in general, music was always highly valued; it is in one's blood, it comes naturally to people: they can sing.

The program being so demanding, there was a lot of competition. You really had to work hard and fight, because there were so many gifted singers. That was very positive, because it made you stronger. There was pressure to excel in all music-related subjects, such as counterpoint, theory, harmony and so on.

That was a big plus, as opposed to today, when singers don't take those subjects as seriously. You don't really see that need to excel in music theory now in Europe, in countries like Germany, Switzerland, or Austria. The truth is: this very detailed music education is not really supported financially, so singers mainly concentrate on singing and instrumentalists on their instruments.

But the big advantage in Eastern Europe was that all of us came out as very well-rounded musicians with an ingrained discipline and work ethic. That was true in Bulgaria, and from what I know from Angela [Gheorghiu], in Romania, too. We both studied for five years, everyday, until we were able to get on the stage and sing professionally. I also think that, with life being so difficult around you, there were few temptations and distractions, so you really had no choice but to study. There was hardly anything else to do!

You began your career in Bulgaria, at the Sofia Opera.

Yes. I was eighteen when I switched from piano to opera. Then, after studying voice for four years at the Academy, I stepped on the stage for the first time. I didn't rush to perform right after my first year! So I had a very solid technical base.

How did you decide to switch from piano to voice?

I accompanied singers and worked with them, and sometimes sang along in these coachings, so my colleagues asked me why I wasn't studying voice. I realized I liked to sing and decided to see if I could do something with my voice—but I never even imagined I would get to where I am today.

Your recent CD is called *Bulgarian Soul*. How important is it for you to be a cultural ambassador for your country?

Extremely important! With this CD, I wanted to show what kind of music we have, because so few people even know where Bulgaria is. They have no idea about the richness of Bulgarian culture, about its enormous history. Because of the Iron Curtain, there was hardly any cultural exchange between Bulgaria and the world. This music is beautiful and full of longing, just like the people. The Bulgarian people can be cheerful but they have this underlying melancholy.

Tell me about your experience as a voice student. √

One of the most important things I understood was [this]: there are no teachers in this world who can make a student perceive what technique means within two days! There are books and different theories, which indicate the same principles, but you have to discover it for yourself.

What is technique? You have to work with yourself, and with what you have, in a very detailed way. It has to do with intuition, talent, and intel-

MARCO BORGGREVE

ligence. You have to think about it—not wait for a teacher to tell you everything, and suddenly, the next day, you think you know how to sing! There is nobody who can do that for you.

Of course, you have to believe in yourself, and have strong nerves. You have to work with different people, so you need to be flexible. What does the conductor want from you today? You should be able to adapt, but never ever change your technique. It's a very delicate line.

In the beginning, I worked a lot, especially with my middle voice. I had very present high notes and low notes. The question was: Am I a soprano or a contralto? But mezzo was the perfect Fach in the end, because I could use both my vocal height and depth.

I was lucky that I only had one teacher. You shouldn't change teachers all the time, anyway. The rest of my development I owe to the people I worked with: conductors and singers. They enriched my imagination and helped me discover what I can do with myself.

Did you ever follow a method, like Marchesi or Vaccai?

No. The most important thing is you have to get to know your voice exactly as it is. That means you have to sing on the bad days. The irony is, the voice is at is best when you don't sing! There are so few perfect days! But that's why you have technique and knowledge of breath support. Today there aren't many singers who sing on the breath. Some sing naturally, and after ten years, the voice gets tired and says, "Please help me!"

When you sing, your voice has a radiating energy that is almost palpable. Are you conscious of that?

Well, I try not to be. It is not a good idea to consciously think of putting energy in the voice. You can only sing with this energy if you have the *Grundlage*—the technical foundation. If you think of energy without foundation, you begin to scream. A singer has to project this energy; that is perhaps what gives singers their charisma, but that should not be associated with driving the voice and forcing it to the point that you can't sing *piano* on the high notes. At the end of a performance, you should have the feeling that you can repeat the whole role.

Those are tricks of the trade, as I call them. The public doesn't need to know them. Actually, *piano* is not just there for effect; it's a mechanism of protection for the voice. To go into *piano* and *mezzo forte* protects the voice from giving too much, so that when you do need to give, you have a whole reservoir of voice and you don't get tired.

I don't understand those who need to sing loud all the time. Your voice is your treasure; you have to protect it! For example, I don't sing everyday. I'm happy when I don't have to sing. When you are a *Profi* [professional singer], you really need the rest, because silence is the best medicine for the voice.

How do you prepare a role?

I listen to a CD. It doesn't matter who sings, because I just want to hear the orchestra. The orchestras have become so big today that people hardly sing *piano* anymore. So the size of the orchestras takes away this beautiful mechanism of protection, of having the option to sing softly! Every *piano* becomes a *mezzo forte*. And you see triple *piano* in the score, but you can't sing it like that, because the orchestras are like huge avalanches over your voice!

Some orchestras are tuned higher, as you know. In Vienna, I sound like a soprano, because it's almost a whole note higher! My body feels differently, too, when I perform in Vienna or in Salzburg. Today, between pleasing the conductors and the stage directors, whoever survives, survives!

That's why I listen to the orchestra first, so I can tell if the role is for me or not. I usually learn very fast. I don't have time to give two years to studying a role.

Then, once I have learned everything, it's crucial for me to work with the stage director. In Europe, there is much emphasis on acting. In America, it's a bit easier for us because the performance follows a more classical line. But the Regie [stage direction] in Europe demands that we work with every detail, every word. Then I develop the notes, the expression, and everything comes together. It's not easy but, in the end, it's important to have fun with it, too.

Tell me about singing one of your specialties: Bellini.

Bellini has the most difficult repertoire for mezzos, because you are very exposed. Overall, in bel canto, I combine two techniques: from singing Rossini and Mozart. For Bellini, just like in Mozart, you need a good ensemble. You can use the same technique as for Rossini, in the coloratura, and the same principles of legato from Mozart. I always say: if you can sing Mozart, you can sing anything, because Mozart demands that you have control over your voice.

We all have our weak spots in a certain part of the voice—that's normal—but the problem comes when you have absolutely no control over the voice. Control includes being able to handle the weak spots. If I lose control, it's over! The emotion rises so high, on top of the technical challenges, that you can't let go, even for a second.

The stage takes a lot out of you, too. That's why technique is so important in keeping a balance between emotion and singing. When the emotion is at a high level, I have to think, "What do I do? How do I breathe?" That's like math, almost. You can't just let go completely on the stage; you have to be aware of what is going on. For that, you have to work the technical aspects of a part early enough, so that you don't come to the rehearsals and try it out onstage, because the stage will surprise you every time.

At every performance, I have to deal with different things. I have to adapt to everything without panicking. That has been my experience in my fourteen years of [this] career.

I think everyone will tell you, regardless of how many years they have sung: in the beginning, everything is easier. Maybe you can let go completely and be guided by emotion. When you're young, you're full of energy and confidence, so you can do everything. That's why singers often accept roles they shouldn't sing, because at a young age, the voice works, no matter how they use it, and that gives them confidence. But it can be dangerous.

When you record, what are your priorities?

Not to be boring. Not just to sing clean in perfect style and intonation. I strive to be as close to the reality of a performance as possible; to be believable and to tell stories with each lied or aria. I'm aware that the listener gets bored after the third aria, in a solo recording.

This danger comes also from the fact that we must repeat so much during the recording. Sometimes, it's a wonderful take for me, but a violin comes in too late or too early, so I have to sing it again, and the right expression can be lost. I learned a lot from recordings about what I can or can't do. We don't really hear ourselves as singers. It was a good school.

Do you find the right emotion in the text, the music, or both?

Both. If I believe in the words, in the story I'm telling, then the public will believe it, too. But to me, the music is the strongest. As I said before, I think like an instrumentalist. They have to tell a story without words.

Also, I believe singers should learn early to maintain their freedom in singing. A rest means something, too. We feel the music, breathe it in, and then we sing it. If you observe pianists or violinists, they use the rests to take a breath in, to feel the coming phrase, and then they play. They don't rush rests. That applies to singing; you can't just pant your way through an aria, it's a process that needs freedom. Some conductors really don't understand that.

How do you deal with such conductors?

That's a good topic for discussion! I say, in general, when you are young, you have to adapt. When you already have a name, the conductors have to be more careful with you! You should be able to ask diplomatically, "Can we do it this way or that way?" You don't gain anything by being arrogant. We all work together and we should have more respect for one another. Then it works wonderfully.

No one should be extreme in imposing his or her point of view. It's the same with stage directors. You have to be able to communicate. No one is perfect in this world. As a singer, no matter how intuitive I am, I don't always make the best dramatic choices, and I need good suggestions. We can't see ourselves, our acting, our bodies.

What is important for you when you sing in concert?

That is a more intimate experience. It shows more of the singer. It's important to keep a balance between the acting and that intimate connection.

Would you teach?

I have already, a little bit. I like it. It makes you less selfish. Maybe I'll teach more in the future.

Do you have any hobbies?

I have no time. My son is five years old! And this profession takes up everything. Yet you have to be able to enjoy life, too, as much as possible.

What roles do you envision for yourself in ten years?

I don't really know. I would say fate has led me to so many different roles, so I trust in the natural flow of things. Perhaps I will do more French bel canto repertoire, and some Verdi, like Eboli, for example.

I can't really think ten years from now; living in the moment is too important. But I keep in mind not to strain the voice, so that I will be able to sing ten years from now!

I'm really enjoying the present and I'm happy with my repertoire. There's always a new opera coming my way: *Rosenkavalier, Ariodante*; every year, there is something else. One day it will be Carmen, but I would certainly love to sing Eboli. That role can't come too late, because there is some coloratura in the "Veil Song"; you still have to be able to do that. But I think mezzos have enough repertoire. We're not always the title role, but throughout all these secondary roles, we can develop slowly and have a long career.

Would you speak technically for a moment and share some of your principles?

My principles? Practice, practice, practice!

Well . . . we take in air and are like a reservoir of breath. Then when I sing, the air comes out and then back in. I have the feeling that everything turns around; it recycles. It's not that you actually breathe in while you sing, but the air comes back in somehow, indirectly. The way I say that sounds impossible, but I have to think that way, so that at the end of a phrase, I still have air.

It took me three years, working every day for one hour, to understand that principle. When I first tried it, I would breathe in and try to speak while continuing to breathe in, but I wasn't letting any air out, so I would choke and turn red.

The idea of breathing in while you sing is more a metaphor to help you circulate the air so that nothing gets stuck. Like in swimming, the breath must be deep and last a long time, if you let it out slowly. Then the support is the sensation you feel—please excuse me for this imagery—when you sit on the toilet and push! It gets the lower abdomen involved. However, in doing that, you have to be careful not to strain the throat; the throat must stay free.

Then there is the question of taking time to understand everything. I saw this in Italy: After just two years of study, they throw the students on the stage; everything is so fast! Directors or conductors pick young, good-looking singers with a role in mind, but no one really thinks about the voice, or the long-term effects on the voice. These beginners do not know the tricks needed to protect the voice. You don't sing directly, on the voice, which is the tendency for young singers. It's hard to put into words. It's like David Copperfield! You have to use these tricks—like going into *piano*, *mezzo forte*, messa di voce, so that you can sing for many years without hurting yourself.

There is another problem, too. When you have a naturally good voice but you sing without knowing what you are doing, you sing without protection. The psychological pressure on you will get stronger and stronger, and there is nothing to lean on, because sooner or later the instinctive knowledge will need technical support. From your first student days, you have to make sure you understand what the teacher is asking you to do, not just say yes and imagine it will come by itself. It won't.

I always taped my lesson and listened to it, then I discussed with my teacher. Then, I would listen to Giulietta Simionato, and I understood that mezzos should not darken their voices on purpose, because that only shortens the range, and then they can only sing "Habanera"! I understood I had to sing *schlank* [slender]. This vocal slenderness helps to cut through the orchestra. You have to show your colors without artificially darkening. The richness and darkness in the voice comes with age and experience, but they should come naturally.

Any words of advice for young singers?

To believe, to keep working and thinking, "What more can I do? How can I be better?" This profession requires a lot of discipline, patience, strength, and good nerves. It's never easy. It's hard in the beginning, when you're fighting to get work. Later, when you get work, it doesn't get easier, because you want more. Even when you are well known, it's far from being simple, because you have to keep proving that you can maintain that level. The public expects you to be better every time. That kind of pressure applies to all professions, I think; the higher you are, the bigger the expectations. So, you have to know what you are getting into as a singer and be prepared to fight.

On the other hand, don't lose your sense of play, of fun, and don't live only for this profession. Yes, singers are more or less egocentric; they have to be, because this profession takes everything, but they have to know other things, too, and try to enjoy life. And one last piece of advice: You have to develop what you have. You should never imitate; just use your "material," explore your own characteristics, develop your qualities, and don't try to sound like anyone else. You have to simply be yourself!

Gregory Kunde

Recorded January 2004 in New York City, USA. Published in Classical Singer, *April 2004.*

Were you a voice major at Illinois State?

I was a conducting education major, but I had to take some voice. I'd never heard of opera until I was nineteen. I was an American kid, [a] lead singer in a rock band and growing up with rock and roll in the sixties and seventies.

When you first became aware of vocal technique, what challenges did you face?

The top and the passaggio. When I was going to school in the mid-seventies, repertory was not really discussed. You took Schirmer's *Operatic Anthology* and picked whatever you wanted to sing. I didn't know the difference between Wagner and Mozart! Both had some arias that didn't go very high, so I would sing "Dalla sua pace" followed by "Nessun dorma"!

Tell me about your apprenticeship at Chicago Lyric Opera.

In the late part of my college years, I did the Met auditions and won a regional audition at Chicago Lyric. Someone who worked there said, "You should audition for our apprentice program." So I persistently called back until they gave me the audition.

Chicago was a spectacular experience! That's where I met my mentor, Alfredo Kraus. I actually had no idea who he was, and I got a couple of recordings to at least know his voice.

Once I started covering Alfredo's roles, Carol Fox, the general manager at the time, encouraged me to approach him. He was very kind to me. He listened to me and said, "Our voices are very similar. You don't have a big voice, so you have to be very careful in what you choose to sing." I never really took it to heart until about eight years later. As a young singer, you take anything that comes your way because you need the work and the experience. I was doing a lot of *Bohème*s and Pinkertons in *Butterfly*, also

Rigoletto, Traviata in regional opera companies. But I finally took Kraus's advice when I was asked to sing *Puritani*, in 1986 in Montreal.

What were the technical principles you learned from Kraus?

The most important was the placement of the voice. He advised me that I have to really become an instrument and place the voice in the perfect spot so that every note will be heard. Kraus said you have to become

like the woodwinds. You always hear the oboes, even though they're not the biggest sound. So, he would have me imagine a little pinhole at the top of my forehead. He said, "The more closed the vowel, the smaller that pinhole gets. You have to concentrate there and bring the sound out in that point." His perception of the voice was way up in the top of the head, and you could hear every sound. That unbelievable focus of the voice has always helped me.

He also told me not to think so much. Now, the only time I get really analytical is when I am learning a role. Then I listen to myself on tape or CD and make sure everything is even from top to bottom. But onstage, I want to concentrate on the character. Especially in bel canto, since the characters can be such uninteresting people, if you let them. It's up to you to make them human, and relate as much as possible to everything happening on the stage. I've been singing bel canto since that *Puritani* in 1986. This music is naturally refreshing because it can be different every time.

Do you make your own variations and ornamentations?

Always! The challenge is in doing different variations for Bellini, Donizetti, and Rossini, because they are not the same. There are some variations Rossini would have done that would never fit with Donizetti. Just by listening to the overture of a piece, you know how a variation should go. This is something hard to teach. It comes with experience. You can point out to people that Donizetti would have never done a certain variation because he didn't use those series of intervals. That applies to

ANTONIO BARBAGALLO

cadenzas, too. For example, you can hear someone singing Donizetti and doing a cadenza and you think, "That's a Verdi cadenza!"

Does it help you to hear other interpretations of the role you are preparing?

It helped me in college. Now I only listen to get a feeling of the orchestration of a piece. Take *Les Troyens*, for example. There are many interpretations of *Les Troyens* by Wagnerian singers. I have nothing in common with them. To be influenced by their interpretation would be wrong. My challenge was to give this a fresh interpretation.

Of course, the center of the voice is much more used in *Les Troyens*. Aeneas has a couple of top notes you just touch on, but most climaxes of phrases are at about A-flat or A. You can carry the chest voice a little higher to reinforce the middle.

But if you use the middle voice too intensely, it might take you away from the stratosphere.

That is a danger. If you emphasize a different part of your anatomy—voice or body—and neglect another, then the emphasized part will overpower the unused part. The only way to get around that is to mix things up as much as possible. Now that I did *Les Troyens*, and recently, *Benvenuto Cellini*, my next opera is *Cenerentola*; so you couldn't get further away from Berlioz!

Tell me about your coloratura skills.

That is a phenomenon that has come to me. I try not to make coloratura a hurdle I have to get over. I play with it. The best music for me is the serious Rossini, like *Tancredi* or *Ermione*. I've done both roles in *Ermione*: Pirro and Oreste. Pirro has coloratura all over the place, but it's different from Oreste. When Rossini wrote for two major tenors, there was the florid tenor and the heroic tenor, sometimes called the "baritenor."

Rossini has such drama in coloratura! When Oreste sings, the florid part is more romantic. But when Pirro sings, the coloratura is more declamatory and harsh. It's wonderful when you can let the public know that there is a difference in emotion between two characters' coloraturas. Then you've given the audience something they enjoy much more than if you have two singers showing off agility that sounds the same.

Do you ever run into technical difficulties?

At one point last year, I was doing *Sonnambula*. One day, watching myself in the mirror, I saw my stomach go the wrong way. My stomach would always go in while singing and now I was starting to push out. It felt okay, but I realized I wasn't letting any air out. So, I went into the practice room every day for a week and had to completely relearn how to breathe! I had been sick and tried to sing through the cold for a couple of performances, so I did something improper, which stayed with me for four months after that! I kept wondering why it was getting harder to sing. An oversight like that can cost you, if you're not careful.

What are your own dos and don'ts of bel canto?

The most important thing is to make the performance your own. In this day and age, there are so many recordings that it can be very tempting to copy other singers. Make your own variations, if you can, staying true to the composer and serving the music. Bel canto can be something of a showoff thing, and that's okay in certain situations, if you're doing an aria by itself. In the context of a whole opera, it's different.

When I worked with Richard Bonynge for the first time, I copied another singer's performance, and he asked me why I did that. I said, "Because so-and-so did it." He said, "Make it yours. Do you really think it needs that high note here or that variation there?" I said, "I don't think so, but it's a tradition."

"Well, make your own tradition!" he told me, and that got me to thinking that this is what the art of bel canto is about: making the piece yours, so that we know when we hear the performance that it is not you doing Pavarotti's interpretation, it's just pure you.

Do you see bel canto as alive, always moving and changing?

Of course, the basic principles of legato and beautiful singing stay the same. But the freedom to invent your own variations and make the phrases different is thrilling because each performance becomes unique. I'll probably get into trouble for this, but the Ricci cadenzas? They're great—but they're Ricci's! They are very good to get a sense of what the art is all about, but once you become an experienced performer, it has to be you, not Ricci! It's a fine line when you invent your own.

One of the very first Rossini bel cantos I did was *La donna del lago*, with Riccardo Muti. There's a famous trio, with two tenors and a soprano, where all three singers sing the same phrases. The second time through, we needed to make variations. Muti is known for sticking to the score, so if you want to change something, it's better not to tell him beforehand; just do it.

I'll never forget the look on his face when I sang my variation straight at him. He smiled at me! But then the next thing I did with him was *Don Pasquale*. When I tried to do some showy variations, he said: "That's not Donizetti. You have to be much simpler in Donizetti bel canto, not as elaborate as in Rossini."

. . . Another "don't" of bel canto involves high notes. Don't do them to show off, but only if they work dramatically. Always push yourself to the next level. If you think that's as fast as you can take that coloratura, you could probably take it a little faster! It's not to go past what you can do, but to go as far as you can, because that's what really makes it exciting.

I think that sometimes people don't appreciate bel canto as much, because it can be just a lot of pretty notes coming from not-so-credible characters. The music is so vocally self-indulgent, and many singers are very well rehearsed, but the performance can lose its edge and become beauty without drama.

Sometimes it's hard to find conductors who welcome the vocal freedom of bel canto. Some conductors want to know exactly what you are going to do . . . I had an incident last summer. I was doing a piece for the first time and I decided to do something different at the dress rehearsal: to make a phrase a little longer, hold one note and come down. The conductor went right through it! I stood there and said, "Where are you going? Wait! I'm not done yet!" It was probably a little embarrassing for all of us, but my colleagues loved it!

Let's talk about the unexpected turn your life took nine years ago. What happened to you?

I was diagnosed with testicular cancer.

What was going on at the time?

I was in Madrid doing *L'italiana in Algeri* and I started to feel a little bit uncomfortable. There's a self-examination you can do for testicular cancer, although I didn't know this at the time. But when I was showering, I felt a lump on one of my testicles.

When I returned to the States, the doctor told me straight out that it was cancer. So, I went into surgery to remove the testicle with the growth. They told me it was stage one out of four. This is the best prognosis you can get. If you're a stage one and you follow the protocol, you can be sure that you will be cured.

There were a couple of different protocols. One was the Indiana University protocol, which saved Lance Armstrong's life. But that one had a history of lung scarring, so you wouldn't be able to use part of your lungs. Of course, I said, "No way, that's not for me!" I wanted to sing again.

The doctor was very accommodating, so we did the other protocol. The whole process itself lasted about six months. Looking back, it wasn't even that long, but when you're in it, it seems endless!

What side effects did you experience from chemotherapy?

They were very tough. Chemotherapy basically tries to kill off every-thing bad in your body. Consequently, a lot of good stuff goes with it, too. They push you as far as your body will go without killing you. So I went from having one uncomfortable little lump to feeling much sicker than I could ever imagine.

What sustained you mentally and emotionally during this time?

My faith in God. There was never a question that I was going to get better. It was just going to be a hard road, but I was determined to get there. I didn't ask, "Why?" All I asked was, "How can you help me?" I kept telling my agent, Robert Lombardo, that I really wanted to sing again. At the beginning of this whole ordeal, he actually advised me not to say anything about my illness. You are the first person I am officially telling about this.

Why did he advise you to keep it quiet?

There is too much prejudice out there. You don't want anyone to know you have cancer because you will not work anymore. That's just a fact of life, not only in our business but almost everywhere. I kept quiet not because I was embarrassed or scared about it, but because I wanted to come back after not singing for so long, without having anyone throw preconceived notions at me. If people I worked for didn't know it, then they wouldn't cancel on that. So, I wanted to prove that this was not so terrible, that it is possible to recover from it, to go on, to live my life and continue my career.

Do you believe that if you had told the truth, and then explained that you've recovered, you still would have met with discrimination?

Definitely. I've seen it. Unfortunately, people today still believe that the word *cancer* is another word for *death*. But many more people survive cancer today than die, especially if it's detected early enough. The doctor told me, "Yes, you're going to die, but you're not going to die of cancer!"

However, in our business, you have to sign contracts sometimes two or more years in advance. If they have even the slightest notion that you may not be around two years from now, they won't hire you.

If you look at it from the general managers' point of view, it's under-standable. They need to have a guarantee that you will be there. But it is terribly morbid. I heard stories where general managers said, "I was told I shouldn't hire you because you were sick and you probably wouldn't be around for very long."

If I had come out right away to say, "Yes, I had cancer but now I am cured, everything is fine!" . . . so what? That is just what I say. I had to prove that it was actually true, and that nine years later I am still singing. What happened is in the past. So send good thoughts to all those who are going through similar situations.

It was so hard not to have my colleagues' support! I couldn't tell them! When you're in a rehearsal period for six weeks, you get to know the other cast members very well. For that period of time, they become a surrogate family, your support system; you tell them about things that happened to you. When you're not able to talk about something like this, it's just horrible!

What was the explanation you gave for disappearing from the singing circuit for all those months?

I said I had a stomach ulcer. The good thing in our profession is that you don't have an everyday, nine-to-five employer to whom you have to explain why you won't be there for the next six months. I had to cancel four jobs. Ironically, the job I came back with was in Madrid! When I look back today, I think, "My God. I must have been crazy!" After not singing for six months, I came back with *Don Pasquale* and then *Puritani* with Eve Queler.

Did chemotherapy affect your voice in any way?

I received great advice from the doctors taking care of me. Chemotherapy kills every red blood cell in your body, so the vocal cords become extremely vulnerable. If you as much as shout or speak loudly, you can do a lot of damage, because the cords have no protection. So, for the whole time I did chemotherapy, I hardly even talked. After it was all over and my hair started to come back, and all [my] blood levels were normal, I saw my laryngologist. He looked at the cords and said, "Perfect!" The six-month nonsinging, barely speaking rest had rejuvenated the whole mechanism!

How long did it take you to recover your vocal shape?

Vocally, I came back rather quickly. I practiced every day and the voice came back in about three weeks. It felt really fresh, and it was fantastic to sing again. The body, however, responded less fast than the cords. I did physical therapy daily, not just for the stomach muscles but for my arms and legs. I had lost muscle tone and I was pretty much incapacitated for a while.

The most exhilarating experience was being onstage again and having my life back! Colleagues asked me, "What did you do to your hair?" Eve Queler said, "Oh, my God! Your beautiful hair! Where is it?" because I had about a quarter of an inch of hair! I said, "Well, I lost a Super Bowl bet and I had to shave my head!" I didn't talk about it. The rumors would fly around, of course, as they always do. You try to ignore them as much as you can.

So, this is really the first time you are opening up about this?

Yes. My family and people in my community knew, of course, because I did some support things for the hospital that took care of me. But people in the opera world don't know, because I have never told anyone personally. My God, to be able to say this now: "Yes, I really did have cancer and I am cured!"

I'm honored . . . Thank you for sharing your inspiring story.

I appreciate that. It's been nine years! It was time to talk about it. I believe singers will be very sympathetic; hopefully general managers will understand and not be swayed, not only by cancer but [by] everything: "Oh, so-and-so has a heart problem. So-and-so has AIDS." I mean, if you have the goods, you've got to be able to work! You should be hired. Don't discriminate against anyone because of their health or what you assume their health will be in two years!

How did this experience affect your perspective?

Something like this can't help but change your whole attitude toward life, if you take the right path. It could have gone two ways. I could have said, "Why me?" but I said, "What do I do? How do I beat this?" Getting better became my job in those months. For five or six years afterward, I thought about it constantly. It made me appreciate everything around me.

What I do for a living is a privilege, and I thank God every day. Of course, having our child was the absolute miracle! You know, when you do chemotherapy, you can't have children anymore, because there are certain things in your body [that] never come back after you kill them, and one is sperm. So, your reproductive function is gone.

Then how did you . . .

It's a secret!

Come on; share one more secret with us, please!

Well, before I started the chemotherapy, the doctors said there was a thing called "banking," which means storing the sperm, so we did that. Our only chance then was in vitro fertilization, you know, your test-tube baby! For me it was easy to say yes, but my chemotherapy was nothing compared to what my wife went through in this process. They had to do it three times, until it was successful. There were all these shots and hormone things, the stress, the emotional ups and downs; it was all incredible. But when we went to the doctor after the third try and he showed us the

little embryo growing inside her, we were ecstatic! We were just hoping for a healthy baby, but I have to tell you: she is gorgeous!

Tell me about the Gregory Kunde Chorale.

It's really become its own animal. We used to sing in a local church choir. I had the summer of '99 free, and I asked the choral director what she thought about the choir coming to my house once a week to do some choral techniques and learn different music other than church anthems. I hadn't done any conducting since I was in college. But they began coming to my house, thirty-five of them in my family room, and we started having a lot of fun. They were all amateurs and about 70 percent of them didn't read music. That was a wonderful challenge for me, and our first concert was very successful.

Afterward, they wanted to keep [going], so in the fall of 2000, we began as a real group. We had five concerts this year alone. It involves a lot of work, but it's a rewarding, new experience for me, to be able to teach amateurs and see them successful. All I do is just stand there and wave my arms! They are great, and the community has really taken to them.

So far, you've only had one or two Met appearances. Are there any scheduled?

No. The Met is kind of elusive to me. I'm not sure why. I was always given the excuse that I had too small a voice. When I sang *Cenerentola* there once, I was told: "Oh, we didn't realize your voice was that big!"

I would love to sing there. But I guess they have other people who sing my repertoire.

Any words of advice for singers?

I know this sounds very trite but: Know your voice and be true to it! Take care of it and let it grow naturally. Think long term. It can be very exciting for ten years, but don't burn yourself out!

Alfredo Kraus was singing *La fille du régiment* at age seventy. He maintained his wonderful sound his whole life. That has always been my model, and I wish that for my up-and-coming colleagues.

Have a long career and never push your voice where it doesn't belong. No matter what anyone tells you, and how much money they offer you, it's not worth it!

Anna Netrebko

Recorded August 2008 in Salzburg, Austria. Published here for the first time.

**You look radiant. How are you feeling with three weeks
[of pregnancy] to go?**

So far, it's been very easy for me and I like it. The boy is doing very
well.

You know that it's a boy . . .

Oh, yeah. I knew this from the beginning. He showed immediately that
he is a boy!

Right now you're taking a break from singing.

Yes, of course.

**Do you feel any difference in the voice now, when you're
singing at home?**

I'm never singing at home.

Never?

Once I stop . . . my concerts and performances, I fully stop [singing].
I'm singing only when I'm practicing, rehearsing, and performing, but
never at home for pleasure.

**I grew up in Romania pretty much around the same time as
you were growing up in Russia. Those were tough times on
the Eastern bloc. What was it like for you?**

It wasn't that tough. I mean, right now when we know what was
behind all that, we think, "Oh, it was tough," but when I was a kid, I
was very happy. I had a great family. We weren't rich, we weren't poor; it
was just enough to have everything we wanted. I mean, we thought so.
And the house was always full of friends, lots of parties. Back then I was
singing a lot at home.

So you had music in the house.

We did. It wasn't opera because in the city where I grew up, there
was no opera theater. It was musical theater, operetta. Mostly I liked

music from the movies, lighter stuff. Yes, music was surrounding me all the time!

Do you remember your first contact with opera?

I don't remember my very first contact. I just wanted to sing, I wanted to be on the stage. I wanted to sing operetta, actually. And I went to study in St. Petersburg. Already during my first year of study I was able to see performances at the Mariinsky Theatre—now the Kirov. That's how I fell in love. I think the sound of the orchestra, the voices, the whole feeling about it when it's live, it really captured me, and I said, "That's what I want to do!"

Then you actually worked at the Mariinsky, washing floors . . .

Yes. That was a job I got because I wanted to see the performances. The Mariinsky is across the street from the conservatory, and I worked there my first two years in the conservatory. It was actually lots of fun. I had the possibility to see everything I wanted. Not only opera rehearsals, but also the ballet, the concerts. Sometimes, it wasn't possible to get tickets, but I was there all the time. These were really important years for me.

You had mentioned that in the conservatory, many of your colleagues were not too encouraging. But you said you found something so clean and pure in your voice and you thought you may be better than they think. That grain of unshakable trust in yourself, that faith is worth more than anything to a young singer. It's so easy to get discouraged by ill-meaning colleagues. What are your thoughts about that now?

It has to be somewhere in between, I think. You should not think too highly of yourself and be too proud, saying, "Oh, I'm the best!" Once you start to think that, it means that you will never grow as an artist. But on the other hand, you don't have to punish yourself and see your level lower than it is, because that it also stopping you. So it has to be somewhere in between. Actually, my voice teacher . . . she was very, very smart. She never let us go in either of those two directions. If you sang a very good exam or concert, she never said, "Oh, my God, you were excellent!" She would say, "It was good. We need to work." And if she saw it was a disaster, that you couldn't bring out on the stage what you wanted and you were very upset, she would say, "No, it wasn't that bad. There were some good things . . . " She'd always keep this balance, which was very smart.

This was Tamara Novichenko?

Tamara, yes.

Was she your first voice teacher?

I'd been studying before with a couple of people, but she was my main teacher with whom I really started my vocal technique.

How did you end up studying with her?

She was the teacher in the conservatory to whom everybody wanted to go. All the sopranos wanted her because most of her singers started to have a career after [their studies with] her. I thought immediately: "Okay, I have to go to this woman because she will teach me how to sing."

Did you do a lot of vocalises?

Oh, yes! I was working a lot! And because I was the youngest one for two or three years, I was starting at nine thirty!

In the morning?

Yeah. With all these coloratura arias which I hated. I wanted to sing something *big*! Like, all the dramatic repertoire!

What were your favorites at that time?

Of course, when you're just starting singing, you're listening to Callas and Tebaldi and all these dramatic arias that are just driving you crazy! And I said, "Ah, I want to sing this and that; I want to sing Gioconda and Mimi," and [Tamara] would [roll her eyes]. She said, "You know what? Maybe you will sing these. But right now . . ." She gave me Lakmé, Queen of the Night, and said, "Study these! You have to!" I have to say thanks to her, because she pushed me to study this difficult music.

So she was encouraging you to keep it light, while your sound also has a darker quality. Did she get into that darker quality at all?

No. She wanted me to sing lighter. Always. It was always good that my voice has this dark quality because it's different from typical coloraturas. I had an advantage. Maybe still now . . . I don't know . . .

Definitely! I hear that—it's like a dramatic color that lies underneath, very alluring and tempting!

Which is good . . . and different!

Do you remember from your lessons with Tamara, if there was any part of your voice that was difficult for you to master?

Everything was difficult because I didn't have any technique. I just had a diapason (range). A big one! It was very easy going to the high notes. But there was no technique. When you don't have breath control, it just doesn't work. So I kept working and working and working. I was never satisfied. When I went for my first competition . . .

Was that the Glinka?

Yes, the Glinka.

CHRISTOPH RÜTTGER

Which you won.

Yes! Surprise for everybody! First of all for me, then for my teacher. That was absolutely . . . Nobody thought this would happen!

What did you sing?

I sang *Sonnambula* and Queen of the Night. So we went to this competition and [Tamara] said, "It's very good for you to try. I'm sure you will not go further than the first two [rounds]. They will eliminate you because you are not experienced and it's the first time. But we'll try it." So when it was my turn, and I sang the big aria from *Sonnambula*, I think that was the first time when I felt something like a drug on the stage. I felt this energy and I almost started to cry. I was almost the last to sing. I saw the jurywoman, the very famous mezzo-soprano, Irina Arkhipova, taking off her glasses and looking at me amazed. And the audience was, like, "Wow!" After that, they came and said, "Oh, my God, she is the best; she will get the first prize!" And I said, "No way! That's not possible, because I can't sing!"

Oh, you did not say that!

No, no, but it's true! I didn't have any technique. There were singers who were much more prepared than me! But maybe they saw something different, and that was the reason why I won this competition.

At that time did you have the interest in fashion that you have now? Looking good onstage—was that always in you?

That was always in me, because, you know, I'm a girl! My sister was a model. And I won a beauty competition in Krasnodar when I was seventeen. That was very funny! But, of course, I didn't have money at all at that time. I was already starting to look at dresses. I designed a dress by myself. My first concert dresses were my designs!

Do you know the actor Stanley Tucci?

I've heard [of him].

Well, I bring him up because I recently heard him say in an

interview that when he memorizes a part, he feels the words in his body. He has to connect his lines to his physical being and that's how he best remembers a role. If I understood correctly, he said he learns his lines by associating them with different areas of his body, where he feels them.

That's interesting!

I just couldn't help thinking that when you're singing, it is also so physical, so integral—as if you too would associate your lines or rather musical phrases with parts of your body. Do you ever think about the physicality of your singing or is it simply natural?

The physicality comes naturally to me. I don't think about it.

Which is probably best . . .

No. Sometimes I need to think about it, like I was thinking that I should move much less. Especially at the beginning, when you cannot really sing, the arms are the first to help you, but it's a very bad habit. From the beginning you have to learn to sing in a relaxed way.

But when you sing, it looks relaxed and natural. You don't make any unusual movements with your mouth.

I'm trying, especially when I know there are cameras, then I really work at keeping my face relaxed. But it's not always like that.

Especially when you are in many movie theaters, thanks to the Met.

That's so important because I know the camera is so close . . . and it's stress[ful]. It's very scary.

But it looks great! So, there are many schools of singing teachers and students; some tend to overintellectualize the process of singing, some find it helpful to have principles put into words; others don't want to talk about it so much. I've read that you don't like to talk technically. But do you have a philosophy of singing that you'd be willing to share?

The simpler you keep it, the better it is! In singing, thinking has to be very little. I mean, for me. The less you think about singing, the better it is. Of course, when you prepare a role, you have to put it in a certain geographical and even choreographical structure, but after that, everything else has to come naturally. I immediately recognize the singers who are thinking too much. It has to be spontaneous. It has to be intuition. It has to be, let's say, talent. Or just some gift. Maybe not talent, but something that is very personal, which appears suddenly during singing. If it's too structured and too intellectual . . . no! I have also met many singers who are speaking so smartly and so wonderfully, you just think, "Oh, my God, you can write a book!" But then they go on the stage and it's like . . . "ugh!"

You said that you are not very much in favor of young artist programs.

No. I think they can destroy young singers. Some are good. I did the Merola in San Francisco—two months—that was perfect. Very good for young singers. They have everything you need. You develop a lot and you're able to perform some things. But if you're stuck in a theater for two years sitting on your ass—excuse me!—and covering . . . *covering*! . . . this is horrible! This is what really stops your development. Young singers have to go and sing on the stage. That's the only thing that can help them learn how to do that. The experience! And the theaters have to do something about that. They have to put on main-stage performances with young singers in big roles, announce that they are young singers' performances, and make the ticket prices cheaper. I'm sure it would be full of people who would love to see a performance with all young singers.

So you think that the idea of covering is not very encouraging psychologically for a young singer . . .

It's horrible! I was once covering for a great, great soprano, actually. And I was sitting the whole day there, and after that when I had a little rehearsal, I couldn't do anything because I only heard her in my mind and nothing from me. I cannot imagine these poor singers who're sitting there for years and doing nothing. It's just so wrong.

Do you still work with Renata Scotto once in a while?

Not recently. I'm very busy and she's very busy. I have worked with her. I prepared my second CD, *Sempre libera*, and I also worked with her on *Capuleti*, on my bel canto roles. And she was great! She is really amazing.

Did she work with you artistically?

Artistically and on the style of bel canto. Not technically.

What did you get from her?

Oh, I got many things from her! The development was very clear. I sang my first Giulietta in *Capuleti* in Philadelphia. I was very inexperienced. It was the beginning of my career and the role wasn't going well. There was something I couldn't catch. And I went to New York to study with her between my performances. By the end of the performance run, the quality of the singing and everything grew, and even the response of the audience. That was amazing, it was so clear! And I know this is because of her.

What was it that made that switch to a higher level?

She told me the great things about how to approach bel canto. Because it's not just "ta, ta, ta, ta, ta, ta"—following the rhythm of the arpeggio-like accompaniment. She taught me how to find the colors in every single phrase, how to make them different, where to do diminuendo or fermatas, where to speed up—all these little things you have to fulfill your singing in bel canto. And it was an amazing difference.

Valery Gergiev is another great mentor for you.

Oh, yes. This is a very important man in my life. We are very good friends. He just called me yesterday; we were talking about the war [in Georgia], unfortunately. But he did so much for me! He was the one who let me sing these big, important roles on the stage when I was twenty-two, twenty-three. He said, "Let her work! Let's try!" We didn't do so many things together because the music he's conducting and the music I'm singing are different, but we did Prokofiev's *Betrothal*, we did *Ruslan and Ludmila*, and *War and Peace*. That was wonderful. I mean, he doesn't have to say anything; you just have to look at him, and everything is there.

Did you do gymnastics as a kid?

Oh, yes. I was an acrobat for many years!

And you were good at it.

I was okay. I did lots of sports when I was a kid. I also did athletics for two years. After that, I was dancing. This really helps.

Do you identify with any role in particular?

One of my favorites is Natasha from *War and Peace*. It's so close to me somehow. When I was her age, like fifteen, sixteen, I was exactly like her. Silly . . . I love it! I love all the other roles though, otherwise I wouldn't sing them.

So you sing only what you like?

Yes, because if I don't like the role, it will never be good. I have tried a couple of roles I can sing vocally, but if I'm not feeling anything, it doesn't sound good. That's why I'm not singing some roles anymore.

We touched on fashion before. What styles appeal to you?

I like many different styles. I like colors.

It looks like you prefer a mix of classical glamour with some funky, hip touches.

It has to be a little crazy and a little messy because I am not a "classical" person. If I wear a little black dress and pearls, it's just not me. I need something crazy. But maybe in five years I will be different. I will get older, so I will be more precise in my style. Armani is definitely not my designer, even if I like it. I love American designers. The best shopping is in America!

In New York.

The *best*!

You've brought much hope to the future of opera by revitalizing it, injecting energy, youthfulness, and fun into it. Do you feel that this has become your mission?

I don't think about it. Somehow I was given an opportunity because of Deutsche Grammophon and all of the attention from the press. I have an opportunity to speak about my work and be known for it. But there are lots of young singers who act well and look great. It's not my mission.

It is associated with you because you have done that on a great scale. You've widened the audience range in terms of age and backgrounds.

You think so?

Definitely! And tell me about your relationship with Rolando Villazón. You seem to have so much fun together onstage and backstage.

Oh, we have a wonderful time. He is a fun person. It's fantastic to be onstage with him! Because the soprano and the tenor are always partners. So it's very important to have a good tenor to sing with. Otherwise you cannot come through the performance. I mean, you can, but especially in performances like *Roméo et Juliette*, *Manon*, *La traviata*, you're always together. If the tenor is weak, it is kind of like he is sitting on your shoulders. If it's the opposite, if he's better than you, then you are climbing; then the performance is at a completely different level.

Did you ever have a bad experience with a tenor?

All of my stage partners have been very good. I'm very lucky. Sometimes it can just happen that you're expecting a little more with the energy, but overall I have great partners.

You have different musical tastes: Amy Winehouse, Christina Aguilera, Robbie Williams . . .

Because I'm watching MTV! I hate TV. But if I'm in a hotel alone in another country and I don't know the language, I put on MTV. It's fun.

Do you get any ideas for what to wear from the MTV videos?

I get some ideas for fashion. I know some designers, too. I went to Fashion Week in New York several times. I love it! And I'm so happy that lots of designers know me somehow. That was very surprising. Like Zac Posen, Donna Karan, and Vera Wang . . . They said, "Oh, it's a big honor for us that you come." And my jaw was dropping, "My God, how do they know me?" They all go to the Met, I think. They always invite me; it's very nice. And I'm so happy with Escada, my God! They came at the beginning of my career and just offered that I wear all these beautiful dresses for concerts and it's fantastic!

Escada is like a sponsor for you?

They give me my concert gowns. All those gorgeous dresses are from Escada.

So many people enjoy what you do in the open-air concerts: stepping away from the microphone so the audience can hear your voice without amplification.

It's my trick! They like it! So at least they know that I have a voice.

How did you get the idea to do this?

I knew everyone would hear the high notes even if it's in a huge space, so I tried it once and it worked.

You've been asked before about doing crossover and said you're not interested. Would you not even consider it?

It could be interesting, who knows. My English is maybe not good enough, but you never say never.

I think it would be so much fun to see you do that—especially with your dance background, too.

I can do something if some interesting project came along, but I would never switch my profession to that, even if it would be more popular or bring me much more money.

What is your best remedy for colds?

Vodka! If the cold just starts—if it's not the flu—this is the prescription! I always recommend it to everybody. Drink one hundred grams of vodka straight in one shot and immediately go to sleep under the covers so you sweat, and next morning you're much better. I did this and it really helps. Don't exaggerate. Don't do this too often!

Do you see teaching in your future?

No. I'm horrible; I don't have any patience.

Have you ever had the opportunity to hear a beginning singer and help him or her in some way?

I have ears to understand what is good and what is wrong there. But to teach someone how to do this . . . I have no idea, because everybody's different. It's very hard to teach singing because everything is inside you. And you have to use different images for everybody.

If you had one advice to give to a novice singer, what would it be?

I would say, "Don't listen to too much advice!" And that they have to believe in themselves, but not to overdo that. Always work, always search for something else.

And keep the balance, as your teacher said.

Keeping the balance is very, very important. Don't go to one side or the other. If you have too many complexes, you will never go through them, because on the stage you don't want to have any complexes. You're there, that's it!—"I'm the king! I'm here with all my power!" But after that, you have to be a regular person again and say, "Okay, that was fine, but I have to do this, this, and that now."

Any upcoming project that you would like to mention?

We did a movie of *La bohème*. It's coming out in the fall of 2008. It's beautiful! It's like a traditional movie. We did the recording before. In the movie we're still singing, but we're using the soundtrack.

Did you enjoy working on camera?

I liked it very much. I couldn't imagine being pregnant and at thirty-six that I [would] be on the big screen like that, looking not that bad, actually. It was fun and interesting; different work from being on the stage, because the camera is close and [the acting] has to be more personal, more intimate, a lot with the eyes. That was very cool!

Gayletha Nichols

Recorded June 2002 via phone. Published in Classical Singer, *November 2002.*

Ms. Nichols, what is the age limit for the [Metropolitan Opera's] Lindemann [Young Artist] program?

There is no age limit. We take it on an individual basis and hope to catch the artists at a time when we can help them most.

How do you find the singers? Do they audition for you?

They do audition. We often find them through the Metropolitan Opera National Council auditions. There are district and regional auditions, and then the finalists come to New York. We do pick some of the singers from there.

Where else do you find them? Do you attend musical events?

Yes. I happen to be in Aspen now for a few weeks, because I am also working on the festival. But I attend eight or ten festivals every year between June and August and hear the apprentices in these festivals sing, so I have an idea who is out there and, given time, who might be appropriate to audition for the program next year. In addition to that, we get a lot of recommendations from our colleagues across the country.

What does the program offer?

You know, a lot has to happen for someone to have an operatic career, so we try to evaluate singers and help them in areas where they might be weak. For instance, if their languages are not so good, they immediately get to study language one-on-one with a teacher of French, Italian, German—we've even expanded that to Russian now. Languages are a very important part of our training program, so singers who need it will receive that kind of training on a weekly or even daily basis. Of course, they all receive musical coaching every day for their own audition repertoire, or for roles that they are learning, not only for the Met stage but for other places where they are performing. We also have a dramatic studies program: acting classes, dance—a lot of guest directors come and work with the singers individually. We also have an Alexander Technique person on our staff who spends enough time with us each week so that everyone will have an individual session with her.

Would the singers still have to work to support themselves, or is this similar to a full-time job?

I guess you could say a fellowship with us is a full-time job. We have a thirty-thousand-dollar living stipend, as we would call it, and that's the minimum that a person in the young artist program would make. They all start with that. And if they sing roles onstage, they would be paid additionally for the roles.

For how long can a singer stay in this program?

It varies. People often stay two or three years, but it is a year-at-a-time commitment, both on the part of the singer and the company.

And are they evaluated? Is somebody responsible for their progress?

Yes. They are evaluated more or less constantly, I am afraid. We try not to make them feel like every time they open their mouth they re-audition for the job. That's not fair. Our commitment to them is stronger than that, but they do get daily input about their work. For instance, if they sing in a master class, I often talk to them afterward about how they felt it went—if they were at their best, or if something did not go well. They also audition for outside folks—meaning people who are holding auditions for summer programs, managers, artistic directors looking for singers. I try to attend the auditions so I am able to talk to them afterward, [to] help them evaluate it and make it better next time.

Do they ever go on to a career at the Met?

Oh, sure they do. There are a lot of people from the program that are now singing at the Met very regularly.

The most common concern of *Classical Singer* readers was that information about this program is so inaccessible. It is not advertised anywhere. So, to sum up, the only way a singer can audition for this program is if someone hears them and recommends them?

Yes, you need to be recommended by somebody. We have in the past done auditions where singers sent in information, but it became very time consuming. Before I convene a whole panel from the members of the Met artistic staff, I need to know whether this is an appropriate candidate. The best way to do that is a verbal or written recommendation from someone in the business whose opinion bears some weight. We do not have one set time of the year for auditions. We are hearing people for the program all year long. Hardly a week goes by without hearing someone. So, it is pretty accessible.

Do you look for experience?

We are looking for the potential, really, and it is not about just training singers for the Met, it's about training singers for opera. So it's not just about Met potential, it's about real talent—how big the vocal gift is. The singers auditioning have to communicate, to say something with their music, to have that spark, to show they are going to be a commanding presence on the stage.

Do you enjoy this job?

Very much.

You get to hear an enormous number of singers . . .

Oh, gosh! Close to a thousand a year now.

And you are musically trained as well . . .

I was a singer before this. There were plenty of times in my early work with young artists, when I thought, "Wow! I wish there were something like this when I was their age."

I take great joy in really being able to help them and be there for them. There was nobody around when I was their age to talk about these things. I have worked with young artists for ten years now. Before I came to the Met, I worked in the Houston Grand Opera Studio for eight years.

Is there any communication between the different young artist programs?

Constantly. Right before you called, I was on the phone to Houston. Diane Zola runs the program now. We were comparing notes about singers she is interested in; she is looking for some extra information on them and I just heard them recently. So, I talk to my colleagues all the time in San Francisco, Chicago, Seattle, Florida, and elsewhere.

Sounds like a huge network.

It is very much so. It's always funny because the singers never think that we are talking about these things, I guess. So if they do something in another part of the country and it's good, I will hear about it. If it is not good, I will hear about it, too. It's pretty easy now to get this information, between your cell phone and your e-mail . . . You know, when they do well, it's to their advantage. Often someone will call me and say, "I know you are not taking so-and-so for your program. Do you think they would be good for our program?" I have found a lot of work for people I was not interested in for the Met. I have been able to place them in other situations that they were able to grow from.

Do you choose mostly American singers?

Not intentionally, but most of our singers are Americans. However, in the last season we also had two Russians, a Belgian, a Canadian; and maybe five other countries were represented. So, it's quite diverse, provided we can get visas for these singers. It is not a student visa. Those are pretty easy. But a training visa, where you are getting paid as well, is a very tricky matter. Sometimes we cannot get them. It depends on the country, what the procedure is, and how much time we have.

Samuel Ramey

Recorded January 2005 in New York City, USA. Published in Classical Singer, *March 2005.*

What did you want to do when you were a kid?

It was always a dream of mine to be a professional baseball player. I was okay, but not that talented in baseball. Then I got interested in singing. When I first started to sing, I thought I'd be a pop singer, because I didn't know anything about opera, growing up. Then, when I went to college, I had decided to study music, but with the idea of becoming a teacher.

Where did you go to college?

I first went to Kansas State University in Manhattan, Kansas. I was studying voice, working on "Non più andrai" from *Le nozze di Figaro*, and my teacher suggested that I find a recording just to get an idea of the style. So, I went to a record store and found this old LP of Ezio Pinza. I listened to him, and that sparked an interest. I started going to the library and listening to opera more. Then one summer, a friend of mine told me about an opera company in Central City, Colorado, which hired young singers to sing in the chorus. So I made a tape, sent it off to them—and they hired me.

Then I went to Central City. That was my first experience in opera; I'd never seen an opera until I was in one.

Who discovered that you actually had an operatic voice?

I think it was my high school music teacher, who also gave me voice lessons. She thought I had some talent. And then, when I started studying seriously in college, I got very good encouragement.

Was your family supportive?

Yes. Almost everybody in my family was talented in music: everybody sang—my brothers and my sister sang just for the fun of it. My mother always hoped one of us would have a career, and I was her last chance—so she was happy I decided to pursue music professionally.

When you started to study voice, what challenged you most?

Well, the high notes were never really a problem. I always had good high notes. I don't know why! I think the big challenge for my voice was [to achieve] a concentration of the sound. My teacher, who I'm still with—Armen Boyajian—had me concentrate on focusing the sound. When I first started studying with him, I tended to spread a little bit, so that also affected the quality of the voice. It is important for a bass voice to be very focused.

You can get as technical as you want.

It's difficult for me to talk about the technical [aspect].

What is your mission when you sing?

Oh, wow! That's hard to put into words. I think it's just giving . . . I like to think of giving the best total performance that I can. I don't think very much about technique.

What I love when I see you perform is your stillness—but at the same time, it is obvious you emanate this huge energy from inside. It's really difficult to separate the stillness from the energy, and to balance them. How did you find that balance?

I've always tried to think of my performances as being very compact. I think overly done movement or gesturing is silly. A lot of the drama in opera is in the music; it doesn't need a lot movement. I think all the acting has to be very compact; everything has to have a meaning. You can't just flail your arms because it helps you vocally. Everything you do should mean something. Within this compact idea, the energy is then channeled in one direction and not scattered all over. Then I can maintain the stillness and not waste any energy on unnecessary movements.

Where does a bass's passaggio lie?

For me, it's D-flat, D, E-flat—right in there.

Is there anything you do differently when you sing in that area of your voice?

No. I don't think about it.

What do you feel in your body when you produce those really low notes?

I feel all the resonators, not just the chest but all of them. Some people make the mistake of losing the head resonators when they sing low notes. The low notes feel predominantly in the chest, but you still feel the other resonators.

You made your Met debut in 1984 in *Rinaldo*, which requires a lot of agility. How important is agility for a bass and for heavier voices?

I think it's very important, because as bass voices get older, they tend to get overdark and woolly sounding. For that reason, it's very important to always practice keeping a voice agile. I always do agility exercises to keep the voice flexible and light, not pushed or heavy.

Do you still see your voice teacher?

Oh, yes. When I'm in New York, I try to see Armen as much as my schedule allows.

What do your lessons with him consist of now?

Basically, repertoire. I'm still doing new roles, so anything new that I do, I always take to him to prepare.

This has been a very long teacher-student relationship for you.

It will be thirty-five years in November! Election Day of 1970 was my first lesson with him.

Do you think it's better to stay with one teacher?

I think it's a mistake for singers to change teachers constantly. But I can't really speak for other singers, because when I found Armen, I just knew he was the best for me, and we've had such a good relationship.

What has kept you going to him all this time?

He takes a real personal interest in his students. He goes to performances. If you're doing something new, he's always there the first time you do it, and sometimes comes back again. He's one of the few teachers who really do that.

How do you stay in such great physical shape?

I try to exercise. I don't run because my knees don't let me run. I like to do power walking as often as I can. I work out a little bit, sometimes at the gym. I lift weights, but I'm careful not to overdo it, because it can be bad for singers, as you know.

You don't do any other sports?

I play some golf, but that's all.

You're an amazing actor, and you bring credibility to such a variety of roles. How do you prepare a role?

Well, it's not something that I really do much on my own. I usually wait until I work with the stage director—unless it's a role that I'm not doing for the first time and I go into a production without much rehearsal. This is very often the case in some European theaters, where you get two-day rehearsals. In that case, I have to call on my own resources. But generally, if I'm doing something new or something I haven't done very often, then I just like to develop the character while working with the director, getting his ideas, coming up with a few ideas of my own, and combining them.

CHRISTIAN STEINER

What do you do if there's something you don't agree with?

You know, that really hasn't happened. Well, maybe a few times in my career. But I haven't really had big problems with directors. I've been lucky in that way, I guess.

Sometimes you see one-dimensional performances of Mephistophélès—your specialty—in *Faust*. I've seen basses who try to do the role as purely evil.

Well, that's not the whole character. He has a few evil moments. But by and large, he has to have a lot of charm, I think. Mephistophélès is a very multifaceted character. He has a little bit of everything in him. In fact, I've done productions where in each act he's almost a different character, with a totally different costume. He has to be very adaptable. He can't be always evil. If he comes on the stage and he's just evil from the outset, how is that going to persuade Faust to sign the contract? He has to be seductive to win people over. In the end, he doesn't win, of course, but he does in the beginning.

Another role I really loved you in is Philip in *Don Carlo*. How do you approach an aria like "Ella giammai m'amò"?

This is the moment when Philip is most fragile. I think the moments when someone is alone and reflecting on his or her life are the most tragic moments in a character. That's really the only moment in the opera where Philip is by himself. The music before Philip even sings is just very lonely sounding. That could be almost like he's sleepwalking or just unable to sleep, and he could be pacing the room. I've never done it staged that way, but it could be an idea. I just think the music in this aria gives you everything you need to know about how to approach it.

You've been performing for more than thirty years. What would you say is the secret of your longevity?

I don't really know. I've been very fortunate, I think, that my voice has remained in good shape. I mean, it's not where it was ten years ago, of course, but it serves me well.

As a bass, you have to constantly sort of reinvent yourself, looking for different repertoire. Now, I could no longer do *Don Giovanni* or *Nozze di Figaro*, some of the roles that I've been known for in the past. You have to think repertoire changes, and looking at new things that suit your voice as it matures. A couple of years ago I did Gianni Schicchi for the first time, in Los Angeles.

And you also did Scarpia recently.

Yeah. I do Scarpia a lot the next few years. I'm also looking at things like Don Pasquale.

How did you approach the role of Scarpia? Sometimes you hear people just aggressively barking it out.

Yeah, I know. And I've seen a lot done that way. It is a part I've wanted to do for a long time. I did it the first time in London, eleven or twelve years ago. Then it didn't come about again until last year at the Met. So more than ten years went by without doing it. I had a big success when I did it in London. But now, in the next couple of years, I do it quite a bit. But Scarpia can't be just brutal and aggressive. Just like Mephistophélès, he has to have a little bit of charm, magnetism, and seductiveness, I think.

And it helps when you are so handsome.

Does it? I don't know . . . it doesn't seem to work with Tosca!

Tell me about working on recordings.

Well, in the beginning, when I first started doing recordings, I recorded a lot of things that I'd never performed. That's difficult, because you just learn the music and you're just singing notes. When I finally got to start doing recordings of things that I had done a lot—the staples of my repertoire—then, during the process of a recording, I can sort of imagine myself in the production, and I think that really makes a difference. It can take on more of a theatrical performance. That's important to me when I record.

What singers of the past were your idols and inspiration?

Ezio Pinza certainly had a very early influence on me, because a recording of his is what really sparked my interest in opera. I think I have most of his records. Cesare Siepi is also somebody that is really up on a pedestal for me. There was also another man who sang mostly at New York City Opera: Norman Treigle. He was somebody that I admire very much. Nicolai Ghiaurov was also one of my favorites.

What do you do when you're not singing? Any hobbies?

Well, in the last few years, I've started playing some golf. I have a lot of singer friends who play. If I know I'm going be working with somebody who's a golfer, I'll take my clubs along, so that can be fun.

You do around seventy performances a year?

Yeah. I never really sat down and counted. I'd probably be shocked if I did!

Do you ever take breaks?

It usually works that I have a couple of weeks here and there. I don't purposely just set aside time. For instance, this past summer I had about six weeks off, which was nice.

When you take breaks, do you keep singing?

Most of the time, I do, because I'm usually learning new things. So, most of the time off that I have, I'm studying, preparing things. But once in a while, I'll take a break.

Do you ever teach?

I am starting to teach. In fact, I'm on the faculty of Roosevelt University in Chicago, this coming year. It's on a very limited basis because I'm still very busy with my singing. Lots of times, wherever I'm working, young singers will always come up and ask me, "Would you listen to me and give me some advice?" And I do that quite frequently.

How is that experience for you?

It's nice. To start really teaching intimidates me a bit right now, you know. I've not really done that. I'm going to have to go to my teacher, Armen, to get a lesson on how to teach. He told me, "When you start wanting to teach, you come to me and I'll help you." I've done a few master classes, but not a lot.

Lots of times, when I go places to do recitals, someone on a university staff will ask me if I'll do a master class, so I've done it a few times. Master classes at a college can be kind of touchy, because you're listening to singers who have teachers, so you don't want to say anything that's going to offend the singer's teacher.

Who came up with the whole idea of the "A Date with the Devil" programs?

This was about ten years ago. I had a contract to do a concert with the St. Luke's Orchestra here in New York. About a year before, I was talking to the man who had been my first agent, Matthew Epstein, and he came up with the idea. He said, "Why don't you put together a program doing arias from all the devil roles that you do?" Then he said, "You could even call it 'A Date with the Devil.'"

I put together the arias, but he came up with the idea. I've got two or three of these concerts this coming season.

What do you normally do on a performance day?

I just take it easy, and I vocalize a little bit throughout the day.

Do you sleep a lot before?

No—unless I'm feeling very tired—then I'll take a nap. But usually, I'm awake and I take it easy. I go to the theater early, and once I'm in makeup and everything, I vocalize a lot, for about a half hour before the performance.

You're a bass and a bass-baritone. How does somebody decide whether they're a bass or a bass-baritone?

I used to call myself a bass-baritone, but that can be confusing. People have different opinions about what a bass-baritone is. I always felt a bass-baritone was somebody who was a bass, but maybe had a little baritonal extension. Some people say a bass-baritone is a voice that is neither a real bass nor a real baritone. It's something like the Germans say: *Zwischenfach*—an in-between Fach. I think it's just what you're comfortable with, and what sounds good in your voice.

Do you consciously keep in mind the differences in style when you sing Mozart as opposed to Puccini or bel canto?

No. That's not something I think about. In the eighties, I sang a lot of Rossini. My voice has gotten heavier and it doesn't want to move as well as it did twenty years ago, so I'm not singing Rossini anymore. But at that time, I never thought, "Oh, I'm doing Rossini, so I have to do this or that." It's not like you're switching gears. It comes from the music.

You sing a lot in English. Any tips on how to sound good when you're singing in English?

English is a difficult language to sing in. I'm now singing *Billy Budd* in Washington. I'm always told that I have very good English diction, but I don't do anything special. I think maybe because it's my native language, or maybe [that] in the beginning I used to sing a lot in English in college. We did everything in English, and even when I first began at New York City Opera, I did Figaro in English in *The Marriage of Figaro*. It wasn't until 1977, when I did a new production of *Figaro* at New York City Opera, that we did it in Italian.

Any words of advice for aspiring singers?

I know that lots of times the hardest thing for a singer to do is say no to a role that's too much too soon. Many singers are too much in a hurry. As soon as they get out of college, they want to start a career. I know that's a difficult transition, from college to the real world, but I think young singers now have it a lot better than when I was beginning, when I first came to New York. Now all the major opera companies have these fantastic young artist programs, which didn't really exist when I could have used something like that. So, if singers have a chance to keep studying, they should take it and not rush.

I was offered some things I had to say no to, in what I considered early in my career. But I started much later than a lot of singers do. I was fortunate in that I found a good agent in the beginning, and that I had my teacher, Armen. Whenever I was offered something, and I had any question about it, I would always go to Armen.

I think one of the most important things for a singer is you need to find a teacher you can trust completely. Once you've found your teacher, stick with him or her and listen to their advice. When you are not sure about repertoire, ask and listen, before taking a step that might be damaging to your voice.

Julius Rudel

Recorded November 2002 in New York City, USA. Published in Classical Singer, *May 2003.*

You are known for being a "singer's conductor." What is your definition of this term?

A "singer's conductor," in my opinion, is someone who understands how music is produced by a singer, how the voice works, what one needs to sing a phrase, how to breathe . . . The voice obviously has to be handled differently than other instruments. It has to be understood. The greatest conductors worked with singers one-on-one to understand their voices.

Some conductors now compete for the limelight with dictatorial stage directors to the detriment of the voice; not to mention the fact that many orchestras are tuned higher to sound more brilliant. Where does that leave the singer? If the voice is most important, shouldn't conductors be more protective of their singers?

Yes, but that depends on a lot of factors. If you have your own orchestra, you can control its tuning, for example. If you are a guest, you must conform to the preestablished tuning. However, that is less of a problem than what actually happens on the stage and how it affects the voice. Many stage directors come from theater and don't understand how a singer functions best. The drama, the characterization are very important; they belong to opera, but the voice is the main reason for an opera's existence, and sometimes that is forgotten!

You have encouraged several well-known singers throughout their careers. Samuel Ramey, Frederica von Stade, Catherine Malfitano . . .

[Plácido] Domingo, [José] Carreras . . . a lot of singers! I worked with them musically on roles, and especially as general manager I was able to give them practical advice, too.

I just attended the dress rehearsal for *Eugene Onegin* at the Juilliard Opera Theater. How was it for you to work with these young singers?

Well, the stakes are higher in a production with young singers because they don't have extensive experience; they're just beginning to get used to performing in a professional setting. So, they need guidance in the phrasing, in breathing, pacing, expression. They need more attention than experienced singers.

For this production, did you work with singers one-on-one first?

Yes, I had to. I always work with each singer separately, then we put it all together with the orchestra.

You must have learned a lot about singers when you came to New York City Opera as an accompanist.

Yes, of course. But even when I was a student, I used to play in voice teachers' studios. So I heard and saw and learned a lot.

Did you like accompanying singers?

It was fun . . . and it also paid my bills! Then, a year later—this was 1944—I made my conducting debut with New York City Opera.

Your musical education began in Vienna. How did these early years influence you?

Vienna is very important to me. I did a lot there. I also love the music of Austrian composers and perform it with pleasure.

You went back to Vienna in 1956 with *Kiss Me, Kate*.

Yes, this was actually the European premiere of *Kiss Me, Kate*, and the first American musical ever to be performed in the Volksoper in Vienna. It was an interesting time because there was some opposition to bringing an American musical there, but it ended up being a great success.

You conduct a lot of genres: grand opera, contemporary opera, musicals. Do you work differently with the singers in each category, or do you have a similar approach?

In more popular repertory, the technique is different . . . more chest, more emphasis on text and character . . . I would say, the basis is the same in the way I approach these genres, but the style is different. Even just in opera, Bellini is sung differently than Puccini.

Do you believe singers should specialize? Is singing "cross-over" a healthy path for a singer?

That is so individual! It depends . . . Some can do it and it's healthy for them, others cannot. A lot of the so-called serious singers go into musicals, and it's not true anymore that only those who cannot sing opera should stick to musicals. It's a much more open world, musically, and it becomes a personal choice.

DON HUNSTEIN

In 1957, you became general manager of New York City Opera, a tenure that lasted twenty-two years! Tell me about crossing from the artistic to the administrative side of the coin.

I was lucky that I grew up with this opera company. We were located in City Center at first, and in 1966 we moved to Lincoln Center. I was in a great position, because not only was I qualified as a musician, both accompanist and conductor, but I had extensive experience with singers and agents, too, so the administrative know-how came easier.

I think that a lot of the same qualities a conductor needs to lead and hold together an orchestra could serve a general manager to keep an opera house under control.

Exactly.

In 1971, you opened the John F. Kennedy Center in Washington DC and became its first music director.

I conducted the opening program there, the world premiere of an opera by Ginastera, and Handel's *Ariodante*. I had commissioned a Mass from Leonard Bernstein for the center.

There are so many "firsts" in your career: premieres, inaugurations . . . Looking back, what do you think about these remarkable achievements?

I think back very seldom. I always think forward. There are incredible moments. It's an interesting time, musically.

You lived in an era that produced spectacular voices: Callas, Tebaldi, Kraus, Corelli . . .

Caballé . . . oh, there were so many!

What do you think was the secret of their greatness?

You know, people always attempt to come up with theories about what happened in the past. In life, there are waves—sometimes they go up, sometimes down. There are amazing singers today as well, but musical life has changed, so we have a different perception. Life has changed in general. In those times, records were very important for a singer's career. Singers had to record and then go on tour. Today, recording is important, but it's not enough. TV, video, and DVDs have taken over, and there aren't too many of those huge personalities. There used to be much more emphasis on creating a larger-than-life personality, and that came largely from recording and going on tour with the records. Not every singer could record; it wasn't as accessible as today.

Did you have very difficult moments in your career?

Oh, who doesn't have them?

But it looks so perfect!

It looks that way. But there are always problems—artistic, financial—the times when you struggle and don't have money, when you're pressured to make the right decisions, especially as general manager of an opera house—what kind of repertoire to schedule, what singers to hire—it's not easy at all.

Hiring singers a few years in advance involves a certain risk.

Yes. You always have to think ahead. I was lucky that the company [NYCO] worked on a shorter-term basis than other companies. We could allow ourselves to hire someone only a year before.

There are so many stories about great relationships between singers and conductors: Callas and Serafin, Sutherland and Bonynge. Do you believe in this type of intense artistic relationship?

It depends. There are always some singers with whom you come into perfect understanding without saying a word . . . Yes, I do believe in them; there have been many singers with whom I worked very well and had good contact in making music. Carreras, Domingo . . . we had the same artistic opinions.

How do you work during a recording?

It has always been important for me to have the recording sound as close to a live performance as possible—to capture the drama, excitement, and expression of stage performances in the studio. Sometimes that happens fast, in two or three days. But normally in a session, you can get fifteen minutes of acceptable material. The practical issues always slow down the process: Is the balance good? Are the singers close enough or far enough away? Is the mike working? Sometimes the singers sing better one day and worse the next. It also depends on whether you've conducted the piece before with the same singers, or if you've conducted the piece at all. Whenever I recorded pieces that I had already conducted for the stage, it was much easier to capture the dramatic colors; the work had dramatic unity.

Do you expect more vocally in a recording session? In a performance, not every single sound is beautifully and perfectly produced . . .

Right. In a recording you demand the beauty of the sound, while in performance, sometimes the beauty can be sacrificed for the sake of artistic expression. If it makes sense dramatically, it doesn't have to be perfect.

How about in concert . . . should singers act?

Oh, yes. At least a little bit! Through their faces, some gestures, body language . . .

What do you look for when singers audition for you?

There is always the first general impression; the details come later. Is the voice beautiful? How big is it, where does it go, and where can it develop? Then, of course, does the singer have theatrical talent, expression, stage presence? You do look over the details, but the whole package counts. I look for expression, something that tells me these are not just notes sung by a beautiful voice. Sometimes, however, the voice is so beautiful that you can't say no, even if the singer lacks artistic expression. Then you try to work with them.

Do you give singers freedom to express themselves, or do you adhere to the credo of "com'è scritto"?

Yes, I do give them freedom. They should express what they want first, then I give my suggestions, and we work within the confines of what is written, or, as you said: "com'è scritto."

What would disturb you most in a singer?

If they are not musical! A singer who has no idea of the markings in the score, of their meaning . . . a singer who has not taken the time to analyze the music . . . that disturbs me!

Do you have any words of advice for young singers?

First, be careful not to sing things that are too difficult in the beginning, so you don't ruin your voice. Second, become an all-around musician—know every detail of the piece you are singing, the markings, the meaning of the words, and be prepared. Never present any piece of music that you haven't gotten to know very well first, because uncertainty will make your life even more difficult when dealing with conductors and stage directors!

Erich Seitter

Recorded June 2003 in Vienna, Austria. Published in Classical Singer, *September 2003.*

Singers from more isolated parts of the world don't have access to much information about auditions for European agencies. They have asked for suggestions on how to proceed in obtaining information and approaching an agent.

Everyone would have access to everything if they checked the Internet. After finding out addresses, all they have to do is write a letter to the agency. They must include information about their performing experience, education, repertoire, a photograph, and also which arias they are offering at the audition. Now it is also very important to add a tape, a CD, or even better a video of a recital or performance. In this respect, the women are at a disadvantage. When yet another soprano—there are so many!—sends materials, it is more helpful to include a video, because that gives the agent a better idea: Is it a young singer? Does she have a routine already? Is she still building her performance style? Avoid sending the overly glamorous, Hollywood-style photos, especially if you don't look like your picture. That is why a video is important, because less-than-perfect looks can be compensated for by a beautiful and solid performance.

In Europe, of course, one of the audition arias has to be in German. I ask for five arias; one has to be Mozart and one in German, so if you come with a German Mozart aria, you have already fulfilled two requirements. The singers I decide to invite for an audition have a choice of possible dates. If someone comes from very far, and is good, they should give themselves three weeks' time, and then I can organize an audition tour right away.

One other suggestion I have for young singers is to take part in competitions. Of course, it is not a requirement, but a competition with agents and general managers as part of the jury is ideal. It is not important whether some retired opera singer judges you. Yes, she may know about the voice, but what can she do for you? Perhaps she can make a phone call to a conductor . . . Singers should look for competitions judged by those who are on the business side of this profession and could hire them.

In some ways, I am not a fan of competitions; they can be unfair . . . and you must have money to travel and participate in them. Asian singers have more money than someone from Siberia, or some parts of Latin America, for example, and they are also very stress and travel resistant, so they constitute a large number of competition candidates . . . Going back to auditioning for agencies, the best months for central Europe are October and November, because that's when the bookings take place for the next season, unless you are a heldentenor or some rare Fach, then you can come in January or February, too.

Speaking of rare Fachs, what voices are in demand in Europe?

Good voices! Well . . . worldwide, there is a lack of low bass voices: Sarastro, Osmin, the type of voice Kurt Moll, Kurt Rydl, or René Pape has. Italian bass roles are sung by Russians a lot, but the beautiful German repertoire bass voice is missing. As for women, dramatic sopranos, real spintos, are badly needed! From Senta onward . . . Chrysotemis . . . In the Italian repertoire, a voice that can sing Amelia in *Ballo*, then *Trovatore*, *Forza* . . . She doesn't have to sing *Turandot*, but we need the real Verdi soprano . . . what Tebaldi and Antonietta Stella were, and Maria Chiara.

Now you have someone like Maria Guleghina who can handle these roles, but the Italians complain of her strong Slavic accent.

We actually have tenors at the moment, despite the general idea that there are no tenors. The young Italian cavalier baritone is also in demand—what Piero Cappuccilli was ten years ago. We need a young Bruson or a young Nucci, who can really sing Posa in *Don Carlo*, di Luna in *Il trovatore*. I sound like Jonathan Friend from the Met when I ask, "Who can sing the role of di Luna today? You go to Florence and see *Il trovatore* or *Ballo*, and where are the Italian voices? All you find is Russian, Russian, Russian!"

When a singer auditions for you, what qualities do you look for right away?

Most important for me is technique. The beauty of the voice comes second. There are singers who don't have a beautiful voice, but an excellent technique: a clear, even voice with no wobble, bleatiness, or obvious register changes. The voice has to seem like one smooth register from top to bottom.

I am old-fashioned . . . In former mass auditions, I would always ask a lyric soprano (Now you're going to say, "How mean!") to sing Pamina's aria. The first six measures tell you if she can sing. How she begins is crucial, as well as the jump from "es" to "ist"! Once I hear that, I already know how well she can handle her register changes. That was so wonder-

ful about Mirella Freni—the high passaggio register between E-flat and A, so important for the soprano repertoire!

Freni always had this purity in what I now call the "Freni *Lage*" (the Freni register/spot)—she could color these notes and do anything from soft to loud. That is what I expect from a lyric soprano.

If the technique is excellent, the singer can sell himself or herself very well, and the image is not that important. Singers who are unattractive in real life step on the stage and the artistic miracle happens: they transform

themselves due to a complete control and mastery of their technique. That is all. Timbre is a matter of taste. If someone sings without a wobble, screaming, or tightness, that pure sound spreads throughout the body and endows the singer with an aura of grace and elegance like a dancer with a great technique, what do you care if the singer is cross-eyed? My father would have said, "It doesn't hurt a woman to be beautiful," but it is not as important in this profession as many make it to be.

If someone displays technical security, they can transport you to a place of beauty. Believe it or not, art comes from this technical control.

Is age important?

Well, today there is this obsession with youth. It depends on the Fach. If a lyric soprano is thirty-three, and has only studied until now, there is something strange there. I would wonder. But age is not the determining factor. When a Blonde or Olympia is just beginning at thirty-five, I have reservations, but if a Tosca comes to me at that age, that is not so strange.

I think the age group between twenty-five and thirty-five is very important for a singer's career development. The career should start sometime in this period of your life. Below twenty-five, I would say you have time, above thirty-five, I don't know . . . it can be a little late.

Do you ask the age at auditions?

Yes, especially if they are beginners. If someone is thirty-four and has only sung three roles, I wonder what they have done the last nine years. But again, when someone sings well, everything comes together at once: personality, charm, confidence, artistry. It's like a puzzle that just fits together.

Do you work with beginners as well?

Of course. We try them out, and if they give good results, we continue. People are so interested in new singers today. "Don't you have a new singer for us?" is a common question.

What is your definition of a beginner?

A beginner to me is someone who has finished their studies, and preferably participated in an opera studio or young artist program. These are important because they teach you to work with partners and listen.

Is it important for you that a singer has worked with orchestra before?

Helpful, but not required. I look for ensemble work. The ability to listen even if you have nothing to sing in the scene is important. If you are in a good opera studio or young artist program in a big house where you sing small parts, you can learn from the great singers there. That is, I can't cook yet, but I go into the best restaurants. I can't afford them, but I order a salad and observe what the others are eating! Quality can be learned! It is not always an innate characteristic.

So, you don't think it is detrimental to a singer's future marketability to sing small roles in a big house?

No. It also depends on your circumstances. If you come from a provincial town where you have no cultural activities except your TV, and your own voice lessons and coachings, I suggest you try to get into a big opera house young artist program for two years. Then you learn so much from the established professionals, even if you just sing "La cena è pronta." However, if you grow up in a big city and have the chance to attend many opera performances and hear the great singers from a young age, I would say, try to go to a smaller house where you can sing—perhaps not leading roles right away, but roles like Marcello or Musetta. Then after three years you can ask yourself, "Where am I? What are my possibilities? Can I be freelance? Can I go one step higher? Am I the type to audition?" The first five years in a singer's career are a crucial period. You must discover if this profession is for you. It is not a matter of having success or not in those initial five years, it is answering the question, "Am I made for this profession?"

When you decide to work with a singer, what is the next step?

Well, I don't draw a contract in the first three years, but only when we realize we can do something together. Each agent has their own nose for a singer, their own instinct. You begin to know what singers fit in what theaters, but as an agent you have to know your limits, too. So, when you arrange auditions for singers, you have to be very aware of the needs of the particular theater or casting director. Then if the singer actually gets hired several times, that builds a trust between agent and singer. There are situations in which you have to say, "I can't do anything for you. You are good but there is no chemistry between us." Or, "I have tried everything possible and you never get a job." Then sometimes, the same singer goes to another agent and gets a contract! The contrary is also possible. Someone leaves their agency, disappointed, comes to me, and starts getting hired. It's the right thing, the right theater in the right moment! In the beginning, that is always very hard. I always refer to it as, "Who will turn the light on for you?" It doesn't matter if there are three or four light-bulbs, once the light is turned on, that is the most important step.

Do you hold auditions only in Vienna?

Yes. I also pick singers from competitions, and then they don't need to audition for me. But I have to state it clearly: I don't hire, I deliver. I can only take you by the hand and lead you to the opera house. Your duty is then to maintain the contact with that house, and once hired, to build yourself a good reputation there. That reflects on my reputation as a good agent. Whenever things don't work, we have to ask, "What did you or I do wrong, and what did the theater do wrong?"

What happens after the first three years of working with a singer, assuming everything goes well?

Then we sign a three-year representation contract. Now you have someone to represent you and the theaters are aware of that, so when they need you they call me. It makes it easier for them.

Is this contract exclusive?

Well, it is not prison . . . when someone is established and other agencies or theaters I don't work with call me, then I am prepared to collaborate with them.

What about the competition between agencies?

Yes, well, it's just like between singers! You can work together when you have to, but you don't put all your cards on the table! Now this business has become so "tight," everyone knows about everyone else, especially through the Internet. When another agent says, "I know a theater doing

Berlioz's *Les Troyens* in England, but I won't tell you where it is," all you have to do is search the Internet and you find out it is the Scottish Opera! However, auditioning directly for the opera house is harder; it's all very much under the control of the agents. The theaters trust us more than they would an individual singer going there on his or her own.

So, your responsibilities as agent are . . . ?

To be in constant contact with theaters—to know what they need. I travel everywhere I have singers performing, mainly to check up on their development. If they are growing, I take them to the general managers directly and say, "Do you have something new for this singer?" I have to get jobs, openings, to check the singers' schedules, to be part of this whole network. A good agent needs to put pressure on the theaters all the time: "I can take my singers to three or four other theaters, if you don't give them the premiere next year or pay them better!" It's a constant persistence.

I imagine this can be tiring work . . .

Very. And you are always guilty for what happens. If singers are successful, of course, they are proud of themselves—as they should be—but if not, it is always the agent's fault!

What about getting your singers to perform in concerts?

I don't produce concerts, but when some producing organization asks me for a singer for a Mass or a requiem, I deliver. The singers are responsible for their flights and hotels. The producers and theaters used to help with travel arrangements before, but they don't have the personnel anymore. We have actually become a travel agency for some singers! In the last five years, the work of the agent has doubled, because it's not just about where there is an opening and how much money can I get for the singer; now the agent has to be a promoter as well, and take care of photos, publicity, everything.

But you earn more money with more responsibilities, don't you?

Truthfully, the income has been frozen at one level for the past ten years. I make the same amount as I did then in proportion to the number of singers I have. The poor singer has to spend so much more, too, for his or her promotion. They need a Web site now, especially after the first five years. It is more practical for the theaters, too, to get information about you from your Web site.

Is there a tendency here to cast one Fach heavier?

It's a big trend. The orchestra sound has become higher, more concentrated, more brilliant—I don't want to say thinner—but more transparent. Even the stages in general are less crowded than thirty years ago.

Voices too are lighter, clearer, fresher, and more lyrical. A soprano that is hired for Isolde today would have never even been considered for the part twenty years ago! But with this change in orchestral sound, a lighter voice would be hired for a heavier part, yes.

Why do you think the orchestral sound has evolved this way?

Because the dramatic voices are missing! It's a vicious cycle. Even the appearance of human beings has changed, in general. They are thinner, taller, better looking . . . My nephews are two heads taller than me, but thinner . . . such a body build cannot hide a big voice. But this Fach issue is very tricky for singers. For example, when you sing Isolde in a small house and are successful, you might be bombarded with offers from bigger houses, so you would force yourself because the jobs are tempting.

Do you obtain both Fest and Gast contracts for your singers?

Yes. It usually depends on the theater. We can also get a part-of-the-season contract. A freelance singer lives from Gast contracts. A Fest contract is important for the first three years in a beginner's career. Being Fest, you can also have a Gast permission, which means you can sing somewhere else occasionally, but you are a member of your particular opera house and get a monthly income whether you sing or not.

In a smaller house you can earn in a month as much as a colleague at a bigger house earns in two evenings. It's a discrepancy, but I believe it is important to go through the Fest contract because it is a way to build repertoire and test yourself. I perform on Tuesday night, let's say. Can I sing full voice in an orchestra rehearsal the next day at 11:00 a.m.? Maybe I went to bed at one o'clock after my performance . . . These tough experiences give you confidence, so when you are freelance, you know what you can handle.

Is there a problem with the reduction of funds in Europe, so that foreign singers are not hired as much?

In the theater/acting department, that is more likely; in opera, not really. If someone is good, nationality does not matter.

Your agency is focused on opera . . .

Yes. I have conductors, designers, stage directors, and of course, singers. I don't deal with musical theater.

What about operetta?

I am the top casting agent for the Mörbisch operetta festival, where we have almost 250,000 visitors annually. However, we only do one operetta a year. It's fifty kilometers from Vienna, outdoors, a very popular festival. But there are no more specialized operetta singers, really.

I am surprised there is a lack of interest in this field, especially here in Austria.

Actually, these operetta performances are always sold out, but I suppose it is not in fashion. The older generations attend them.

There are cases in which so-called agents do nothing for singers but take advantage of their hunger for work, promising much and delivering little, while somehow managing to take money from them. Do you have any comments on that?

If you fall into the hands of such an agent, you must simply trust your instincts, which will tell you from the beginning and from his behavior not only what kind of a professional but the type of person he is. I can't imagine what kind of agent would promise things and do nothing. Then he is a terrible agent. They should not ask for money or anything else from you at the start. The money will come with the contracts, not before. All I have to say is: Keep your eyes and ears open. Do not believe everything!

A singer-agent relationship is like a marriage. If you feel there can be no trust, because your instinct tells you so, go to someone else. Do not get pulled into anything you feel uncomfortable with. There are many agents around; you don't have to settle for anything you feel is not right.

A good agent has the duty to tell the singer, "I tried, but your Fach is not in demand at theaters." The responsibility of a singer is to notice if they don't do well in a theater—if they are not getting any roles, for example. Then the agent would have you change the theater. Honesty and the ability to communicate openly with your agent are crucial . . . But sometimes, it is all very subjective.

As a Fest singer, you can perform all the main parts in one year, and then they hire a new stage director who doesn't like you—perhaps you remind him of his ex-wife—and all of a sudden you are on the sidelines, not singing anything. Well . . . that applies more to theater, but it can happen in opera, too. However, if you are excellent, even a hostile stage director will be forced to give you a good part.

Sometimes you have to fight for yourself and say, "I have the right not only to get my income but also to get time onstage, to be heard and seen!" You must have at least two roles per year!

I heard about a case in which a singer was exclusively signed by a famous agency, and now she does not get any work. How is that possible? Why would an agency sign someone and then keep them on hold?

Perhaps she is too passive or not building a good reputation. Sometimes when I hear that one of my singers is not doing too well, I am disappointed and pull back. However, I don't just keep them on hold; I try to find out what is wrong. It can also be an unlucky time; all singers and agents go through that.

How are American singers viewed in Europe?

They are fast learners and very practical. They buy a Eurail ticket and travel everywhere. Ask a Viennese, "Today is Tuesday; can you go to Hamburg on Friday?" and they complain they are so tired . . . The Americans would say, "Okay, no problem! Tomorrow!" They know, "If I don't grab this opportunity, there is a huge line waiting behind me!" But the Americans are not coming as much now as they did in the fifties and sixties. Now there are many more opera companies in the States, so they can actually start their career there, too. The road from America to Europe is not as traveled as before.

Do you work with American opera theaters?

Of course. Just this week, I got a German tenor and Italian bass engaged to sing at the Met. Interestingly enough, I have had more luck with the Met than with Chicago and San Francisco. I get a lot of requests for singers for the German repertoire.

Do you like your work?

Yes. There are many happy moments . . . when you sit in the fourth row, look up on the stage, and think, "No one believed in this singer; no one wanted to give him this part! And now look at him or her!" That makes me very happy.

Patrick Summers

Recorded October 2004 in Houston, USA. Published in Classical Singer, *November 2005.*

What are your responsibilities as HGO's [Houston Grand Opera] music director?

My chief responsibility is the maintenance and administration of the orchestra and the performances that I conduct here. But I'm also involved in deciding the future repertoire [and] the casting; all of the artistic decisions in the company involve me.

Do singers audition for you?

Yes.

What do you look for in an audition?

I look for a very individual timbre, someone who doesn't sound like anyone else, a beautifully produced voice. I'm looking for someone whose voice is inseparable from who they are. I'm looking for a person's relationship to music through their voice. I want to see that their voice is the utmost expression of who they are, and thus, who the character is.

So they don't sing something as separate from their selves . . .

Right. I can't bear artifice, and someone who sings something that they think I will like, or sing something in a manner—you know, that sort of sculpted and manufactured kind of product. I'm looking for honesty.

Any advice for singers when they audition?

Never sing music you don't like.

What if a piece you sing is very well suited to you but it's out of your Fach?

I think that's fine! Artists aren't machines with labels. Maria Callas sang *I Puritani* and *Die Walküre* in the same week. She didn't do too badly!

What makes a bad impression on you?

Artifice. Any kind of fakery. I want to know who you are when you audition for me. I don't need you to tell me that in words; I want to see it and hear it: "I love this music more than anything in the world; that's why I'm singing it," even if it's something nobody knows.

Then you don't really look for résumés, and experience, and teachers, and so on?

No. I could care less.

Describe your experience as music director of the San Francisco Opera Center.

I was fortunate to be at the San Francisco Opera at a very young age. I was studying there myself when I was twenty-two, and I worked there for fifteen years before I took my position in Houston. I was music director of the Opera Center for five of those years. The Opera Center is the umbrella organization over the Merola Program, and the Adler fellowship program, and Western Opera Theater, which is now gone.

I was exposed to a great era in the company. There were a great many young singers who auditioned for us. Sometimes the greatest talents are not the most finely put together at a young age, so I learned to develop discernment and trust, as well as a strong aesthetic sense. Some singers who came to us were young and "green," but you could see their incredible relationship to music, whether they could or couldn't express it at that time. That's what you train. Then you find that core of imagination in them.

Of course, they have to have the voice first. You cannot create a great voice from a mediocre voice. You can make a great voice greater by training it.

Do you teach?

I don't any longer. I taught at the Opera Center and also at the Shanghai Conservatory, through an exchange program.

How was the Shanghai experience?

It was probably the most influential part of my life, as far as my real relationship to music. I first went in 1987, and I was last there in 1992. China is very different now, but the conservatory students of the eighties had grown up in the Cultural Revolution, so their entire formative years were shaped by it. The idea of a singer's going to a conservatory in China and being entitled to a career was absolutely foreign to them.

These conservatories were populated with the most incredible talents and the most enormous amount of desire. Look at the obstacles they had to overcome to get there!

The two major conservatories in China—the central Conservatory in Beijing and the Shanghai Conservatory—actually date back to the Victorian era.

Did the students study only Chinese opera and traditional Chinese music, or did they also study Western music?

Now, you can do either.

But you couldn't study any Western music during the Cultural Revolution.

Oh, no! During the Cultural Revolution, the voice department head of one of the conservatories hid her records under the floorboards of her house. When students would come over, she would play Caruso records at this tiny, tiny volume. All the kids would gather close to the LP player so they could hear it. But then she was sent away, as were most intellectuals, to work on a farm.

I'll never forget a night in Shanghai; it was in the spring, very warm. At that time, Shanghai didn't have enough electricity to light the entire city all night, so they had periodical blackouts, and everyone was accustomed to this. I started a class in the evening with twelve singers, and lots of people attending. We were just going to work on some music like always, and the lights went out, so all the students went to get candles and gas lamps.

So there we were in this classroom, three stories high, over a completely black Shanghai—I'll never forget it. And on this particular night, I heard a young soprano who I've now lost track of—but I remember her on that candle-lit evening. She was singing "Ruhe Sanft, mein holdes Leben" from *Zaide* by Mozart. She had a wonderful voice, and I asked her through my translator, "What is this about?" (In that era, it was rare for them to speak English.)

I had worked with this girl before and she had a beautiful, creamy voice. When I asked her this question I was expecting a sort of translation of the aria, or a setup of the scene, but she spoke to me in English for the first time and said, "In this aria, Mr. Mozart wish peace on whole world!" And it suddenly dawned on me that there were forces at work here that weren't necessarily career oriented! That is what attracts me in a singer! The career comes if you have that impetus inside of you, and I don't think it's the other way around.

You developed the Pacific Voices program for the San Francisco Opera Center. Tell me about that.

Pacific Voices was a San Francisco opera program. It was meant to celebrate and utilize San Francisco's position in the Pacific—San Francisco Opera being the oldest cultural institution on the Pacific Rim. So we decided to go to as many countries as we could, on the Pacific borders, to see what kinds of special talents were out there.

The aim was to do a miniature Merola program, for about two weeks. We took two singers from each country and brought them to San Francisco, and it was a process we hoped would be ongoing every two years, but the San Francisco Opera didn't take that up.

GREG BARRETT

It was an absolutely amazing experience, and it resulted in some singers who have gone on to careers, like Alfredo Portilla, Vassily Gerello, and others. There were people who went on to musical careers that weren't classical.

It was unusual, very outside of the box and very heartfelt; it's something I wish I could do more of.

You conducted the first ever *Tosca* **produced in China. What was that experience like?**

That was in 1988. It was extraordinary! We had a cast in Mandarin and one in Italian. We were performing *Tosca* for an audience that didn't know it. It was a real melodrama for them: They didn't know she was going to kill Scarpia, or that she was going to jump. They screamed when it happened!

It was really visceral. I kept thinking, "This must have been the experience of seeing it in Italy for the first time!" Their participation in the performance was not to see how the B-flat is at the end of "Recondita armonia." It was the story itself, which was very exciting for them.

Now Shanghai has its own opera house and they produce Western opera all the time; they're a big international city. Then, they were certainly a big city, but that kind of Western culture was not so common.

What do you think it was about opera that appealed to them?

It's just amazing how opera appeals to every culture. Operas are grand statements of emotion; that's why they appeal to all of us, no matter where we come from.

Do you do any master classes?

I have, very often in San Francisco. I sometimes still do them.

How does teaching singers enrich you?

Of all of the ways to express oneself in the classical arts, singing is the most personal, and the one from which you cannot separate yourself, because it's coming from inside of you. As hard as a lot of singers try, they can't separate that.

The exciting part of teaching is watching singers gain confidence in themselves and thus in their vocalism. As you know, classical singing is a very physically demanding art form, because your ability to sing—the technique of singing itself—is the art form, and you're living through it. When you get a score, you've got all of these things you have to fulfill, and it is your technical ability to do that which makes you an artist. That takes a huge amount of courage and personality.

Do you give freedom to singers in tempo, phrasing?
Absolutely.

What would you tell singers who are faced with impossible stage directors?
I'd ask: "Are the singers participants in the production, or are they puppets?"

A lot of singers, especially in the German Fest houses, don't dare to speak up because they're afraid they might lose their jobs.

And they probably would. But they have to stand up for themselves. And isn't part of our attraction to the operatic world to go see personalities? Why else would you go to a live performance?

One of my favorite types of work is working with the stage director; that's one of the most rewarding things in my life—when it works, and when they're really collaborative and wanting to work out what it is today, here and now! Conversely, when they can't do that, when they can't collaborate, it is hell! It really is hell! So you try to avoid those situations. But as a singer, you have to assert yourself.

What is it like for you to conduct so many world premieres for which there is no precedent for performance, where you can give it your own personal stamp?
By nature of what we do, whatever I conduct has my personal stamp—but my purpose in conducting is to say what the composer needs to say, not to put my personal stamp on a work.

Conducting premieres is a wonderful thing to do. But that's the same creative activity that should inform *La bohème* or *La traviata* every time we do those operas: like you would do it for the first time. You have to think, "What does an opera mean in the context of all the people who are in this rehearsal room today?" That approach is harder to do than it sounds. But I think the more work you can do on new music, the more able you are to transfer this fresh approach to standard repertoire.

How does it feel to be part of this innovative and ground-breaking company?

One of the great attractions of HGO is that we're sort of in perpetual festival. The company tends to approach all the works as new, because even our standard repertoire doesn't come around nearly as often as it does in bigger companies. For us it's every six or seven years between *Bohèmes*. The higher percentage of your activity that is devoted to new works, the greater chance you'll have that everything in your company will be new. Every time we rehearse *Traviata* or *Rigoletto*, it's new. We haven't just done *Rigoletto* last season and we're reviving it this season—which happens in a lot of companies, and that has its advantages, too—but here, it's rather an event when we do *Rigoletto*. And it should be. All operas are events.

You went to Indiana University. How did your education there influence your future?

The big influence that shaped me at Indiana University was Margaret Harshaw, in whose vocal studio I played at an early age. And it was Margaret who first told me that I was a conductor. She said, "You play the piano like a conductor, so you should be one." I played orchestrally, and I'd never even thought about it. So, at her encouragement, I got involved in the opera program at IU, played a lot of operas, and eventually auditioned for the Merola Program, where I went as a coach in 1986.

I had a great education at IU and many teachers had a big impact on me. The depth of knowledge and experience there in that era was absolutely remarkable. I owe a lifetime debt to that organization. But Margaret was the reason I have this career.

I wanted to be a musician. I started out as a pianist, and I had not been allowed to dream about conducting to that extent until it was suddenly in front of me. That is, after all, what major educational institutions should do: provide you the ability to dream and imagine something that you didn't know was available to you.

Margaret was a remarkable pedagogue. She was not for everyone; she was very controversial. She was tough, old-school, New England, screaming—you never knew what you were going to get in there, but at the heart of it was a dedication to this art form that you rarely see today.

Unfortunately, that's happened in every art form. Are we going to see forty-year Hollywood careers anymore? I'm not sure the aesthetic is to find a young Katharine Hepburn and follow her through her life as an actress. And she was rare. There were a couple of dozen Hollywood careers from the thirties and forties that lasted a lifetime and the public followed them on the screen for forty years, not for five—like Henry Fonda and Jimmy Stewart. You went to those movies because they were in them.

I think in the operatic world, too, we're now post-Sutherland and post-Pavarotti, all of these long-career singers. There was an event around those singers taking on a new part. That's what everyone focused on. That has disappeared. We don't focus very much on the activities of singers—but then we turn around and say there aren't any stars. The nineteenth-century pieces, especially, are written for great star personalities. You can't pretend they're not. Just as you can't pretend that Hamlet isn't for a grand star actor.

How does a conductor expand and improve his orchestra? I once heard a conductor say that the success of a conductor depends on how good the orchestra is. So, you can have an average conductor, but if the orchestra knows how to play, can a mediocre conductor get away with sounding well anyway?

Is the point of our work to "get away" with something? Sure, the Met orchestra can get through *Bohème* no matter who is on the podium, and it's still a Met orchestra performance. Our orchestra here can get through a piece with quite a lot of aplomb now, no matter who is up there. But that's not what we're doing.

What do you do as a conductor? You chip away at bad habits. You greatly encourage the musical things that are in the direction you want to go. You have to be very clear technically with the orchestra, so that there can be flexibility in a piece like *Madama Butterfly*, because it's very flexible music. What you need in performance from the orchestra is creating a really tactile response to the beat. It's very complex because most of that special connection that happens between an orchestra and a conductor is something you never talk about. If you talk about it, you don't have it anymore.

You don't get along with everyone and you can't please everyone. If that's your goal, you've set yourself up to fail. The approach does not have to be, "This is how we're doing the following ten things."

I am not a screaming totalitarian. The approach is to create the greatest amount of flexibility so that the conductor can just privately address those ten things. I'm not only training them to perform with me; they've got to perform with other conductors. So, they have to be able to respond to a wide variety of people. Then the bigger issues, like sound and intonation, don't take care of themselves; you have to address those things. But they are all positively affected by a response of being in the moment.

**You're a musicologist; music to you is not just performance—
it involves a level of intellectual analysis and understanding.
Singers can get trapped sometimes into too much analysis,
which may inhibit the performance instinct. How do you combine the intellect with the visceral experience of music making,
and what would you say to a singer in regard to that?**

I think you've got to do your homework and know what kind of stylis-
tic things you're dealing with. But when you go in to rehearse, you've got
to forget about that; they are two separate acts. Musicology is part of a
conductor's technique, but not the technique itself. Then you can make
an informed choice. You can't make an informed choice if you've never
educated yourself about what the choices are.

Working with a singer, you're trying to find out what the piece is, between the two of you, which is different between different people. We're
supposed to be striving for the highest level of creative activity, and that
is what, not when, nor even how. "How" is your technique, and that has
to be done, you can't ignore it. I'm going to conduct *Trovatore* for the first
time in January and I'm studying away on "how": the history and the
performance practice of the piece. But that is so I can rehearse at a higher
level. You've got to do that work.

What words of advice do you have for singers today?

Don't build your career. Build yourself and the career will come along.
It's yourself that we want, so work on that, and the career follows. Don't
start with the career in mind. That will work for three or four years, but
how long do you want to be here? Are you so dedicated to this art form
that you want to do it for the rest of your life?

If you want to do it for the rest of your life, you've got to work on
yourself, because you can't keep up an artifice for thirty years—and why
should you? It's not rewarding. There can be a very short-term reward.
You may get in there and all the right people will listen to you, and famous
person A and famous person B will tell you things, and maybe you'll get
an article in *Opera News*. That's all noise. Who are you? It's yourself that's
going to propel the career.

A career cannot bring you along. It's the other way around.

Ricardo Tamura

Recorded July 2003 in Vienna, Austria. Published in Classical Singer, *October 2004.*

The Zurich Opera studio was the doorway to [begin your tenor career in Europe]. Tell me a little bit about this program.

It was mostly an audition preparation program. You had three months to prepare repertoire for auditions according to your type of voice. After those first three months of audition preparation, we auditioned for agents from Germany, Switzerland, and Austria.

About four agents took me; the one that worked with me the most was Inge Tennigkeit. She sent me to my first auditions in Germany, in Kassel and Lübeck. Both houses gave me an offer. In Germany, they have A, B, C, and D houses, and Kassel was an A house.

What is this rating based on?

It's based on the size and salary of the orchestra. So, theoretically speaking, the A houses have the best orchestras, and the D houses have very bad orchestras normally.

In the A houses, you'd expect to find the best singers; in B, the second best; and so on. That's not always the case. So since Kassel was an A house, and Lübeck was a B house, I decided to go to Kassel, as a beginner with a Fest contract.

For how many years was the contract?

It was for two years. The first two years you work in Germany, you are considered a beginner, unless you come as a guest, but you can only do that if you have a name already.

As a beginner, you don't do much. You learn the language, you coach a lot and you do some small roles. You get paid per month.

What happened to me was that I was put to work right away, to do the main role in an operetta—*Maske in Blau*—in German with a lot of dialogue.

Then I had to do the Rossini Stabat Mater. My second production was *Zar und Zimmermann*, where I had a main part again, and I was supposed to do Don Ottavio in *Don Giovanni* right after that. I got completely overwhelmed!

I couldn't speak German, so I had to memorize the dialogue for the operetta, but you have to interpret, not just say the text!

So, it was a lot of work. It was all choreographed, so I had to dance, learn the music, struggle with German . . . just everything at once! I had never had dance lessons before, so I couldn't handle it!

Because of that, rumors started that, "Yeah, he has a nice voice, but he cannot move onstage!" I did the operetta anyway, but because of this rumor, all the new stage directors that came already said, "You cannot move, so we have to do something else with you." I started becoming angry about that.

I also had some problems with colleagues who were not nice to me in the beginning, and I had a coach there who didn't like me and never really taught me any role. I was scheduled to work with him many hours, and everyone expected I would learn the parts, but he never taught me these roles musically.

But what happened during these coachings?

We repeated the same bar for the whole hour! So I had, like, forty coachings with him, and we just did the first page of an aria! I came unprepared for the next productions. Then the rumor was as well, "Not only can he not move, he is also not musical, because he is slow in learning his music!"

But there was nobody to help you besides that coach?

They have three other coaches, but nobody knew—including myself—that what was going on was wrong.

You thought the way he worked with you was normal?

Yeah. I thought he was really precise and wanted everything to be

202 | The Interviews

right, and we had plenty of time, but we really didn't have that much time.

Why do you think he held you back? Was it that subjective?

I cannot exactly say what happened; it was probably a chemistry thing, but it never worked. When he was in a good mood, we would do two bars, but never more than two pages of any role in all the sessions I had with him.

So, there you were in the middle of Germany with no knowledge of the language, no idea of how a coach in an opera house should work with you, and creating an undeserved reputation for yourself! Tough beginning . . . but a good warning for other singers who follow the same path, not to get stuck like that.

Oh, yeah! And also, when you are a beginner in Germany, you have to learn—and I am still learning, although I am not a beginner anymore—to set your territory. Once you get there, you have to make your own space. That means you cannot let people walk over you. Say you make a mistake and you apologize, and that happens several times, then at some point, you become the idiot who only makes mistakes. Other people, even when they make mistakes, always have a reason to shout back and say, "Yeah, I made a mistake, so what?" When they do that, people somehow respect them.

Then you can't be too nice and apologetic.

Not at all! If you are nice and apologetic, people start thinking they can do anything with you because you are not going to shout back. You have to fight back! At some point, you have to learn to put your foot down and say, "No, that's not the way it is! It is this way!"

You don't have to be mean, but you have to be strong and say, "What is my right is my right, and I'm not going to let anybody take my rights away!" There was a colleague there who was not very nice to anybody, but when I came, new and inexperienced, I was the perfect target for him to torture.

Every time he said something bad to me, I always laughed, but I never shouted back at him. The same with some stage directors—they shouted at me, and I said, "Okay, sorry, it's my problem!" but I didn't react. I had learned that even if it is not your fault, you just assume it is; it is a rule of good education in Brazil. But in Germany, you don't do that!

The stage directors are also part of the theater ensemble?

Not necessarily. Some, yes, but most are guests.

And they can be so aggressive?

You have all kinds. Some are the nicest and most supportive people. I learned a lot from one stage director, and I am grateful for the work he did with me.

But you also have lunatics. Sometimes their psychological problems make them good stage directors, so you have to put up with the fact that they are not stable, but if they are not stable and they are also not good stage directors, it's a nightmare. Then, especially, you have to fight back!

So, I actually got to the point in Kassel where I couldn't sing anymore. It wasn't a technical problem; I just didn't have the nerves. I felt that every time I moved, everybody was watching me, and even if I did it right, they were going to blame me anyway. I couldn't learn my music anymore. I was at a dead end!

How did you manage to go on?

Well, there was one person there who said, "I've got to work with you!" He was the first Kapellmeister, Bernhard Lang.

In Germany you have the general music director, and his assistant is the first Kapellmeister. Our general music director was never there, so the first Kapellmeister filled that position as well. I started working with Bernhard at a time when I couldn't do anything in the theater, just very small roles, because I had been hired for two years and they had to put up with me.

Although Bernhard is a conductor, he has a lot of ideas about vocal technique, and he has worked with singers all his life. So, he did some vocal work with me and preparation of arias plus the musical preparation of the roles, which I wasn't getting from the coach I mentioned before.

Was he charging you for this work?

No, because we had a deal: I didn't have to pay anything until I got a good job. He does that with some people. When I start being paid more for singing, then I should give him 10 percent of the first ten performances of each role that is really well paid.

Moreover, he went to the office and got himself assigned to me as my coach, so most of the hours we did were through the theater. At the beginning of the second season, I was doing small roles. But gradually, I started getting more confident, and they decided to risk giving me bigger parts.

So, I did a couple of main roles again. Then, all of a sudden, I could move and I could sing, and it was a shame I had to leave, because at the end of the first year, they had decided they would not renew my contract after the second year.

The problem was that when you start as a beginner in an A house, you cannot then go directly to a better house. If I had had huge success in Kassel, and done all of the main roles, maybe someone from a bigger house would have heard me and taken me.

But the rule is, after those beginning two years, you should continue in the same level house, then later on try for a bigger house.

So, is there no rating above the A houses?

No. Above are the top international houses. But you could say, there are the A, the A-plus, and the A-minus houses. Kassel was an A-minus.

So from there, I had to go to a smaller house. And that was also what I wanted. When you go to a big house and don't have a lot of experience, you don't learn that much, because there are three or four people who sing exactly the same roles you sing.

So, being triple cast, you get very little rehearsal and very few performances. If you go to a smaller house, you are the only person in your Fach, so you are the lyric tenor of the house, for example. You have no double cast; you have to do all the roles, all the rehearsals, all the performances.

It's the best school you can get, especially if you have not performed a lot in your life. So, I went to a smaller house, to Osnabrück, which was officially a B–C house. But of all the smaller houses, it has possibly the best standards; they really want to have a good-quality ensemble and productions. In many C houses, they don't care. They just want to put something onstage.

But in Osnabrück, I would say they have standards as good as or better than some A houses. I didn't know that at first; it was an accident that I went there. I auditioned in many houses, and Osnabrück took me.

First, I went there as a guest for *Butterfly*, then I became part of the ensemble.

And your status changed.

Yes, because when you don't go as a beginner, it doesn't matter what happened to you in the past, you're immediately seen as a professional singer.

So, you have to go through those first two years no matter what happens, and how hard they are . . .

Yes. That is normal for Germany.

What was the difference in treatment, when you achieved the status of "Profi," or professional singer?

As a beginner, you are expected not to be good. As a professional, you are expected to be good, and if you are not good, if you have any problems, it's, "What can we do to help you?" If you are a beginner, it's more like, "Why the hell do you have these problems? You shouldn't have problems!"

Of course, your behavior has to be different, too. As a professional, you really can't give anyone a chance to step on you; otherwise you will be treated as a beginner again! You have to say, "No, I am a professional now, and I am doing my thing, so you take care of your own things, and let me take care of mine! And if I sang the wrong note there, it was not because of me. It was because the light wasn't right or the costume was too tight." Of course, you can't do that if you keep making the same mistake; then it is obvious it's your fault. But do not apologize if you happen to make a little mistake that you won't make again! So, in Osnabrück I did main roles in many operas, as well as small roles. When you are Fest, you also have to do small roles, because you are the only tenor in that Fach.

What is your Fach?

Lyric to spinto. That means roles from Don Ottavio up to *Tosca*. But in Osnabrück I also did roles that were beyond my Fach, like Ernani, which is considered a dramatic tenor role in Germany.

They gave me the chance to do that because they thought it was a good role for me.

Are they somewhat flexible with Fachs, and cater to your individuality?

In Osnabrück, yes, as in all the good houses. But there are many houses in which you are just put in a drawer with a label and you have to do everything.

There are theaters that even do it in an evil way! They write in your contract "tenor" or "soprano," and they don't put down any Fach. And if you are hired as a tenor, it means every opera that has a tenor role is for you—Rossini to Wagner!

I have heard of a soprano who had to sing everything from Zerbinetta to Butterfly in one season, because it says in the contract that she is a soprano.

What a dangerous trap! Then you'd better examine these contracts very carefully.

You have to have a good agent. If you don't have one, there is always in the theater one singer or actor who represents the union, and he can help you not only read the contract but find the tricks written there. It is a very tricky situation; there are many sentences you read and think, "Well, there's no problem there," and it turns out, that in a particular situation that can be a very strong weapon against you.

Don't get enthusiastic, don't sign; get someone to help you read it!

But why would the theaters do that? Is it not in their best interest as sellers of art, that this art is high quality, and therefore that you sing your best in the roles most suitable for you? Why would a theater make you sing Tosca if you are a coloratura?

There are two problems. One problem is that there are many houses in Germany that don't have enough money.

So, if they have to do a production, it doesn't matter how the production comes out. They cannot do any better, because they cannot afford to hire different people, and they have to deal with what they have. So, "It's your problem how you are going to sing that, but you are in, because we are doing that production, and we don't have anybody else!"

The other problem is that in many cases the production decisions are controlled by the stage directors. It doesn't matter for most of them what singers they have. It's just, "I want to stage *Otello* next season. If we have the singers or not, it's not my problem! We have a tenor, a soprano, a baritone, so we can do it!"

So, it's between the Intendant who wants to stage certain operas, the Operndirektor who is also a stage director and wants to stage other operas, and the guest directors for the operas the audience wants to see. Sometimes the GMD [general music director] wants to conduct his preferred operas. So, they put all of these in a season.

If they don't have the singers, they just get a guest. But it might turn out later that there is nobody to guest, so they either have to drop the project or force the house singers to do it anyway.

If your Fach is specified in the contract, you can turn down a part that is not in that Fach, but if it is not specified, they might force you to do it.

What if you refuse?

You can get fired, because you are breaking your contract. It's not that they do it on purpose; it is mostly money related. There are many situations.

Sometimes they already have a guest who is a friend of the house and will do it for less money. But if that guest cancels, to get a new guest would be more expensive, so they get the person in the house who doesn't have a specified Fach.

But in houses like Osnabrück this doesn't happen a lot. That is why I stayed there for so long, because I like the way they work. But I have heard many nightmare stories from other colleagues, just because they didn't watch what was put down in their contracts.

So the houses don't have every Fach filled?

They normally don't. Not even the big houses. For example, a coloratura soprano is a Fach that doesn't appear in most operas. You can do a whole season without needing a coloratura; that's why in most cases coloraturas are guests, and there are very few houses that have a Fest coloratura.

Every opera house has to do two or three German operas, one Verdi or Puccini, sometimes a Wagner opera, as well as a modern piece.

Who dictates what repertoire they have to do?

Well, they have to keep a certain balance to serve all the tastes. That's why it is harder for coloraturas to be Fest. But they can make a living just singing Queen of the Night in all of the houses, because they do *Zauberflöte* everywhere. Same thing with basses.

I actually heard that basses are badly needed.

They are. You have three different Fachs there: the high basses—let's say, the Mozart bass-baritone—the low basses, and the comic basses—the buffos. But in the small houses, you are never going to find all three.

They have one, maybe two, and one of them covers the third Fach. There are some bass-baritones who can do buffo parts; if not, they get a guest. Then they have a light and a heavy mezzo.

They have a light, a heavy, and a buffo tenor, and two baritones—lighter and heavier. In the soprano category, they have a bunch of them, for all possible Fachs, except coloratura. The lightest is called a soubrette.

Would the soubrette Fach cover coloratura as well?

Sometimes. If you have a soubrette who sings coloratura, it's great! But most of them can't sing coloratura. The soubrette appears very often in German operas before Wagner. They always have stuff to do—that is why there are always Fest soubrettes. Then they have a lyric soprano who can do Mozart as well as some Italian operas.

Like *Bohème?*

Well, Mimi is considered a little heavier than a lyric. The whole concept of Fachs in Germany is a bit different from Italy and America. They have a book called *Kloiber Handbuch der Oper*. It's an opera guide like any other, but *Kloiber* writes for each opera what Fach should sing each role.

This book was adopted as the Bible in Germany. That means what is in the book is the law. It can be problematic. In Italy, for example, in the tenor Fach, you have the leggiero, the lyric, the spinto, and the dramatic—you could even add the heldentenor. But Kloiber divided the tenors into lyric, *jugendlich* [youthful] heldentenor, and heldentenor.

So, because you have only these three categories, that means a lyric tenor in Germany has to go from the leggiero—which includes coloratura—up to *Butterfly* and *Bohème*.

So, when I was a lyric tenor, I was supposed to do coloratura roles as well—that's why I also had some problems in Kassel. I was never a leggiero; I am a lyric, but according to *Kloiber*, if I am a lyric I have to sing Almaviva in *Barbiere* and other Rossini parts.

They tend to follow that guide blindly?

Yes. In my case, I have arranged to change. They do that sometimes; you can create a new word—and get them to write that in your contract—that describes your Fach.

A sort of sub-Fach?

Right. In my new contract I have something like "Italian spinto." This is not in the *Kloiber* guide, so they cannot force me to do anything because there is no definition of *spinto* there.

So you can beat them at their own game. If they can trick you by writing just "tenor" in your contract, you can trick them right back with undefined terminology!

Yes! You have to, to protect yourself! So, this new Fach would mean I can sing roles belonging to the spinto Fach in Italy, like Cavaradossi, Andrea Chenier, Ernani, Turiddu, Hoffmann—well, Hoffmann is more spinto dramatic, but I've done it before.

According to *Kloiber*, the heldentenor sings all the Wagner roles, some other German operas, and the really heavy Italian stuff like Otello, Calaf, and Radames—although Radames I wouldn't consider a heldentenor. The Fach I did in Osnabrück more or less was the *jugendliche* heldentenor—from *Bohème* to *Andrea Chénier*—although the contract was for lyric. The *Kloiber* guide was out of print for many years; now it has come back out again. Any singer who wants to come to Germany should take a look at this book.

So, for example, if you are a lyric soprano and audition in Germany, don't do an aria that you think is for you, if it is not referred to in the *Kloiber* as a lyric soprano aria. If they want to, they can create problems for you if you don't stick to one Fach.

They don't like to have people do more Fachs, at least in the beginning. (When you are famous, you can do whatever you want!) You might think that singers covering more than one Fach is a good thing for the theaters; some theaters even like that! But most directors think that if you are doing two Fachs, you don't do any one of them well.

When you audition as a beginner, does it count if you list roles you've simply studied?

No. Of course, if you have a good résumé, that's better, but it's actually not that important. And it's not good to lie!

Many people like to show off. They are not going to believe that if you have done so many big parts, you are now auditioning to be a beginner in Germany. Even if you have a résumé that doesn't show much, the audition is the most important.

What counts most is when you walk on the stage, when you introduce yourself, and the first three bars, unless they wait for a high C or something.

But they don't stop you after the first three bars . . .

No, but they have already made up their minds. That's why the arias that have a long introduction are not advisable. Or an aria like "Che gelida manina," for example, where the first bars are not that interesting, so they need to wait for the high C. The problem is that once they get bored, they don't hear you anymore.

Your image plays a huge role as well.

Image is very important, which doesn't mean that you should dress up. You cannot give the impression that you desperately need the job. For example, I started doing auditions in a suit with a tie, like a schoolboy!

They looked at me and said, "Yeah, he's a good boy, but that's not what we need. We need an animal!" Normally, the spinto tenor roles are very passionate. So they want to see the lover in you! You have to show the animal, you know, chest hair, and open shirt . . . just kidding, maybe not that extreme, but along those lines. I've seen some baritones audition in T-shirts and jeans, and Wagnerian tenors in leather!

Of course, everyone has to dress as they like, and it should be comfortable, and not look like you are begging for the job or dressed especially for that occasion. You are there, and if they don't hire you, that's their problem. You have to be—what's the word?

Cool.

Right! You dress like you normally would, maybe a little finer. I see a lot of sopranos come in evening gowns with the makeup and the hair. The Intendant and opera director are sitting there in jeans and T-shirt, thinking, "What is she going to look like as Giorgetta in *Il tabarro*?" for example. It's just like being a model. They are going to pick you as a top model if they can change your look in any way they want.

So, as a singer, if you come natural and they can see everything they can do with you, the chances are better they will take you than if you already present an image.

There are some people who have a way of walking on the stage so the directors think, "He is going to play verismo—I need somebody who walks like a peasant!"

So acting during your audition is not recommended?

Well, everything I am telling you is not universal. There are some stage directors who appreciate it when you move; and for some Fachs, it is even desired.

A buffo tenor has to show he can move without being a clown, because in every opera he'll be doing, he'll be dancing and jumping. But in most auditions, for most types of voices, you should not move or act. Just stand and feel everything that you sing; they should see in your face that you experience what you are saying.

In Germany, whenever they do a new production, it is usually what they call a modern staging, not a traditional staging with old costumes and old movements. So, you can do *La traviata* in jeans, and you are not going to be a courtesan but a biker or a mermaid. If in the audition you show that you can only do Violetta as a courtesan, they will think, "But our production is not like that, so I am going to have a lot of work changing her image, so I don't want her."

Then you have to get rid of set gestures or movements and be sort of tabula rasa, so the directors can then draw their own concept on your slate, so to speak?

Yes. You just have to be you, so they can see if they could imagine you doing that part.

You mean, their vision of that part.

Yes. I've seen people used to singing an aria sitting on a chair, so when they go to an audition, they ask for a chair. So, the stage director thinks, "But in our production, he is not going to be sitting on a chair, he's going to be hanging from the ceiling, and if he can only sing that aria sitting, I don't want him!"

Mark Belfort always said, "When you sing, if you have an urge to do a movement or a gesture that it comes from inside of you, and you are going to die if you don't do it, then you do it. But never do a movement because you think it is right, or someone has told you to."

Who listens to these auditions in the theaters?

It's different. Normally, the Intendant, the GMD, the Operndirektor, and the stage director who is going to do the production.

What is the difference between the Intendant and the Operndirektor?

Every opera house in Germany has three departments: opera, theater, and ballet. That is called a *Drei-Sparten-Haus*.

The Intendant is the boss of all departments. Below him, you have a director for each department, so the singers' direct boss is the Operndirektor. Parallel to him is also the GMD [General Music Director], who is a conductor.

In some theaters, the GMD has the same status as the Operndirektor; in others, he is above and can have almost the same status as the Intendant. If the GMD has the power to make the decisions in a particular house, they are going to listen to your voice and your musicality, and not care so much about your looks.

But in general, the Operndirektor makes the decisions, and in most cases, he is a stage director, so he is going to base his decisions on your looks. Of course, he will hear if you are really bad. But if you look good, and are not extremely bad, he will take you. This then becomes a problem, because if he has an image of the person he wants, that means everybody else who walks in and doesn't fit that image is already out.

But what about the Intendant and the GMD? Can't they overrule decisions?

Yes, they can. If they like someone very much, they can persuade the Operndirektor maybe to try them out for one year. But the Intendant is also a stage director, normally, so he has the same views as the Operndirektor in most cases.

Then it is up to the GMD, who can veto decisions. If the GMD says no, then most of the time the person will not be taken. But if he says yes, then it is between the Operndirektor and the Intendant.

Do they make decisions based on age?

Well, of course, they prefer younger people, because they are less experienced, they require less money, and they are easier to persuade to do things they don't want to do. Older people are harder to bend.

When you say "older," what age are you referring to?

In Germany, it is very hard to find singers below twenty-five. So, twenty-five to thirty would be young; thirty to thirty-five, even thirty-seven, would be medium young to mature; after thirty-seven, it's already older. Over forty-five is old.

Would they hire somebody over forty?

Yes. If they are good enough, even at fifty they can be taken. But unfortunately that mostly applies to basses.

I would think the agents would be the first problem for mature singers.

Many agents don't want to work with older inexperienced singers because they need to know that these singers will be engaged so they can make money. It costs the agents money to represent someone, so they like to feel they have a guarantee that the singer can be hired.

So, the solution for a mature singer with little experience would be to audition at the opera houses on his or her own.

Yes. The problem is that you never know who is looking for what; the agents have control of that. Unless you have some money put aside and you just go and audition in as many theaters as you can.

What about being overweight; does that play a huge part in auditioning?

If you are overweight and can move, it's okay; but if being overweight causes you problems moving, you are going to have a hard time, because most of the productions in Germany have a lot of movement. The stage directors will want you to jump or do other things. But there are exceptions.

In Osnabrück, we have had people who are overweight because our Operndirektor does not have a problem with that. But it will be tougher with the agents because they know what most directors are looking for. The rule is, if you are extremely good, it doesn't matter what you look like; you will be taken.

If you are good, but the agents don't want you because you are overweight or mature, the best thing to do is to try the opera houses directly and keep auditioning until someone takes you. There is always going to be some opera house among the hundred-something theaters in Germany looking for your type. You can call the theaters directly and send your materials. Some theaters prefer you to have an agent, but most are open to direct contact.

What is the normal percentage that you pay the agent once he gets you a contract?

Well, first of all, you have to know that no agent in Germany is going to ask you for money or an exclusive contract in the beginning. They might ask you to sign a paper where you agree to give them a percentage when they get you a job. If you get a Fest contract, the agent gets 10 percent of your salary for the first one or two years.

If the theater renews your contract after that, then the agent doesn't get paid anything. I stayed over that period of time in Osnabrück, so I don't have to pay my agent anymore. He would have to move you to another theater to get more money. Of course, the agents will also watch how you are doing, and if it is not going well, they are going to try to push you somewhere else. If they get you a guest job, they take about 12 to 15 percent from your guest contract pay . . . it varies.

Sometimes the theaters pay for your hotel and trip, but you have to have that in your guest contract, otherwise you will have to cover the travel costs yourself. What happens sometimes is that they pay for a certain hotel which might be very bad, so if you go to a better one, you pay the difference.

Is it true that as a guest you get paid in one or two evenings what you would normally make in a month as Fest?

Yeah. As a Fest you get paid every month plus vacation—thirteen months in a year.

Thirteen months?

Every theater closes for about forty-five days in the year. So during that time, you get two salaries: the normal monthly salary and another extra holiday salary, so technically you get thirteen salaries in a year.

Now they have changed that; you get two thirds of your extra salary for vacation and one third at Christmas. You get medical insurance, paid partially by you, partially by the theater; retirement funds; as well as other insurance you share half and half with the theater.

So, when you have a Fest contract, you don't make too much money, but you don't have anything to worry about.

What would be the average monthly salary for a beginner?

According to the law, the least you could get as a beginner used to be twenty-four hundred marks; that's about twelve hundred dollars per month. But since the Euro came, things have changed, and I think it went up a little bit.

Can you get by in Germany on twelve hundred dollars a month?

Well . . . When you get the minimum wage, taxes are smaller. But if you get a little bit over that and you are single, after all the insurances and retirement costs are deducted plus the taxes, you are left with half of your income. So that means if you are making fifteen hundred dollars a month, you are going to get seven hundred and fifty dollars at the end of the month. And you have to pay your rent, transportation, food, clothes. It is very little money.

Everybody who goes to Germany has to take that into consideration. You have to have some money saved.

I would also imagine it is hard for a beginner to get a guest contract right away.

Right. A beginner can count on a guest contract only if it is in a very small theater or if they have done a certain role many times.

Nobody is going to hire you as a guest for a role you have never done in your life, unless you have already been singing in Germany for a while, and they have heard you and really want you. The exceptions are, in most cases, singers who come from the States and have a great agent there, so they come directly as a guest in a big house, although they have no experience. Sometimes that can be overwhelming—but once you do a guest production in a big house, then you can be a guest in any other big house.

However, most beginners start with a Fest contract . . . Now, if you are married and your spouse is with you and doesn't work, then you get about 65 percent of your income after taxes. But if your spouse stays in America, it doesn't matter if they work or not, you are considered single in Germany, so you pay the higher taxes.

If your spouse is with you and works, then one of you pays less taxes and the other much more than if he or she were single. If you don't have a Fest job, and you work as a guest, then you are going to be taxed normally, as single or married.

But if you already have a Fest job and you get a second job as a guest, when they deduct the taxes, you will be left with about a third of what the guest contract promised you. So, it is true that as a guest, you are offered for a performance what you would normally get in a month as Fest. But from that you lose two thirds to taxes—either they deduct it immediately or you pay at the end of the year.

So, that's why you are paid so much! It doesn't matter if you are married or not. If you have two jobs, the first job is taxed normally, and the second job falls into the worst tax category! So you have to be a really well-paid guest to make money. Or, just [a] guest!

But the only possibility for that to be profitable is, in most cases, to spend a number of years as Fest, to get well known so that more and more theaters call you for guest jobs, then after five, six years, you could go off as a freelancer.

So, those initial two years would not be enough?

I would not risk going completely freelance after only two years, because that can go well for a while, but you never know. You have to give yourself a number of years as Fest to make contacts and guest all over Germany.

Please don't quit your Fest job too soon to become a freelancer, because you're going to starve! And this is very important, too, unless you are really well known—when you are a freelancer, you will not be listed in the book of singers from Germany. They have a book with the names of all the singers who are working, so if you are not there, how are people going to call you?

I suppose, also, you can't get too enthusiastic if one month you get a lot of calls.

Right. That happened to a lot of people I know. They started getting a lot of calls to guest while they were still fresh in their Fest job, and they quit. In a year, they made a lot of money, but that was it. Then there were no more calls, or not enough.

Does your income increase with your years at the theater?

The first contract you get at an opera house, whether as a beginner or not, is going to be limited for a certain number of years.

So, in those years—usually two—the contract says how much you are going to make. My first contract didn't have the amount written for the second year. That's a mistake, because then they can pay you less in the second year. According to the law, it has to say how much you will make each year, and normally it is already a couple of Euros more for the second year.

Then, the theater has up to October from the previous season to fire you. So, if I have a contract that goes to 2004, if the theater hasn't fired me by October 31, 2003, my contract extends automatically for another year. So, in 2004 to 2005, the income I will receive will be the same as the last year of my contract. And so on.

When you are there a certain number of years, your salary goes up a certain percent. If you move to another theater, you keep the income from the last year of your contract at the previous theater and you have to negotiate with the new theater to get more.

Let's talk about these modern stagings. How difficult is it to deal with them?

Very. The less you know about the opera you are doing, the easier it is. But if you are somebody like me, who really cares about the background of the opera and what you are saying and why the composers wrote it that way, then you get angry most of the time. There are many stage directors who do modern productions totally different from the libretto, but they still make sense and are very logical. It is still very hard to work with that, because you expect *La bohème* to happen in Paris with a girl who has tuberculosis and a guy who doesn't have a job, right?

But when they do a production where suddenly you are an astronaut and Mimi comes from another planet, or if it is wartime and you are some SS officer and Mimi is a war prisoner, how do you deal with that? Most of the time it is a logical new take on the libretto, but there are always those productions where the director doesn't really care if [his concept] fits the libretto. So, you have to play dumb and work exactly with what is in front of you—unfortunately. That is the only disadvantage of working in Germany.

There are many stage directors who are just beginning to stage operas, and they don't really understand what the spirit of a modern production is, so they might ask you to do something totally inappropriate to the story.

Do the stage directors explain their concepts to the singers?

The ones who know why they are doing that production are going to tell you their reasons. But if somebody doesn't have a reason at all but just wants it like that, they won't explain. Then you have to find a reason for yourself so you can decide how you are going to act.

For example, if the director sets *Bohème* as a TV show where all the characters live together and know each other, that doesn't make sense. You know at the start of the opera that Rodolfo doesn't know Mimi, so how would you play that? They give you some stupid reason, that you are drunk or on drugs, or something, and that's why you act as if you just met Mimi. But try to sing your text and give some emotion to it and act as if you are drunk!

What does the audience think?

The audience normally doesn't like that. Normally, they love the traditional productions, or at least those productions where nothing extreme happens. But then there is a group of audience members who classify themselves as "intellectual" and want to see something modern.

However, it has to make sense. But because in Germany the state finances art and culture, then you can do with art and culture whatever you want. The more extreme you get, the more art you are doing! A traditional thing is considered kitsch; it's not art because it's old-fashioned!

If you do a Wagner opera following the pages of descriptions and indications he wrote, that's not art! To make it art, they have to modernize it and give it their own interpretation. If it is a good interpretation, the audience might like it, and the singers might have fun doing it. But if it's a bad one, it's your problem as a singer—you have to do it.

Is it true that a lot of directors come mostly from theater, and they don't have an understanding of vocal production?

Yeah. Most stage directors come from theater, but normally, they are not beginners. They already have experience with what the singers need. It might happen that you get somebody who is doing his first opera.

But unless he is a real jerk, he will ask for your help. If you say you cannot do it, he will usually understand and try something else. This problem of understanding the singer is also true in the sense that directors don't want to make the singer the star of the show.

It is very rare that a director will put the singer downstage center and let him or her sing from there. Usually, whenever a singer has to sing an aria, he is all the way in the back. It can get physical, too; you have to jump or dance or move. Or they do stupid things—they don't make you move, but all the time while you are standing there singing, there's some clown doing crazy things on the stage.

That must be annoying.

It's very annoying, but it happens sometimes. But no stage director is going to force you to sing to the back, or in a position in which you cannot sing. It is not going to be a problem that will damage your voice. As a singer in Germany, you have the right to protect your voice and your body. You might have a problem with heights, for example, and then you can refuse to sing five meters high.

Tell me about the rehearsal process—the day-to-day work as a Fest singer.

Working in a small house in Germany is very hard, but it is a good school. Before coming here, I had a lot of problems with things I could not eat before a performance, and the care I had to take three days before.

Once I arrived here, I had to get rid of all of that. When you are the only singer for your Fach, you have to do all the big and small roles for that Fach. In a season, the small houses usually do about eight new productions, so you might be in about five or six of them.

At the end of a season, you start rehearsing musically for the first role you'll perform in the next season, after the summer break. If you are new in the theater, you are responsible for already knowing that role when you come. The first six weeks of the season, the theater is closed and you rehearse the staging of the first production. They want the production to develop as you work, so they try different things and repeat a lot—that's why they need six weeks.

So you are part of the production from the onset?

Right. Sometimes what comes out is different from what the director started out with. In the big houses, you work six hours a day for those six weeks. That means from ten to one, and from six to nine in the evening.

In the small houses, where you are a single cast, you rehearse eight hours a day, during the day from ten to two and from six to ten in the evening. In the four-hour break, you have to do your banking, shopping, eating, resting, and everything. So, you eat whatever is available, because you have to fit everything in. Then you get over the notion that you cannot eat or drink this or that.

Self-imposed restrictions?

Oh, yeah. You don't have time for them. You have to learn to sleep immediately when you lie down, especially before a performance, because on a performance day, you have rehearsal until one or two. It's not like, "Oh, I have a *Don Carlo* in three days, so I need to rest." No way!

You will be rehearsing up to and including the performance day. And during the stage rehearsals for that first production, whenever you have free time, you get musical calls to prepare the music for the second production. Then, once the first production has the premiere and the performances start, you also begin the stage rehearsals for the second production, and again, whenever you have a moment, the musical rehearsals for the third production, and so on.

You are constantly busy.

Yes. Especially those Fachs that exist in every opera, like a soubrette or a buffo tenor—they have to be in every production.

So, it's normal for a buffo tenor to have up to 120 performances a year! There are 320 days in a season altogether, so that means practically a performance every three days, and eight-hour stage rehearsals and musical calls in between.

When do you take a break?

In the summer and on December 24. On Christmas Day and New Year's Day you usually have to perform, in *La bohème* or a New Year's concert. The summer breaks change sometimes. This season is four weeks longer than last, and everyone is already dying in the house; we cannot keep going anymore! But that's when you push your limits, and you lose all restrictions such as, "Oh, I cannot sing because I need my rest and my special diet."

Oh, please! When you are in a situation like that, where you have performed the whole year, you have four weeks longer to go than normal, and still many performances, you manage to do it. Or you don't. If you don't, at least you know that you are not fit for this business.

That is why I like the system in Germany, because it tests you. Either you die—but you die soon enough to realize that you are not made for this type of work—or you survive. And if you survive, you know you can do whatever you want. You can sing Monday in Sydney and Tuesday in New York, because nothing can disturb you anymore.

What are your plans now?

Well, I'm going into my sixth year in Osnabrück. I've been doing more and more guesting. Last year I did a whole production in Düsseldorf, which is one of the big houses.

So, you weren't "guesting" just for one performance, but for a whole production?

Yes, that can happen, too. It was a *Wiederaufnahme*—a revival of an old production—so I rehearsed with them for two weeks. Once you start guesting in the bigger houses, you start getting more possibilities.

My career is now at a point where I could probably survive from guesting. But because I like Osnabrück so much, I am staying longer as a Fest. I have a new contract now, with reduced activity and many opportunities to guest. I had actually quit for next season to be a freelancer, but then I got a bit scared, and Osnabrück made me a good offer to stay. But I hope that in a year or two at most; I will become a freelancer or get a Fest contract in a really big opera house where they have five tenors that do my Fach.

Then, when you get a contract for only twenty performances a year, it is great to be Fest! You have your monthly income and financial security, but you have more time to guest or simply to enjoy life!

Carol Vaness

Recorded March 2004 in New York City, USA. Published in Classical Singer, *May 2004.*

Did you always want to be a singer?

When I was a kid, I wanted to be a graphic artist. I was always drawing something. I did sing, though. I was raised Roman Catholic and always sang in church choir. In those days, we did lots of good music in the Mass: all the great composers of church music. I was an alto and I could read music because I had started taking piano lessons when I was seven. But I didn't really want to be a singer.

Did you perform in piano recitals at all?

Oh, no, I was terribly shy. Once I played a junior recital for a tenor. But then I kept on studying piano as part of my major.

Where did you go to school?

I went to California State Polytechnic University, where I got my bachelor of fine arts, and then to Cal State University Northridge, where I got my MFA and, later, an honorary doctorate. My first major was English and music, with the focus on piano.

Did you take voice lessons?

I hadn't planned to—but I had a crush on the choir director, a young guy from Southern California. He was really cute, and I took a voice class with him as one of the electives. He started to give me a lot of attention, and when he said, "I'd like to give you voice lessons," I asked, "What does that mean?" He said, "For one hour a week, you'll come in and you'll sing," but all I could hear him say was, "For one hour a week, you get to be in the same room with me!"

You actually started as a mezzo.

Yes. It turned out I was this guy's first voice student, so I lucked out! He encouraged me. I always had high notes but he thought that my most beautiful timbre was in the middle and low voice.

When did you switch to soprano?

I switched in graduate school. I walked into an audition for David Scott and sang "O don fatale." When I finished, he said, "I think you're a soprano," and I thought, "How silly! Anyone can tell I am a mezzo-soprano." Of course, he managed to convince me. I had always done *Zwischenfach* [between Fach] things. I sang mostly mezzo repertoire, but then I'd sing "Leise, leise, fromme Weise" from *Der Freischütz* or "V'adoro, pupille" from *Giulio Cesare*. I think my first voice teacher didn't necessarily know a lot of repertoire, so if he heard something he liked and thought it was within my range, he would say, "You should sing this," but whether or not it was the mezzo Fach, it didn't matter.

What was the biggest vocal challenge for you when you switched to soprano?

The challenge was in trying to make the top beautiful and not get nervous when I sang up there. Actually, mezzos need to be trained pretty much the same as a soprano, because it's almost the same range; just the quality and color are different. My top had always been very bright, so it became a question of adapting the rest of the voice to it, brightening the middle to match the top. The passaggio was not a problem; I could actually sing there very easily and last a long time.

What kind of vocalises did you do?

I did a lot of arpeggio work and anything that would leap over the passaggio into the top. Once the top became comfortable, I did more scale work, fast and slow. But I found that repertoire itself helped my technique the most. By singing "Non mi dir," I learned more than by doing a scale.

What is your basic singing philosophy?

Sing with your body as a whole! There are three places to sing from, and you have to use all three. Your resonance is in the head; your actual mechanism is in the throat, of course; and your support, or your engine, comes from the diaphragm. The throat is the computer; the body and diaphragm are the electrical outlet, the energy provider; and the head is the monitor, with loudspeakers, and all the areas around the computer. It all has to work together.

Your voice is very large and rich, yet you don't get heavy, as some dramatic voices tend to do. You manage to stay slender and flexible throughout your range. How do you maintain that suppleness?

Well, through breath and support. I also keep in mind that even the darkest, biggest voices should be high placed, so that they don't sing down on the mechanism. You have to think of the whole mechanism as a flexible tension, as opposed to just tension and strength. I also think that people can get a funny idea of support as something that needs to be nailed

down, but support needs to stay flexible. It's like singing with your knees slightly bent as opposed to keeping them locked. The reason is: you should be able to move in any direction with your knees bent and still stay strong from the waist down, while allowing your breathing to be free. I always emphasize that with my students.

Do you teach privately?

I have a few students, in California, in New York, in a couple of other places. I'm going to start teaching more and more. I would like to open a studio, but it's a question of having enough time to dedicate to my students. I don't believe in just dumping people, you know: start with someone, get them going, and then [leave].

Teaching is a wonderful experience. Anytime you can explain to a young singer that they are not alone, that we all go through the same things and have the same fears, anytime you can help someone, it enriches you a lot. What you have to give, gives back to you immediately when you're teaching.

You have to be careful, however, to respect the individuality of the student. A lot of problems in America come from teachers trying to teach their own method, as opposed to finding what works best with each singer. I find that a lot of teachers will repeat the same exercises with every student. Some may be valid but you need to see how a student is more comfortable.

I think that, as a teacher, you can have an idea of a method, but you have to adjust your method to each student. The voice is mostly controlled by the mind, so you have to help each young singer get out of his or her own way in order to let the voice go, as opposed to holding on to it and putting it somewhere. But in order to do that, you, the teacher, have to first get out of your own way, so you can be in tune with your student.

You should allow what the student is feeling to come out so that you can realize what he or she needs. What gets them the most concentrated and the least worried? You have to give them courage to try certain things. If you can help them mentally, they can do it physically. Singers search for the right technique, but that only means whatever is right for each individual.

I also love master classes, but I don't believe in demonstrating for the audience. I know people sometimes go to a master class thinking, "Oh, so-and-so will be there; maybe they'll sing!" I don't, ever, because it's not about me. It's a possibility for young singers to take what they do in a private studio and be able to do it in front of other people.

One of your specialties is Mozart. You mentioned once that you love the Da Ponte libretti of Mozart's operas. What is it about the Mozart–Da Ponte combination that inspires you?

I just think Mozart was able to set anything that Da Ponte gave him with great humanity. All of the Da Ponte characters are very real. They're not just one dimensional; they have major faults as well as qualities. The beauty of the Da Ponte libretti lies in the flow of the Italian; it feels like eating rich chocolate. There are many ways you can read the language, and Mozart enhances that by making the music very human.

Do you have any "golden rules" when singing Mozart?

Well, I wouldn't change my voice. The rules apply more to the style of how I use my voice. I think the mistake can be to change the way you sing because you confuse it with changing the style. So I always sing Mozart with vibrato and not with straight tones. There are some people who like it more straight tone. I never use it because that would not be true to my voice. You can't really hide in Mozart because it's so exposed, and if I try to modify my nature in any way, it doesn't work.

I think Mozart was a very direct man. His music is direct, and while the librettos have moments of great ambiguity, because of the interests of the characters, I believe it has to be sung with great honesty.

What do you love about Fiordiligi?

Everything! She is so human. In the end, you forgive her despite her faults, because she has always tried to do her best as a woman, as a person, as a faithful entity. I love her music. It's really difficult. The challenge lies not in the arias—they are hard enough —but in the ensembles. You have to ride on top of these ensembles and still make her not only feminine but full blooded. Riding that high for that long is a little tricky, but not impossible.

One of the most thrilling performances I experienced at the Met several years ago was your masterful portrayal of Hoffmann's three loves. In the span of three hours, you moved from coloratura to lyric to dramatic soprano/mezzo. Tell me about that experience.

Of course, when I was sitting there as the doll, waiting to be pushed onstage, I thought I was the stupidest soprano in the world! I think that *Tales of Hoffmann* gave me the chance to practice what I believe is important for every soprano: to be able to do some coloratura even if you have a dramatic voice. It's so necessary to be flexible. Fortunately, coloratura was always something I had, so I didn't have to work that hard for Olympia. The challenge for me in that production was to be calm enough to perform the doll, because it's not something that suits me temperamentally!

How did you manage to maintain your flexibility throughout the doll's mechanical movements, which might lead to stiffness?

The wonderful thing about that particular staging was that it was extremely choreographed. Once you learn the movements, you need to remain in flexible tension, so you could look stiff but not be stiff. Think of any Asian movement, like in tai chi; there, it can appear that you're not moving much, but you're actually very inwardly active, with a powerful center. You're very connected to the earth and you don't have to move a lot to stay active. You can stand like the doll for a long time, and be actively standing, as opposed to holding yourself still. The stiffness and stillness are going to be perceived by the audience.

Do you do any particular exercise backstage to get into performance mode?

Sometimes, when I don't feel engaged, I focus on breathing and do some panting—not too much. I try not to be too frantic, but just stay controlled and quiet. Some people really like to stay hyper. I am hyper by nature, but I like to hold my hyperactivity in, which is a little painful at times. But the minute I get onstage, I try to really concentrate all that hyperactivity into a single place, staying aware of everything—whether I need to focus on the words here, on technique there, on the breath, or on, "Oh, the tenor is lost," or the conductor is doing a slower tempo— that multilayered cake that is performance. Hopefully, by the time you get onstage, you are able to use everything—your physicality, your vocal technique, your breathing, the words—as the character would use them. So you're not out of character really, it's just that your character happens to sing. That's what I mean about "it has to be all one."

How do you prepare for a role?

If it's something I'm totally unfamiliar with, I sometimes listen to a recording a little bit. But when I actually start to learn it, I just go to a pianist, or I pound out pitches and rhythm myself, marking it, translating it. I start with the bare bones and try not to jump to interpretation before I am technically ready. I have it almost memorized by the time I start to interpret. Roles attach themselves quickly in my mind because I do associate a pitch and a word with that character. So by the time I get to be the character, the music had already moved me to understand what the character really needs.

Of course, it's all in the music and the words. One doesn't have to exclude the other. You should be able to make the words perfectly understood and still sing well. That doesn't mean you have to sing a pure *i* as high as you can go, but you should be able to approximate a good sound close to an *i*, so that the word is understandable.

You participated in the inaugural year of the San Francisco Merola program. What did you learn from Kurt Adler?

He taught me something very valuable: When you take a breath, you don't just take a breath! You take a breath depending on the type of phrase you will be singing. There's no point to gasp and inhale fast, if you're going to sing a really slow phrase, or to inhale slowly if your next phrase is fast.

Breathing and the silences are just as important as the music, the diction, and the support. It's all connected together as part of the Zen whole, so to speak.

He also taught me that you don't have to be the most perfect singer and you are allowed to have bad days. But you need to really work hard at being consistent within a framework, so that you don't have extreme highs and lows. I learned to always think ahead, be prepared, and be consistent in everything I took on.

Another of your favorite roles, besides Fiordiligi, is Tosca. What is it about her that galvanizes you into such inspiring performances?

Her personality and her music. It just suits me physically and emotionally. She is very active, and I like to be active on the stage. I mean, you get to live through everything: passionate love, rape, murder, suicide. What more could a performer ask for?

Moving from verismo to bel canto, I heard a beautifully moving excerpt of your recording of *Anna Bolena*. How do you fit

your dramatic temperament into the more subtle, legato form of bel canto?

Just as with Mozart, I don't make any great difference in my voice to adapt to the style. The words are shockingly important in bel canto, too. I think the mistake people can make with bel canto is when they come to cadenzas, thinking that cadenzas are just pretty. I think that if you remain within the character dramatically, the cadenzas, the fiorituras, the coloratura—all the things you associate with *La sonnambula, Anna Bolena, Norma*—have great intent.

That was the magic of Maria Callas. It seemed as if she invented the cadenzas and coloratura in bel canto, because she made a statement with each one. A long melisma could be like a word, an emotion of anguish, sadness, fear, happiness, anger, whatever she had been singing about.

It's important not to avoid the drama within the long bel canto lines. The long legato lines are part of the style, but the drama must be there, too, or the style has nowhere to go. It becomes a mechanical sequence of long lines. When you come to melodrama or verismo, the long line is important, too, but it is punctuated differently. The utterances may be shorter. There are sounds that are not necessarily meant to be beautiful. However, you can also find that in bel canto. I don't believe that all of Norma should be pretty because that is not her character. When she has the big confrontation with Pollione at the end, it's the beauty of the drama that comes through the singing, but it doesn't need to be perfect. When she says, "Trema per te, fellon!" that is not pretty!

There are some sopranos who believe in making it all beautiful, but I'm not one of them. I think that singing is more attractive when it's full of emotion. There is a lot to be said for perfection, but great emotion is perfection to me.

Another important figure in your career was Beverly Sills. How did she influence your path?

She was just very nurturing. I sang the small role of the Queen with her in *I Puritani*, and she helped me get an audition for Julius Rudel for the New York City Opera. It happened in the middle of my second year at Merola. Kurt Adler wanted me to return for a third year. But when Maestro Rudel offered me my debut in New York, I wanted to do it, even though it was much less secure to go there with only some performances of *La clemenza di Tito* and no other work under my belt. But I sold my car and went to New York. I was very blessed because I didn't have to go through the German Fest system. If you go into that you're doomed to whatever Fach they hire you for, which would have been tough for me, since I always jumped Fachs.

How do you keep in such great shape?

I do a lot of walking; I go to the gym. At the gym, I do the elliptical machine, sometimes treadmill, but no more StairMasters, because I've had back surgery. I also can't do weightlifting because of my back, and it's not too wise to do too much with the upper body anyway. I think you can do enough everyday things, by not overeating and taking care of yourself, so that you don't have to do major weightlifting. Of course, weightlifting can be helpful, as long as you don't engage the throat muscles, so that means lifting very light weights.

What happened to your back, and how did surgery affect your singing?

I had an injury and blew a disk. Of course, I had to cancel singing for a while. Then I had to refind the way to tilt my pelvis forward to make sure I was totally supporting, because I believe in getting underneath my voice, and avoid sticking my butt out. Tilting makes me stay active and aware of support. Initially, my back was very uncomfortable after the surgery. It took me a couple of months to recover.

What do you enjoy doing in your free time?

I enjoy reading, seeing friends, going to the movies, hiking, goofing around, planting things, playing with my dogs, being home, doing normal things.

You are very glamorous . . .

Oh, God! I wish you'd seen me before I put makeup on!

How important is image for a singer?

I think that you have to care for both. You have to respect what houses the voice. It's about the foolishness of being a drinking smoker and thinking you can be a singer; then you clearly have no respect for the instrument. I don't think you have to be the thinnest thing walking around on the face of the earth, but I don't believe it's fair to the world of opera or to your voice to think that it's okay to weigh three hundred pounds, because "I need it to sing!" That's BS and we all know it!

Singing is an athletic activity. Singers should start paying attention to their image from the beginning, when they're young and it's easier to do something about it. Your image doesn't have to be glamorous, but you should be able to go into a room and feel good about yourself. It's about learning a part and transforming yourself for the sake of the music and for your own heart and soul into something for an audience. And if that includes something like *La traviata*, wouldn't it behoove you to be within a certain range, to make it not only believable but also healthy for yourself, so that you have more options?

Of course, there are people who have real problems with weight; they are the exception. But I find that a lot of men and women use this profession as an excuse for saying, "Well, I need to eat; I'm a singer!" We all need to eat to live. But we don't need to overeat. Opera singers don't need to be fat.

Where do you think this cliché about opera singers originated from?

I wonder, too. Singers of the past were not enormously overweight. They were not thin; they were more or less normal. Look at Melba, Patti, Tebaldi, Caruso. I guess people kept looking for louder and louder voices. The orchestras and the houses got bigger, so maybe singers looked for bigger vocal volume in their own weight—fat weight rather than muscle weight. I was heavier for a long time, but I really wasn't happy. My happiness level as a singer went up when I was able to move more. I'm not thin now, I'm a size 12, but I'm thin enough.

Did you start your career thin and then gained weight?

No. I started my career weighing probably around 195 pounds. At my heaviest, I weighed 230 pounds! I was big! At my thinnest, I've weighed 145 pounds. I'm somewhere around there now—but as women, we don't really like to talk about our weight, do we?

How did you lose weight?

As our voices are our discipline, I simply disciplined my eating. When you are aware of your singing, you can become aware of your eating. You have to be aware of your singing to sing well. So, all you have to do is pay attention to your body, as you would if you were singing, and realize when you are actually full. Yes, we all love the taste, but at some point, you have to learn to say, "I really loved this, but I think I've had enough, calorie-wise, and I can have a little again tomorrow if I want." It has to become a discipline, especially once you hit thirty-five or forty, and your metabolism just goes south! You really have to be careful then.

Did you lose weight fast?

No. I lost it over a couple of years. I started to exercise and cut portions down. I saw an immense difference and then I kept it up. I've gone up a few pounds now and then, but I never let it get past the ten-pound limit. If I go up, I say, "Okay, I'll do an extra ten minutes at the gym tomorrow." It requires great control over yourself, but it's worth it, as long as you do it all in moderation.

Do you invest a lot in the visual aspect of the business: Web sites, headshots, business cards?

Me? No. I have the same pictures since ten years ago. But I spent decent money on the photo to begin with. I went to one of the best photographers—Christian Steiner—so I got great photographs. If I get to the point where I really don't look like that, I'll change them.

I think you have to be willing to spend the money on a really good photographer. You don't necessarily need to go for the most glamorous shot. You want something honest that shows who you really are, so when they look at you, they are able to see what you can bring to a character. As for business cards, if you send one with your résumé, don't put "so-and-so, soprano"!

Why not?

That's my personal view. I can't stand that. When I look at such a card, I think it defines you only as that, and I find it very limiting.

So what would you put on a business card, then?

I would put just my name with my contact information, agency, etc. It would be clear from your résumé that you're a soprano or a tenor.

How do you deal with stage directors and difficult stagings?

I first have to get out of my own way and see if I am uncomfortable with something just because I'm being rigid, or if it's really a stupid idea. If it doesn't hurt the music or the character, then I need to try it. I try to always give it a go before I refuse. But if I really find it's going to disturb my character or my voice or hurt me in any way, then I refuse to do it.

You run across directors who put you in those situations. You must have the guts to stand up for yourself without being a dope about it and just saying no because, "Well, I can say no, so I will say no!" I think that attitude is very stupid because it cuts off a whole avenue of being able to grow. If you try it differently, you may actually make progress. But of course, there are times when you really need to say no.

What about conductors?

It gets trickier with conductors. You have to be flexible and have a voice that can do what is asked of you instantly: depth, height, flexibility, softness, loudness. You try as much as you can to do what they ask without hurting yourself. Even if it's not your interpretation, you can learn something. Of course, with some conductors, you just hate their guts! You still have to try anyway, until you want to blurt out, "Oh, forget it! I hate your guts, I'm not doing that!" Of course, you can't really say that to a conductor, even if you want to; it wouldn't be appropriate behavior. It's really meant to be a collaboration, and if some conductors don't want to collaborate, you have to stick up for yourself and take care of yourself, because no one is going to take care of you, but you. Nobody else cares if you sing or not. You have to care the most!

What is your basic philosophy of life?

It's short! So, just remember that!

What would you advise singers to do or not do when in the process of studying?

I would say: Never, ever self-criticize. Don't be overly hard on yourself. Don't negative-speak to yourself. Certainly, be diligent but not harsh. Then, when you enter the professional field, be prepared to continue studying, and don't think you're ever finished. It's always a work in progress. Each performance is a rehearsal for the next performance, which is a rehearsal for the next performance! That's all. Never stop going forward!

What do you think American singers bring to the opera world?

They bring energy and flexibility. However, we still need to encourage Americans to let their voices be individual and not try to sound like someone else. It's important to stay true to yourself, so if you have a fast vibrato, don't necessarily struggle to erase it out of your voice, if it's not a technical flaw or a problem of balance. I mean, if your voice just has a fast vibrato because that is its personal color, well, then that's what you should use, instead of trying to sound like someone who has a slower vibrato. Don't make your voice darker or brighter, but rather find what it naturally is, and make it the healthiest and most balanced it can be. Thus you will be an individual voice. You will not be a clone: "Oh, she sounds like Leontyne Price, and he sounds like Jon Vickers!" You'll be compared to others anyway, but don't aim for that.

The greatest singers have instantly recognizable voices. It's because they are individuals, and that means you get to recognize their flaws as well as their greatness. I'm not saying, "Cultivate your flaws," but don't beat yourself up about them. Just continue to work and try to be better— but don't think you're terrible because you have a flaw.

Above all, we should avoid, in America, having assembly-line singers, all formed to sound the same. No two operas are alike, no two singers are alike, and no two interpretations of a part are the same. Every singer who has the guts to get up and take that first breath to sing deserves to be heard. Whether that person will have a long career or not, who knows? The greatest voices in the world have not had careers, and some minor voices have had major careers.

What do you think is the secret to a career?

I don't think there is a secret. It's fate and preparation, along with how much you are willing to give to it. You have to love it more than anything, because there is a lot of great pain involved, and a lot of stress. There is also a lot of joy that you can't get anywhere else. But in the end, this profession has to fulfill your soul so completely that you can't imagine life without it.

Ramón Vargas

Recorded March 2002 in New York City, USA. Published in Classical Singer, *July 2002.*

On your Web site, www.ramonvargas.com, it is possible to hear you perform a fragment of a Christmas carol with the boys' choir of the Basilica de Guadalupe in Mexico City, at the age of twelve. Tell me about that moment.

It was the end of one of the most important periods in my life, because that was the last time I sang publicly as a boy soprano. I had started performing in this chorus at the age of ten, singing professionally, and exploring a vast repertoire, from Gregorian chant to Bach and Mozart. This experience was crucial in shaping my perspective on music and future development, because from that moment on, although singing to me meant having fun, I took the study of music very seriously.

Several years later, after having already sung at the Palacio de Bellas Artes in Mexico City, you experienced a huge vocal crisis. What happened?

I made my debut there at twenty-two, and a year and a half later, I experienced more than a vocal crisis; I lost the desire to sing. Perhaps I was thinking too much. It wasn't the same as when I was a child and sang with spontaneous joy and pleasure; singing had become a burden. I began to be afraid and lose my confidence. I did not want to sing anymore. I stayed home, depressed, and I even thought of moving on to other things.

After a few weeks, I felt a longing to sing again, so I started to listen to my favorite recordings of singers of the past, and most of all, I listened to myself in that recording, the one on the Web site, and it made me cry. Thus, I became determined to rediscover the natural way of singing I had lost with my childhood. Since then, I have been almost entirely self-taught. With the help of one of my dearest friends, Ricardo Sanchez, I began to experiment with and explore my voice. He was not a teacher yet, but through his knowledge of singing and his strong wish to help me, we worked for a year and a half toward understanding my voice. At the end of this period, I felt I had recovered my confidence and I was able to continue on my own. I understood that working with and by yourself is very important. You should have an idea of what you are looking for in your singing, because no one will be able to tell you. I am convinced that a singer is born a singer. Ideally, a teacher's guidance should consist in making the singer aware of what he or she is and has.

Tell me about your "singing principles."

When I speak of this, sometimes I become too esoteric. I consider singing to be an energy form—a light—that exists in itself and uses us to develop and show itself. I believe we are like a crystal through which singing manifests itself. Our work is to polish this crystal well, so that it could project this light in the most beautiful and brilliant way. The more talent you have, the purer the crystal; the more you work, the better cut and polished the crystal. As the Gospel says, everyone will be called to account for their commitment and duty to the talents they have been granted. Throughout this process, we should be humble before the music, before the composer, the style, and before ourselves. Only those who are humble are capable to learn and develop themselves. There is a Chinese proverb that says: "We must never confuse merit with success." When you follow the basic principles of singing and art, you can't go wrong! Performing "Ave Maria" in church in front of family and friends could be the greatest success for a singer, as important as it is for me to sing a grand premiere at the Met. By the same token, for another singer, performing in an important production at the Met could mean nothing if it is not being filmed or well received by the critics. Everything is relative. Therefore, it is important to follow yourself and believe in what you are doing.

What about technique?

For me there is no "technical" way of singing. However, I believe there are three important principles in singing: spontaneity, flexibility, and depth. If we are able to coordinate these three principles, singing becomes more natural. The voice is not born in the throat; it comes from much deeper inside. It could be compared to a waterfall, which is not created where you see it as a waterfall, but it forms further back through the union of several springs. The same goes for the voice. Singing (and all the art forms) requires a spiritual formation and state of mind.

You always say: "Cantare è un modo di pensare" [Singing is a way of thinking].

Yes. In singing you must have a clear concept of what you are doing. There are singers who have a sensationalist concept; therefore their singing will be guided by the need to create sensationalist effects. Then there are singers for whom singing is a compromise between art and themselves; thus, depending on this compromise, their singing will be ever more real and artistic. And so on. Each individual is responsible to discover what they are searching for in the art of singing, whether they are singers or listeners.

How do you see the teacher-student relationship?

As we know, not all former singers are the best teachers. A singer already has a history with its values, successes, and sometimes its frustrations. Thus, when he has been successful, he will think that everyone must follow his method. When, on the contrary, he has had frustrations, he will try to stay away from certain ideas, to help his student avoid the same frustrations. In the end, despite all good intentions, both concepts are wrong, because none takes into account the nature of the student. There has to exist the same humility on the part of both teacher and student, and thus, create a rapport of loyalty, similar to friendship, since working together has a sole purpose: to create the conditions necessary for the student to discover his or her natural way of singing. If the student does not know what he is looking for in the music to express through singing, he will wander from teacher to teacher endlessly.

You have studied pedagogy and are a teacher by nature. How does teaching help you?

Teaching helps me a lot. Through the students I discover things that I apply myself later. I discover ways to sing or interpret I never thought of. Sometimes, when a student has a problem, in the process of helping him improve, I help myself! Unfortunately, I don't have much time. But every time I give a lesson, I end up enriched from the experience.

If you had a student who has never sung before, how would you begin to teach him or her?

The first thing I would ask is, why does he want to sing. If he knows, it's a good start; if not, he must try to find out. If he tells me it is "because I like it," that is good. If he says it's "to become famous," that is a bad start. Studying singing in order to become rich and famous is wrong! You do it because for you, it is the best way to develop as a person, to grow as a human being. You do it because it fills up an important part of your life, of your personality.

Your attention to detail in singing is remarkable. How do you manage to be so meticulous, and at the same time, manifest an

emotional abandonment that could jeopardize precision? How do you combine the two?

You are right. At first, I was doubtful, because there are some who say that singing is, above all, an emotional expression. Others say that discipline is most important in singing. I believe the combination of both is right. We cannot allow ourselves to be swept away by emotion alone, because art has its limits, its own dimension. Therefore, being guided by passion or sensation alone would produce only a partial form of expression, as would being led solely by the intellect. Going back to the idea of humility before music, if the composers worked so carefully on their operas, we have to respect them. Through our sensibility and talent, we must try to understand and express what they wanted. So, putting heart in it is not enough, it is also important to know much more: the languages, musical styles, history, et cetera. True, it takes longer, but when you build an aria or a role in this way, it is rewarding because once you've analyzed it, you understand better what the composer wanted, and you present it in a more authentic way, in favor of the music, without imitating anyone. Thus, you need to find a good balance between these two aspects and be very meticulous when studying.

You often speak of "giovanile ardore" [youthful ardor] in singing. What do you mean?

This I must be careful with, otherwise it could be more confusing than helpful. I feel that this spontaneity, flexibility, and depth in the voice all create a phenomenon that I call "la voce in movimento" [the voice in movement]. When the voice has all of these three characteristics, well balanced, it becomes like a river that flows constantly. A most clear example for me is Jussi Björling. His voice is "in movement"; it has this vibration. I don't mean the vibration created by the movement of the cords. In Italy, they named this "la lagrima nella voce" [the tear in the voice], referring to something inside that gave the impression of a lament, a cry, a moan. It was said that Caruso and Rubini had it, and then everyone tried to copy it. Perhaps they were referring to what I call youthful ardor because when you are young, you have a special kind of energy. However, the voice can sound old, even if you are twenty, if you don't give it this movement, and it could sound youthful at seventy if you are actively applying these principles.

During your life you experienced various crises, not only in your artistic development but also in your personal life, such as the short, tortured life of your first son, Eduardo, who suffered brain damage due to the delay of medical intervention at his birth, and his death in 2000. From where did you draw you strength during this difficult time?

My son, Eduardo, was born with cerebral paralysis; he was unable to walk or speak. This made me reflect on so many things. Where did I draw my strength from? I don't know! I think that your strength comes from your principles, from your family and the people who have always stood by you, from your morals, from your reality. It is very easy to allow these experiences to defeat us! Therefore, I have a special understanding for those who have such problems—there are so many all around us! Of course, this affected my singing immensely but it was singing that healed me as well, because through it, I could express my pain. My wife and I, with a group of friends, created a foundation to help children like Eduardo. We try to maintain his memory alive by putting a smile on the faces of his other little "brothers" who have the same problems.

With which operatic character do you identify most?

I relate strongly to Edgardo from *Lucia di Lamermoor*. He is a noble and strong character who was willing to sacrifice his ego and fury for love. Love transformed him into a more evolved being.

As we've seen, your principles are more than singing principles. They are a philosophy in themselves. How have they changed you and your perspective on life?

I definitely believe that my work in art has changed me in every way, especially if we look at it from the perspective of the ancient Greeks, who considered art a highly evolved expression of the human being. Artists were respected for this capacity to express a superior human manifestation. I don't feel that I am doing something more extraordinary than anyone in this world. However, the contact with aesthetics in general could make one become more respectful, tolerant, and as a result, a better person. Naturally, I became more tolerant with others and with myself. I would like to sing better and I always try to. But I have to accept my limitations, and I fight against them without frustration or fear and with a sincere desire to become better.

You have performed with outstanding American singers such as Ruth Ann Swenson and Dwayne Croft, and you have come in

contact with many young American singers not only in the
United States but in Europe as well. What would you recommend
to an American singer in the beginning of his or her career?

American singers are very well accepted in Europe. There is practically no theater where there are no American singers on the roster. I think
it is very important and helpful for American singers to spend some time
in Europe, to travel, to learn, to understand other cultures. Performing
La bohème when you know Paris is a whole different experience. Singing
Schumann or Schubert lieder after having been to Vienna becomes easier
in terms of expressing and understanding the music. A singer exposed to
other cultures is a better singer, thus acquiring the individuality needed to
create a great artist. Art is an expression of one's whole personality.

**Where could a singer who seems to have everything go wrong?
When talent, opportunity, and contacts are not enough, what is
missing?**

To be an opera singer, you need many ingredients, and all need to
come together in the right proportion. You need voice, musical talent,
histrionic talent, stage presence, patience, discipline and a pinch of luck.
You must be a good colleague, avoid creating conflicts and dissension, and
keep your feet on the ground. Unfortunately, as public figures, we are subject to the unrelenting criticism and judgment of others, so an essential
ingredient to the mix is having nerves of steel.

**Let's talk about repertory. You are a master of bel canto.
Your Rossini and Donizetti arias CD from 1991 is a jewel, a true
lesson in bel canto. Ten years later, when your Verdi arias CD
came out, you declared that you sing Verdi in the same bel canto
style. Please elaborate on this.**

Well, Verdi is the son of bel canto. He was an admirer of Donizetti.
While he was working on his first opera, *Oberto*, Donizetti was conducting the rehearsals for his own *Roberto Devereux* at La Scala. It could be
my imagination, but I hear fragments of *Roberto Devereux* in *Rigoletto*. Verdi himself used the singers who sang Bellini's, Rossini's and Donizetti's
works to perform. So, it's easy to hear the bel canto influence throughout
his music and thus perform it the same way.

**You are very careful in changing your repertoire. What new
repertoire are you exploring right now?**

I really like Berlioz and French music in general because it suits my
voice. I still have more than enough repertoire to develop. I don't want to
perform anything I cannot sing well. I am slowly moving toward the more

dramatic Verdi; however, remaining faithful to the bel canto roles.

Are you happy with where you are now in your life?

Yes, I believe I am in the best moment of my life so far! On the other hand, besides the tragic events I experienced, I can say I have always been happy because I've lived every phase of my life in a natural manner. As a student, I had my dreams and devoted myself to them without anxieties. Starting my career, being able to live from my work made me extremely happy. Always moving forward, and being grateful, I am as proud and content to be doing this today as I was in the beginning.

But when life deals you unexpected blows, it is so difficult to maintain this elusive inner equilibrium so important to singing well. How do you maintain your equilibrium?

Yes, I am not surprised when I hear that a colleague has stopped singing because he had a problem. To me, singing is like yoga. Before going onstage, I need to calm myself, to look inward and be well with myself. As human beings, we are so fragile. In the end, I think singers are as good as their physical and mental health allows them to be.

What is your fundamental philosophy of life?

Live and let live, respect others, and if you can, help them! The same applies to the voice. Let the voice live, allow the art of singing to grow inside you, respect yourself, and do not force anything.

What is your greatest fear?

My greatest fear would be losing the fundamental sources of strength in my life—family, friendship, and love! Without them, I'd feel lost.

Looking back, did you ever think you would reach this career level? How did you maintain your faith?

I never thought I would arrive where I am. However, I always had the hope and I worked very hard, not to "arrive" somewhere, but because I wanted to be better and this brought me peace. I also maintained my faith through the support of my family and true friends.

What is your message to all the singers who love this art and are fighting to improve and create their way?

Be constant, be generous, believe in what you are doing, and develop the capacity to enjoy simple things in order to grow and learn. Ingenuity, from Schiller's perspective, is a rare quality. It is also important to understand that we are part of a chain of people who serve this art, and if we can be tolerant, and work with ourselves and together, it will not only be rewarding for us but it will be to benefit music and artistic expression everywhere.

Rolando Villazón

Recorded November 2003 in New York City, USA. Published in Classical Singer, *August 2004.*

How did you discover your talent?

I always loved performing, but at first, I wanted to be an actor. I never saw myself as a singer. When I was twelve, I discovered Plácido Domingo on an LP with John Denver. I fell in love with Domingo's voice and started buying all [the] LPs of Domingo singing love songs, not opera. I learned all the songs and tried to imitate him. This was an early school for me between the ages of twelve and twenty. At the same time, I was attending a performing arts academy, where I studied acting, voice, ballet, modern dance, et cetera. At eighteen, I gave a concert in my school and a baritone in the audience told me I could become an opera singer. I took a few lessons with him, but I had to stop because my plan was actually to become a priest! I had a mentor who was supposed to guide me [into] this vocation. This mentor organized a concert and asked me to sing. I sang: "Granada," "Core 'ngrato," and "Una furtiva lagrima." Afterward, we had some tequilas and he asked me how I felt. I said, "Incredible!" So, he said, "I just showed you that your vocation is not with us! You have to sing opera. When you sing at the Met, I'll be there." And he was!

What was your biggest technical challenge?

To become aware of what I do with my voice. I see my voice as a horse. So: to be able to ride this horse, and not let it ride me. Knowing where to put the voice in the high notes, in the passaggio, and especially how to do *piano*. At first, I didn't have any *pianissimo*. I thought it was not in me. This was the hardest challenge for me. I had three teachers. Every time I felt I reached the top with one teacher, I left. After the third teacher, I understood that it's in you; you have to know your instrument. I received that advice later from Domingo. He told me, "The sooner you learn to understand your instrument, and know what you do with it, the better you'll perform and the freer you'll be!"

What is your daily singing routine like?

I often do a five-minute warm-up of easy scales, and then I sing arias. Some days I do nothing. But I sing a lot, even in the shower! I also like to sing out in rehearsals because I can put everything together: voice, energy, acting. For me, it doesn't work to rest the voice too much. Sometimes I take one-week breaks between performances.

Do you still have a voice teacher?

No. I work with different coaches. Singers are very vulnerable. It's a very delicate matter to have someone tell you what to do with your voice. You can create an addiction to that person, which can also be hurtful psychologically. Then, you perform to please that one particular teacher or coach. When you work with more people, you have several ideas about style, phrasing, et cetera. Of course, you have the conductor in each production and hope that he will tell you things. Some conductors don't like to get involved. But I like it when they give suggestions.

Tell me about your basic singing principles.

The beautiful thing about singing is that it's full of metaphors. Here is one I like: The voice is like a sock with sand in it. You grab the sock by the top, meaning the voice has to be hooked to the top (the mask). But you also need the body; that's why you have the sand. The sock has to be filled with just enough sand to remain flexible. You put too much sand, and the sock will fall. This means you lose flexibility and connection to the mask because of too much weight in the voice. So I try to put the right amount of sand and to keep holding it from the very top, so the voice has the body but also the ring by being in the mask.

But it could go the other way, too. You may have too little sand.

Exactly! And then the sock is just flying around without an anchor. It's too light. I need the weight of the sand to have the voice feel natural. When it has little sand, the voice is too ethereal. Talking about being conscious of what you do: a lot of people tell you to put the voice in the mask, because it's healthy. Yes, it is healthier to sing suspended in the mask rather than weighed down in the throat or chest. But it doesn't mean it's the right way. It's the balance of the two. The truth is, I don't think so much technically. I never thought about what to do with the diaphragm. A teacher once told me to put my tongue down when I sing high notes, because my tongue usually goes up. I tried but couldn't produce a sound. She said, "But you are limiting your space!" She may have been right but that

JASON BELL

didn't feel right for me.

Your idol does the same when he sings high notes.

Ah, yes! Domingo! I discovered that some months ago watching a video. I couldn't believe it. He does the same thing. Actually, better said: I do what he does!

And when you get tired . . .

I shut up. I even try not to talk. But I rarely get tired. I think when you find that right way to sing in yourself, you don't get tired. I don't have the special tenor routines because I think you become vulnerable when you do all that. It's all in the mind. I try to have a normal life. What I need is inside me. Of course, if it is cold, I'll protect myself, but I do not exaggerate. I don't walk around with scarves!

Your performing arts academy training must have helped you very much as a singer.

Yes. It's helped me in that I feel very comfortable onstage. It has taught me that, as you try to understand the voice, you need to understand your own body and know what comes natural to you.

How do you stay healthy?

Fortunately, I rarely get sick. I try to eat well and sleep at least eight hours a night. Now that I have a one-year-old, seven hours is okay!

How do you handle family and career?

Our home is in Paris but we travel together all the time. Eventually, the problem will be when the kid goes to school. It's so important for a singer to take care of his personal life. If you are unhappy, your singing will reflect that. Of course, there are singers who struggle in their lives but their singing is very exciting. It depends. For me, it's very important to have stability.

How about stage fright?

I love it! I want to be nervous before a performance because I transform that into energy, like a dragon getting the fire out. Every singer needs to be nervous, I think.

Being so young, how do older colleagues treat you when you begin working with them?

So far, I've been happy about it. Now I just sang with Renée Fleming and Dmitri Hvorostovsky; they were supportive and complimented me. I feel like I am really their colleague. Of course, I understand where I am right now. I am beginning my career. However, while I think it's important not to be arrogant, it is also very important not to be intimidated. If you are singing with a big star soprano and you are Alfredo, she is just Violetta and that's it! Everybody had a beginning. It's a question of balance. Arrogance will also work against you. You have to know where you are standing. If everything is going very well, that's great, but you have to understand that things can change anytime.

You participated in the San Francisco Merola program as well as the young artist program in Pittsburgh. Tell me about those experiences.

First of all, I would encourage all singers to do a young artist program. It's very hard to go from the conservatory to the main stage, so this is a very important step. You deal with everything you get in the real world of opera, you get paid, and the audiences are more tolerant. No one expects you to be perfect. I auditioned twice for the Merola program, which went on for ten weeks in the summer. I did Alfredo with them. In some performances I was singing in the chorus. I think that's good because it teaches you to be part of a team. It's about Verdi, about making music, about being a good colleague. However, you have to be careful not to tire yourself out. After rehearsals as a soloist, then as part of the chorus, after coachings, movement classes, and master classes, you can finish the day with no voice. If you're not very solid in your technique, it can be dangerous.

In San Francisco, you had master classes with Joan Sutherland. What did you learn from her?

What you learn from master classes is the right energy. You are scared to death when you go there, so you have to transform that into energy! What I remember from her was the way she moved onstage and talked about different phrases, her approach to opera, her portamentos, her emphasis on having a balanced weight in the voice.

Then you went to Pittsburgh.

Yes. For six months. That was a very good preparation for my career. I sang in *Lucia*, *Vanessa*, *Onegin*, and *Werther*; two productions with orchestra, two with piano. We had special coaches for each production, and language teachers.

Why did you choose Pittsburgh?

Well, my father was an American football fan, and his favorite team was the Pittsburgh Steelers. I found out there was a young artist program in Pittsburgh during the season, so I thought it would be fun to be there at the same time and invite my father to see them. Actually, that was the main reason! But it turned out to be wonderful. It was a great program and they treated me very well, so I should thank the Steelers for my going there!

You won two national competitions in Mexico, and then you placed second . . . in Plácido Domingo's Operalia. How did you deal with competition pressure and how were these experiences for you?

I have never in my life felt such nervousness as I did during competitions. Not even in auditions. It's terrible! When you sing an opera, you have three hours to develop and show your voice. If you crack the high C in "Che gelida manina," you still have the second and third acts. If you sing well, and act well, people can forgive you. Well . . . maybe! But in a competition, have one accident like that, and you're out! Every single note is the most important thing in the world. Of course, that's the way it should be all the time, but the pressure is unbelievable. That's why it's better to do competitions when you're young and have that eagerness and strong nerves. Even the national contests I did, I had to do one three times before winning. I remember during Operalia, I was so nervous and kept drinking Coca-Cola on top of it! My hands were shaking and I couldn't stop pacing. I was out of control. So, I went into an empty room and just turned off the light. I sat down and thought of every single phrase in my aria. I told myself, "Don't pretend to be bigger than you are. Just go there and do what you usually do." Ten minutes in the darkness, quiet, thinking about the aria made all the difference. I turned on the light, looked at myself in the mirror, and I knew I was going to sing well. Operalia was like a dream come true for me. I met my idol, Plácido Domingo. He had been such an immense influence in my development. He wasn't part of the jury, but he was there all the time. He saw all the preliminaries, and sang in the gala. I sang with him in the *Bohème* duet "O Mimi, tu più non torni" and he sang the baritone part! It was unbelievable! He was so encouraging. And his energy! Everyone was so inspired by it! He seemed a young artist himself, as if he had just won the contest! After that, I've maintained a close contact with Domingo. Every time we are in the same city, we meet. Sometimes I can't believe the singer who inspired me to sing as a teenager, has now become a mentor to me. Going back to competitions, you just have to push everything away from you: the jury, the colleagues, the nerves. It's also very important to choose a repertoire in which you feel absolutely comfortable rather than something very complicated. Sing the things you always sing. I wouldn't act too much, either. The story has to be in the way you sing. Acting can be a distraction in the end.

You're expanding your repertory at a very early age. You're scheduled to sing Hoffmann and Don Carlo. How can you tell you are ready for these roles?

Ah, the big question! And I had to decide on this Don Carlo three years ago! I like to take risks. Don Carlo might be too early but it's only one production. It's a small house and Riccardo Chailly is conducting. I auditioned for him so he knows he has a lyric tenor. After that, if I decide to sing Don Carlo again, it will be after 2007. Hoffmann can be sung with a lyric voice, so it's more for me.

Where do you see yourself in ten years?

My voice has this characteristic: it's dark, so people expect it to be big. Now it's just a lyric voice, but because it's dark, that can be confusing. In ten years, until I reach forty, I'll keep singing my current repertoire: Roméo, Des Grieux, Edgardo, the Duke of Mantua, Alfredo, Nemorino . . . All these roles are so good for the voice and for technique. Eventually, I will add *Ballo*. Maybe I will do one crazy thing like Don Carlo, and people will think, "This stupid tenor; he will destroy his voice!" I don't believe people destroy their voices with one production. Worst case scenario is it won't fit me. The problem is when you insist on a certain repertoire even after you see it's wrong for you. But if you feel the urge to try a certain role once, then just do it and see how it feels.

Any other technical tip you can give singers?

They've probably heard this before: Text is immensely important! Also, consonants are very useful. We tend to think a lot in vowels. But these breaks between the vowels carry the emotion.

So you associate consonants with emotion?

Exactly. The consonants punctuate the emotion and the vowels carry it out. You can find enormous emotion in a well-pronounced *b* or *p* or a rolled *r*.

In other words, you can assign an emotion to a consonant, depending on the meaning of the word?

Oh, yes!

So if you sang "guerra" [war], maybe you could associate the rolled *r* with charging ahead in battle or with a drum roll . . .

You got it. And that will awaken the right emotion in you!

You have a passion for drawing. Your Web site, www.rolandovillazon.com, has some wonderful drawings. Do you find any parallels between drawing and singing?

I believe everything you do is important. I also love to read and go to museums. The more information you have, the better. Even if you don't believe that Alfredo needs information from the Metropolitan Museum of Art. But when you go there and see a position, an expression in a painting; when you see El Greco's paintings in the exhibition going on now, you learn. It's all in the way the painters play with colors. The voice is about colors. Everything is a metaphor in singing, so if you see the sunrise, if you look at trees or watch children play in the park, it might help you discover something. We need to be sponges and absorb everything. I'm an amateur drawer, but this allows me to be creative. I work with lines, proportion, and perspective. It also helps me to take things lighter because I can parody certain characters and productions. It's a release.

A word of advice for other singers?

Lots of coaches may tell you, "Don't sing with your all your wealth; sing with your interest!" My advice is: Every time you perform, sing with all your "savings account" plus the interest. Give everything! But make sure that afterward, you are going to work to put more savings in your account. I don't agree that you should save your voice. Of course, don't overdo it, don't push. Just give what you have as a performer, but give everything. Then you go and coach. You listen to your performances and keep working very hard. Even if you get a debut at the Met and sign an exclusive recording contract. You should be the toughest judge of yourself. You never reach something . . .

You never reach anything, really.

That's life, actually! But in singing, that mentality can be especially harmful. You just have to keep going. The day you say, "I've arrived," is the day you stop singing. You have to search and doubt, and keep working all the time. It's a never-ending journey.

Joseph Volpe

Recorded May 2002 in New York City. The first part was published in Classical Singer, *November 2002. The continuation* dates from December 22, 2008, and appears here for the first time.*

You have devoted more than thirty-five years of your life to the Metropolitan Opera. Your life's journey is a perfect illustration of a true success story created through hard work, patience, determination, faith, willpower, and total commitment—qualities singers themselves need in building a career. Did you have a vision of your future when you started working at the Met?

I had a business prior to working at the Met, and I decided that I wanted to build scenery for Broadway shows. And somebody said, "Well, the best scenery in the world is built at the Metropolitan Opera." So I said, "Okay. How do I do that? How do I get to the Met?" The only way was to take an apprentice test at the union. I took it, scored rather high, and ended up going to the Met. So, I did not have a vision. I mean, I had a different vision, let us say. Then, as I became more and more involved in and familiar with the Met operation and with live opera performances—I was really taken by them—it's hard for me to say when, but at some point during those early years, I decided that this was where I really felt I could make a difference. Probably in the late sixties, I thought that if I worked my way through every area and learned a lot about the organization, it would be possible that—leaving politics aside—I would be able to run the Met someday.

Where did this desire to succeed come from?

I think the question with any young person—I was young at the time—is what they want to do with their lives. Do you want to be involved in something—as far as work—where you can make a contribution to an organization such as the Met or any performing arts organization, particularly if you are a performer, and are you prepared to go through the early stages of that career without really making any money? You also have to make the decision: do you want to go out and make a lot of money in this world, or do you want to do things? So, I made that decision. Everybody has to face that sooner or later.

What kept you going through the various behind-the-scenes struggles for power in the Met's history?

Actually, I didn't feel the struggle, because, as I was working, learning, and doing things, the struggle wasn't in the forefront at all, it was back somewhere else. I was enjoying what I was doing, so, in fact, it wasn't a struggle.

In general, what is the secret formula behind your staying power, and how would it apply to a singer's career?

I think it's determination. In the case of a singer . . . if I was the singer, there would be no hope, because there's no talent. The question is: does the singer have the natural talent and ability first? That's something that they have to find out. Not that those can't be developed and improved, but there should exist a basic, God-given talent. Once they know that they do have the ability to succeed, then it's a matter of having the drive to do it, and that's the most difficult part, because there are a lot of disappointments in life. I've had many in my career, and I'm sure singers have more, because in the case of a singer's career, if you audition for something and are not accepted, that disappointment could really set you back if you don't believe in yourself. So, having a belief that you can succeed is probably the most important.

Your reputation for being direct and tolerating no nonsense did not come with power; you have always been frank in an institution [that] is a mini-political world in itself, and in which frankness can work against you. However, it seems to have worked for you. How so?

Yes, I am straightforward and frank, but I do have the sense to be cautious at times. I think it's a question of balance. I don't run around just giving my opinions all over the place to people who don't want to have them and wouldn't understand them anyway. So, you have to be somewhat political. I guess my reputation is that I'm not. You need to be considerate of other people. I think there is a combination of politics and consideration, and I'm very considerate when dealing with others, although I'm very straightforward.

Do you sing at all?

Actually, I did a few years back, but I don't today. I do hum a lot, and

there's always some melody or something in my head, but I don't sing . . .
Well, you wouldn't call it singing!

**Were you acquainted with opera before you started working at
the Met?**

My mother and my grandmother adored opera, being of Italian heritage, and in both cases, they very much wanted to hear opera. In the case
of my grandmother, those were the days when we had the old record
players—the Victrola—long before your time. The one record that my
grandmother had was *Cavalleria rusticana*, which she played forever. Of
course, she was Sicilian. So, I was familiar because of my grandmother
and my mother. My father was busy making a living, didn't have a lot of
time, and was not an opera fan.

**As general manager of one of the most important opera
houses in the world, you are responsible for all aspects of the
Met's life, a gargantuan task. Nevertheless, you take the time to
attend rehearsals and performances, and especially to establish
a good communication with the artists. Why is that important
to you?**

First of all, knowing your product in any venture is very important.
I'm very involved with what we produce, so I attend rehearsals, I go to
performances; I want to see how singers sing. I won't accept hearing it
from someone else. I want to hear it firsthand. I'm very involved. As far as
my relationship with singers, I have a responsibility to make sure that they
have the best atmosphere in which to perform. That's why I also pay attention to what's happening on the stage. Having a relationship with them is
important, because they need to feel supported by the head of the theater.
That makes it easier for them to perform. I send every one of them a note
when they first start out at the Met at the beginning of the season, letting
them know that if there are any problems, they can either contact my as-
sistants or give me a call if I can be of some help. That's part of the job.

**The Met is, no doubt, one of the most coveted opera houses
in the world. Singers dream of performing on its stage. Yet this
American opera house seems so inaccessible to professionally
capable American singers who work regionally, even nationally,
and have a great deal of experience as well as good reviews. How
does such a singer gain access to auditioning for the Met, and on
what criteria are singers selected? In general, what are you looking for, in terms of "package": voice, looks, experience (in the U.S.
and/or abroad), age, cultural diversity, management, diplomas . . .**

DARIO ACOSTA

First, how does one get an audition for the Met? You make a phone call. You call the Met and, believe it or not, if the singer has the appropriate background, someone in the artistic department would have a discussion with them. They'd send in information about themselves, and I think, in most cases, everybody with appropriate background is heard, as far as an audition. Countrywide, we have the National Council auditions—I don't know how many people audition every year—but that goes on all year round, and then in the spring, the winners chosen from each district come here, and there is a semifinal followed by a final. The important thing is: the singer has to be ready to sing at the Met. They must have performing experience outside. In certain cases, if they know their repertoire extremely well, and they're coached well . . . I think that enables them to come to the Metropolitan Opera. In most cases, it's important for artists to develop a career—whether it be in Europe or in other American houses—before coming to the Met, only because coming to the Met can be a real shock to the system, and it's important that they are ready for that. Audiences are very unforgiving. An artist makes their debut—and I see this quite a bit today—wonderful talent but not really ready, and unfortunately, it's a major setback in their career. That's why it's important that they go through the audition procedure. Also, there is the possibility of working with coaches at the Met, and those coaches could be of great assistance to the singers.

What about looks? Does physical appearance make a difference in hiring singers?

Today, you'll find that many companies will not hire people if they don't have a certain look. I mean, there are many American singers that aren't hired in Europe at all, because of their size. Although, if you have a glorious voice, as we well know, and you really have a lot of talent, you will sing no matter what your size is, and you can sing at the Met. But

I think today things are changing. Audiences want to watch attractive people with attractive voices, rather than just one of the two.

How does one get more information about the Lindemann Young Artist Program? Direct inquiry doesn't seem to help, and there is no advertising for it. Can one audition directly for this program?

The Lindemann Young Artist Development Program is something you can audition for directly. As a matter of fact, I should find out more information from the head of that program and give it to you, so the people can be made aware of it.

What about experience in Europe? Is that more valuable than experience in the U.S.?

Well, I think the best-trained singers in the world today are Americans, quite frankly. However, experience anywhere makes a difference. If it's in European houses, there are certain things you can learn there that you might not learn here. It's important to have experience. That's the key to a career. I don't suggest oversinging, but the more you sing in different places, the more you have the opportunity to learn and become better.

Does age matter?

If it doesn't affect what the singer can do, it doesn't matter. If they have the talent, the ability, whether they are x years old or y, I don't think it really makes any difference.

You have made opera much more accessible to a larger audience, managing to maintain an equilibrium between employing star singers who are box-office attractions and at the same time, reaching out to a broader audience through various programs. Developing the "Met titles," establishing a student discount program, and starting an opera education program for young children have been major steps in attracting a wider audience. How do you plan to continue this expansion?

With the student discount program, we have been active in New York City. Honor students at the City University of New York have a cultural passport program where students have an opportunity to come to some rehearsals, and they have discount tickets. We're reaching out more and more beyond the New York City schools, to universities and colleges.

What would you do to make opera more appealing to future generations?

You mean it's not appealing now?

Well, it's more so than before, but I still see a lot of people in

my age group and younger who are still intimidated by opera.

It's interesting . . . you know, we did *A Midsummer Night's Dream* last year, and I was amazed at the number of young people here. It was really something! What's happening is that there are more young people coming to the contemporary works. So, I think what we can do is enlarge our repertoire and try to balance it in a way that it appeals to varied groups.

What is your prediction for the future of opera in general?

I think it looks very bright. It's expanding even in today's times, when the economy is very difficult. There's been some setback after September 11, but I don't think opera has been affected the way museums have been.

You have a reputation for not tolerating diva behavior . . .

What is diva behavior?

Well, you know . . . tantrums, refusals to comply with aspects of the production . . .

If somebody refuses to come in or does not show up for rehearsals, and it affects the artistic product and the other singers, of course I can't tolerate it. I mean, it's not fair to those that are here. I don't have any problems with [the idea of] a "diva," but there are certain rules and regulations; there's a certain way you have to work with your colleagues. I find that most of the very good, competent singers do that. Now you will have, occasionally, a singer who has a lot of problems . . . there's one specifically that we had an unfortunate situation with a few years back, where she wouldn't work with her colleagues and she wouldn't come to rehearsals on time. So, that affects the product. And if it's going to affect the product, then I can't let it go.

The Mini-Met was an idea conceived in the early seventies that had a short life, and in the early nineties, James Levine decided to revive it. Can you elaborate on the Mini-Met and its purpose?

Jimmy once said that he'd love to have a small facility to perform operas that this house is too large for. But—quite frankly—one, it's not something that we can afford to do; and two, given what we are doing with our orchestra and chorus in Carnegie Hall and elsewhere, our schedule is very tight. So I don't think the Mini-Met in the sense that it was conceived back in the seventies is going to happen, because I don't believe there is a need for it at this point.

What distinguishes the great singers from the good singers?

Their greatness! If you look at the great singers today, one, they have natural talent; two, they have a dedication; and three, you can go to a performance knowing that they are very secure in what they're singing. They don't take on roles they're not sure of, and they give you the best performance they can give. I think that's what makes a great singer. There are a lot of singers today that are very good singers, but I don't think they have the natural talent of the great singers. It's like a great ball player versus a good ball player. It's a question of talent. Now, there are ball players in baseball, for example, where the best is maybe not the most talented, because of hard work and determination. It works the same anywhere. However, I guess if your vocal cords do not allow you to have that range and be able to sing the way one expects of a great singer, then I'm afraid you're doomed. Talent is, of course, very important, and so is how the talent is used. There are a lot of very promising young singers who take on the wrong repertoire and do things that are too heavy early on. So they really shorten their career and never become the great singer they should.

You book singers years in advance. Is there a fear that maybe in three or four years, a singer will not be . . .

It's not a fear. There's always a consideration. When you're booking singers, you have to guess as to what you think is going to happen in their career three or four years out. Most times you're right, and sometimes you're wrong. When you're wrong, you then have to try to discuss it with them and find a reasonable resolution, and that's not easy.

Do chorus members ever become soloists?

There was one chorus member, recently, who sang some solo roles and then moved on and went elsewhere. As a general practice, no. But it happens on occasion.

Is it true that if you sing in the chorus, you are labeled as a chorus singer, and then it's hard to escape that?

There might be some truth to that, I would think.

Does graduating from any particular conservatory or school really matter in auditioning?

No.

Do you ever attend musical events and "discover" new talent?

Last year I was all over Europe attending musical events. What happens today is that we have a talent scout in Europe, Eva Wagner, who is being considered to run Bayreuth. She works for the Met as a consultant. So she's seeing a lot of things in Europe. We have an artistic staff that attends events as well. Is it likely that I would be the first person to see a singer and say, "Hey, Sally or Jonathan or Jimmy, you ought to really hear this singer?" Probably not, because there's a big network. I mean, we're normally pretty well aware of most young singers coming on the scene and singing in European houses or here. However, it could very well be that I would go hear a singer and say, "Well, maybe we should try this singer in some different repertoire." But no, I'm not the frontline person searching for talent.

Is there any hope for an unmanaged singer in today's opera market?

"Managed" meaning by . . . ?

An agent.

Well, it depends. There are agents who are really just booking agents, and there are agents that are managers who help and guide the singer. That's the kind of assistance a singer needs. They need somebody who's knowledgeable—who has experience—because to do it all oneself, I think, is virtually impossible. An agent who manages the career will also protect the singer, so the singer doesn't pick the wrong repertory based on their voice. In fact, not too long ago, we had an audition of a singer who was singing absolutely all the wrong repertoire; it was much too heavy for her. And we mentioned that to the agent. It's a very difficult situation today, because you have to find the right person. Take, for example, an American singer, Risë Stevens—her husband managed her career. Fortunately for her, he was very knowledgeable and spent his whole life doing that. It's important to have somebody really committed to the singer to help them, and not just get a commission every time the singer sings.

A common question of *Classical Singer* readers is about discrimination in hiring musicians and singers. How much of a role does EEO [Equal Employment Opportunity] play in this process?

It's equal for everyone, on the basis of talent. First of all, in the case of our musicians, they audition behind a screen. The shocking thing was that, for years, women never played the French horn. Then we had auditions not too many years ago, and the winner was a woman. Now, if you look at the Met orchestra, you'll see we have more women—I think we have three French horn players—than we've ever had. You'll find that in the chorus today, we have more and more African-American singers than we've ever had before, because there are more and more that are auditioning for those positions. A few years back, they said, "Well, the Met doesn't employ any African-American tenors."

That was one of the questions, too.

It's very simple. If they're there, if they come to audition, and they're good, we'll hire them. It's got nothing to do with where a singer comes from, or with the color of their skin, or if they're part of a minority or not. If you look today, Ramón Vargas, who is Mexican, is performing a lot at the Met. Why does Argentina produce so many tenors? There are a lot of Argentinean tenors around at present. I mean, if you are talented in every sense of the word, and you decide to pursue a career and put yourself out there, race or nationality doesn't make any difference. If you can sing, you can sing.

What exactly are your responsibilities at the Met?

I'm responsible for whatever we produce at the Met. There are people who make decisions up the line. I don't decide on a singer that goes into the Young Artist program. We have an entire artistic staff. But, what we produce and what you see on the stage, ultimately, I have to approve. And then my responsibility is to make sure the place runs correctly and that we don't have big losses so that we can stay in business. It's important that we have a balanced repertoire so we can sell tickets . . . we budget about a 90 percent box office. So, ultimately, as Harry Truman says, the buck stops here!

*It's been more than six years since our *Classical Singer* interview! What are you doing now? Are you still at Giuliani Partners?

That's over. I was with Giuliani Partners for eighteen months. It's a wonderful consulting firm. But that was business oriented, and I really missed being involved with the theater. So I had a meeting with Richard Pilbrow, the founder of a company called Theater Projects Consultants, and we decided that I would go work with him. Theatre Projects Consultants is the largest theater consulting firm in the world. They work with architects in building new theaters and performing arts centers. We have an architect, and our own designers, project managers, and the technical people that do all of the equipment backstage. So we start off doing the basic geometry of the auditorium and the stage. For example, in the Kodak Theater, which we did in L.A., David Rockwell was the architect. We did the actual design of the interior and he did the decoration. It's always a collaboration, depending on the architect. But what we do also is the entire theater, anything from restaurant services, backstage, dressing rooms, restrooms, theater seats—everything. Presently, I'm involved with a project in Athens. The Niarchos Foundation is building a new opera house, a national library, and a cultural park, close to the water. The architect is Renzo Piano. They're supposed to open the theater, I think, in 2014. We have a Performing Arts Center in Orlando, which has a multiform theater—which is an incredible theater, fourteen hundred seats: [it is an] opera house and it converts to a symphony hall. They also have a Broadway theater and a community theater. In Kansas City, there's the Kauffman Performing Arts Center—the Kauffman Foundation has put up most of the money for that. They'll have a proscenium theater [that] will be for opera and ballet, and also a symphony hall. Dallas has a new opera house [that] is going to open in the fall of 2009. So I'm heavily involved in really the oversight of all of the theaters, helping the company because of my experience of many years in the theater. I look at all of the drawings, I consult with the clients, so I'm having a grand time! It's so much fun! We also have projects where we do management studies of theaters; that's developing now also. Many of the theaters will ask about programming and presentations. So, I'm in a way, advising, yet I don't have to stay up nights to worry about fund-raising and budgets or artist cancellations. That's somebody else's responsibility.

So you get to travel a lot . . .

I've been traveling quite a bit. We also have an office in London, and Renzo Piano's main office is in Paris, so there are a lot of trips to Paris. I also went twice to Athens. I had an opportunity in the spring to go to our London office, then I went to the new opera houses in Copenhagen, and in Oslo. Both of these theaters are about fourteen hundred seats. The Athens Opera we're planning will have between fourteen and sixteen hundred seats, which is an ideal size for acoustics. Of course, the Met has thirty-eight hundred seats, and it has great acoustics. But the whole atmosphere in these theaters is so much more different because the performers really have direct contact with the audience, which makes it quite wonderful. Of course, if you have government subsidy and assuming it will continue, you can afford theaters like that. In the United States, you can't because they rely so heavily on the box office for everything.

Looking back at your Met career now, how do you feel?

Well, actually, Cristina, I have not gone back to the Met very often. I went this year to see *Damnation of Faust.* It's interesting . . . I miss the people, the company. But there are many things I don't miss: the fund-raising, the pressures of working night and day, the worries. I guess I look at singers through different ears and eyes now. Many times I find, when you step back, you have a different view of the way people perform. When you're responsible for hiring them . . . I mean you always want to look at the bright side, the good side. I think when you're not involved, you have a somewhat more open and objective judgment. But I enjoy going to performances. It was very difficult for me when Luciano [Pavarotti] died because we were so close. We went to his funeral in Modena. I've known him since he made his debut in 1968. So when I hear people sing what Luciano sang . . . There was a fortieth anniversary dinner for Plácido Domingo, and there were three women singers: Susan Graham, Deborah Voigt, and Patricia Racette, and they sang "Nessun dorma." Afterward Debbie Voigt came to me and said, "What did you think?" and I said, "I didn't. I didn't like it. That's all great for an audience of dinner patrons to pay a lot of money to celebrate, but it's not for me." They imitated the three tenors, they came out in tuxedos. I thought it was quite silly. In a way, it's not what I think opera and music is all about. But anyway, maybe I'm just stuck with the tradition and the beauty of opera itself. I don't particularly like to see people make fun of it in that way. You're gonna have three women sing "Nessun dorma," it's just like the Irish tenors, I mean, who cares? I guess I'm living in the past.

No, I wouldn't like that, either. But then I guess you also wouldn't be too crazy about hearing me sing "Habanera" with a rumba rhythm . . .

Well, no, no . . . That's different. I just found that there are so many things they could have done. But then of course, that being after Luciano's dying and on the Met stage, and celebrating Plácido's fortieth anniversary, which would have also been Luciano's fortieth anniversary year . . . nobody thought of all of that except me.

Do you like the direction the Met is going in?

What Peter has done with television and the movies, that's very good for people who can't go to the opera. However, a lot of these directors that come in knowing nothing about opera—I don't believe that's the right way to go, but the press thinks it's very innovative. I know that singers have trouble with the directors who don't understand the language or the piece. *The Damnation of Faust* was done by Robert Lepage. I had also seen his "KÀ," which is Cirque du Soleil, in Las Vegas. I don't think his kind of interactive video works with opera. The reason was: when Susan Graham was singing, she was projected up on the screen, but it was out of sync. I'm hearing her and looking at her mouth, it's like she's lip-synching. Now maybe people didn't see it out of sync. What happened was, they added some special effects like flames, so by the time it went through the processor, that added a delay. So for me that didn't work. Otherwise, they're doing more new productions, they've gotten the box office up, but the expenses have increased tremendously. I think there's a good side and a bad side to everything.

Some singers told me they feel a lot of pressure because of shorter rehearsal periods, and because of the great increase in radio broadcasts through Sirius Satellite Radio, for example.

Well, I think that adding the number of new productions, jamming everything in, doesn't really provide for the best artistic performances all the time. However, I guess the question is: does the audience really know the difference? And I'm now coming to believe that a few audience members know the difference, but not many, I'm sorry to say. I just think that the mentality today of people going to the theater is: they just want this instant entertainment, and that doesn't work with music. I mean, not many people can sit down today and just relax and listen to music. There's gotta be so much more involved. And that's a shame. Everything is visual. I know that Lepage is going to be doing the Ring, and I am concerned about that, because you have these beautiful passages of music, and you don't need people jumping around or being projected onstage. So that will be an interesting challenge for them.

Diane Zola

Recorded April 2006 via phone. Published in Classical Singer, *July 2006.*

You were a dramatic soprano. Where did you study?

I studied at the University of Michigan, the University of Texas at Austin, and the Mozarteum in Austria.

Did you go on to a career as a singer?

I had a minimal career. I was one of those singers in New York who worked in a law firm and pounded the pavement doing auditions. I did some singing in the States and in Europe.

What made you decide to get into management?

I felt that my career wasn't going the way I'd hoped, and I had the possibility of taking a job at CAMI [Columbia Artists Management].

What was it like for you to be an artist manager?

After CAMI, I had my own management agency, and then I worked at another agency for five years. But I found that being an artist manager wasn't always artistically gratifying. You're never really part of the process. It's a frustrating job, because there is always someone who is never happy with what you do, either your artists or the presenters. It was not fulfilling.

How did you decide to stop being a manager?

I didn't really stop, but I was always looking at other, possibly more fulfilling options. I always loved young singers, and I felt that, having been both a singer and an artist manager, I had a lot to offer. When my colleague, Gayletha Nichols, was leaving the Houston Grand Opera Studio to work for the Met, I was asked if I might be interested in applying for the job. I did, and I am now in my fifth season here.

In what ways did your experience as a manager serve you here?

It allowed me to see how singers need to step outside of themselves and realize that often, when they don't get a job, it's not about them personally. It's hard for singers not to take things personally, because their instrument is intangible and it's part of them.

I always give the example of two different kinds of apples. Some people like Fuji apples and others prefer Granny Smith apples—but they're both apples! We don't all have the same taste.

Singers need to look beyond and always move forward, instead of dwelling on why they didn't get something. They should, rather, try to better themselves by asking, "What can I do to make myself more marketable and more interesting to those who are hiring?"

What can happen is that many singers have too many people they listen to—and often not the right people. Everyone is willing to give advice. That's another thing I learned as an artist manager: As a singer, you need to have just a small group you can really trust for feedback, and know that no matter how difficult it is, they will tell you if something is not working. Oftentimes, singers love to hear what they think works for them, and they can't step outside of themselves to listen and observe themselves. It's a hard life, being a singer!

What would you say are the key ingredients for having a singing career?

First, you have to have an incredible voice, not necessarily perfectly beautiful, but interesting. Then you must have a passion for performing. Everyone sees a certain amount of glamour in being a singer—the stage, the applause, the publicity—but that's such a small percentage of how you, as a singer, will actually spend your time.

Are you digging deep into the text, and always improving your musical skills? Do you read the novel an opera is based on, or other literature from that time period? Do you go to art museums? Do you take the time to translate the entire opera and understand what is going on throughout all the parts?

There is this whole issue of languages for American singers. We can mimic; we can use the IPA [International Phonetic Alphabet], and our diction can be good, but do we really understand syntax? We can understand words, but what about the meaning in the way they're put together? It's all this and more that makes a singer.

What is the age limit for the HGO [Houston Grand Opera] Studio?

There is no age limit. But [last] year, our singers ranged from twenty-three to twenty-eight. One has to be honest with oneself and say, "This is a young artist training program." If you're thirty-five or forty—I'm not saying you still can't have a career at that age, but a young artist training program is probably not the path for you.

David Gockley and Carlisle Floyd founded the HGO Studio as a bridge between academia and the professional life. They found there was a lot that our educational systems were not giving to these young singers. Four years in a university is not a lot of time. This is why these studios were founded.

What does the program offer?

We invite a singer to join us for a year at a time; it's a nine-month period. The pianists usually stay for two years. The singers receive a stipend, voice lessons every week, language instruction—they have to choose from Italian, French, German or Russian—and we also offer English for foreign students. Some study two languages. This is not just about diction or understanding a role; it's pure language instruction.

We bring a lot of guest coaches. There are a number of singers who get a membership to the gym. I also pay for some of them to belong to Weight Watchers, because being physically fit is very important to a singer. It's not just about appearance; it's also about health and fitness.

We're also very fortunate here in Houston to have a very generous community—whether it's people opening up their homes, or coming to help us with our database and entering all the applications before I head out on the road. We have a buddies program where each singer has two buddies, and these people are there to help [the singers] if they need to be picked up from the airport. We have groups that come in and do in-kind work, where they offer their services for free, talk about business, how to manage your money. We try to make this program as complete as possible.

Is the stipend sufficient for the studio singers to live in Houston?

Yes. In addition, we have a lot of in-house and out-of-house gigs they can do for the development department, so they're paid for those as well. I also get calls for recitals, or, for example, someone is being released to sing with Opera Pacific now. We also offer a lot of opportunities for artists to perform in main-stage productions, because they are all involved in studying and covering roles.

Sometimes we have alternate cast performances. It's a fabulous opportunity for them to learn roles, to watch the pros work, to be involved with world-renowned directors and conductors. Some years we do a studio production. [Last] year we repeated *The Little Prince*, which we world-premiered in June 2003, and the majority of the studio artists were involved in that.

We have an incredible music staff here, second to none. The singers get coachings not just for the roles they're singing or covering at HGO, but for their audition repertoire, or for whatever they need to sing else-where, too.

When are the auditions for the HGO Studio?

November—but they take place around the country: Houston, San Francisco, Chicago, Cincinnati, and New York.

How do you manage to stay alert during a long day of auditions?

Well, sometimes we're in auditions all day and it's so depressing. People aren't singing well, or maybe we've made bad choices in whom to hear. Then this one person comes in and opens his or her mouth, and it's like honey. That makes you wake up. This is what I love about auditions, that element of surprise.

What disturbs you in an audition?

Someone who's unprepared. One time, we had someone offer an aria, and three pages of the aria were missing! That's disturbing! Preparing well is also part of the job.

It disturbs me to see someone come in and not be pleasant. Some peo-ple may have an arrogant air about them, and that's most likely a defense mechanism, but that puts you off. The thing is, I wish singers would real-ize that we want them to do well. We want to have a lot of good people to choose from. We, as judges, are on their side. If we didn't want them to do well, what would be the point in going through all of this?

I always tell singers, "Consider auditions and competitions as perfor-mances." Some say it's not possible. I say, yes, it is! You need to set the stage. Of course, I don't want to see overacting, like someone falling to their knees or flailing their arms about. We will always be most interested in the voice, but it helps to see someone display dramatic instincts.

Do education and previous stage experience play a big factor in accepting singers for the studio?

They do. You can often tell where someone has gone to school. Certain schools are better at musical preparation and understanding of styles, as well as giving singers the repertoire that's right for them. In school, you often end up singing roles that you would not be engaged for in the pro-fessional world, so singers get an unrealistic idea of what they should be singing.

Oh, and another thing I find really annoying is when people's materi-als are sloppy, whether it's a written application that I find difficult to read, or a résumé in which opera names are misspelled or names of colleagues are misspelled. It disturbs me when singers don't take the time to prepare their materials well. It doesn't even take that long.

It's much easier now to update your materials than it used to be. I've been to summer programs to hear singers in auditions, and they don't even have that particular summer program on their résumé yet. That should be the first thing to add, even when you're in the middle of it.

People have to take responsibility for these things. This is their career, and they have to invest in these details, too, not just in their voice.

If somebody ever has a bad audition, would you give him or her another chance?

I'm always willing to give someone a second chance. I was there; I understand what it's like. The truth is, we remember a bad audition sooner than a brilliant audition. But with that said, I am very open to hearing someone a second, and sometimes even a third time.

Gayletha Nichols, Lindemann Young Artist Program director, spoke of there being extensive communication between the various Young Artist Programs in the United States. She mentioned you compare notes on singers.

Singers all talk among themselves, but they don't think we talk? If someone is doing very well, I'll get a phone call. If one of our young artists goes out in the summer to Wolf Trap or to San Francisco, I'm going to hear how they're doing. I think it makes for a more cohesive world for these young singers.

I have a wonderful group of colleagues like Gayletha—there's also Leonora Rosenberg at the Met, Richard Pearlman [Editor's note: This interview took place before the unfortunate passing of Mr. Pearlman in April 2006.] in Chicago, Sheri Greenawald in San Francisco, and Felicity Jackson in Florida. We talk to each other and share concerns for someone. A lot of times we all travel to the other company for various reasons and we'll hear their young artists. Sometimes we're all vying to have the same young artists in our program. I think it's great sometimes when we're all interested in the same person.

Do you ever have singers in the HGO studio who choose to go for a steady, less pressure-filled job in the chorus?

I don't think being in the chorus is less pressure; it's a different type of pressure. But none of the studio artists I know do that. We're very proud of our alumni out there working as full-time singers. Some of them leave here with a lot of work for the next few years in their pockets. Others go to New York and struggle like a lot of other singers. There are no guarantees.

I would say that if you get into [a program], especially one of the training programs I mentioned—the Met, Chicago, San Francisco, or us—it's maybe a little easier to have doors open for you. People hear you. Our studio artists sing for artistic administrators and general directors coming to see performances here; they audition for them. They're being heard all the time by a lot of people.

Do you try to cover all Fachs when you pick the singers?

It's different every year; there's no set recipe. Of course, we look at who might be returning, when we're looking to see who to add to the studio. We look at repertoire for the following year, and what roles our studio artists might have the opportunity to perform or cover. Then we might find one or two where the talent is so extraordinary that even though we may not have a lot of work for them onstage, we feel that we can offer them a certain level of training that they're not going to find in graduate school. So we open our doors to them that way.

When did you start as artistic administrator?

I started on September 12, 2005, and I continued as director of the Opera Studio until the first part of this year, so I had both jobs for several months.

What are your responsibilities?

I work very closely with the general director and music director regarding all artistic plans for the future: repertoire, artists, the negotiation of contracts, [and] also for chorus and orchestra. I'm the representative for AGMA; people come to me if they have complaints or concerns about the company. I will still stay somewhat involved with the Studio as far as advice, especially about repertoire for the Studio artists, and also about management.

What plans do you have for the company in the next five years?

I would say we're going to stay on a very innovative, interesting track, both repertoire-wise and with artists. I see us continuing to grow, and hopefully even our seasons may expand to more productions.

Any other words of advice for singers?

There are so many words of advice that I would give. I think number one is to study hard; to cover all of your bases; learn your languages; to remember that in addition to being an aurally oriented society, we are also a visually oriented society; and to make sure that you are in good physical shape and health . . .

Never feel slighted. If this is meant to happen for you, you have to just keep going on, from audition, to audition, to audition. We have to remember how many auditions Beverly Sills sang at [New York] City Opera before she was ever engaged. Everyone wants instant gratification. There isn't any instant gratification; it's a lot of hard work.

When do you think someone should draw the line, if the career is not happening?

I think that's personal. Actually, it depends on the voice type. The heavier the voice, I would say, the longer you can try to pursue the career. But I think you have to step back and take an honest look at your life, and say, "Am I finding the fulfillment and the joy struggling to do this? Is it worth it? Or is there something else that I could do that would bring me more joy and satisfaction?" And look at your options. There are a lot of options out there. The world is endless.

Part 2
Author's Corner

"To Thine Own Self Be True"

"What do you want to do with your life?"

The question stopped me midsentence as I was blabbering on about the various freelance activities that were shaping my existence in March 2005.

I quickly realized I had no answer. And so I stood there silent, facing José Cura while we were waiting for someone from the Metropolitan Opera Press Department to come and take us to an office where we could do the interview—an interview that originated with my looking at the Metropolitan Opera calendar and fixating on the handsome Argentinian's photo.

I knew of José Cura but had never actually seen him onstage. When I discovered that he would be performing Samson at the Met that spring, I jumped at the opportunity to see and hear him live. And what an opportunity! I sat through *Samson et Dalila* breathless, astounded, discovering facets of Samson I never imagined existed. Mr. Cura presented a character so rich in nuance and psychological detail that his portrayal transformed the role into a deeply complex yet understandable human being, tormented by the conflict of passion and duty.

Following my proven method of contact, I left José Cura a letter and an issue of *Classical Singer* magazine at the Met stage door, asking him to put me on the backstage list for after the upcoming matinee of his performance. But as I came to the stage door after the matinee, I found out that I was not on any list. Slightly dejected, I walked back out among the waiting fans. Should I stay or should I go? I had no idea if he'd even received my letter, let alone if he wanted to do an interview. Fortunately, my wavering did not last very long as a mane of black hair captured everyone's attention from the distance and triggered a murmur of excitement among the mostly female "guardians" of the Met stage door. José Cura walked out among them, greeted by a perpetuating flutter of programs and eyelids, punctuated by high-pitched exclamations. "You poor man!" sighed a woman, referring to Mr. Cura's physical ordeal onstage—tied up and grinding at the mill, beaten and thrown about by the guards, he had invested in every physical detail of the role as much as in its psychological and emotional details.

I watched Mr. Cura as he signed autographs, and I pulled slightly to the side next to the man who had accompanied him out the stage door. As Mr. Cura made his way near me, I stepped in front of him, startling him, and introduced myself. Before I could finish my sentence about wanting an interview, he reached out into his coat pocket and pulled out my business card. "You are the one!" he exclaimed. I had a sudden flare-up of the heart that knocked my knees one against the other into a state of intoxicating weakness, and propelled my jaw open—an inevitable reaction I suppose when a dark, handsome, charismatic, larger-than-life male force tells you: "You are the one!" I must have looked like the besotted Tom in those Tom and Jerry cartoons whenever Tom fell in love. I could practically envision little red hearts floating around my head—and was surprised that no one else seemed to notice. Mr. Cura decided it was time to bring me back to reality, and gently added, "The one who wrote me the letter and gave me the magazine."

"Uh . . . I am the one . . . uh . . . who wrote you the magazine and gave you the letter . . . um . . . I mean . . . the letter was written for you . . . by me . . . and the magazine was . . . um . . . left . . . also by me to interview you . . . " I pulled myself together. "I mean, I would interview you for that magazine. If you want me. To do it. Um . . . interview you, I mean . . . " *Shut up, Cristina!*

After my brilliant display of articulate English, Mr. Cura said, "Walk with me!" I followed him and the other man—who introduced himself as Mr. Cura's assistant—onto 65th Street. "I have to get to the airport," said Mr. Cura, urging me to come up with an organized plan for an interview. I told him my time possibilities and he promised to have his secretary e-mail me to set it up for when he returned from Madrid to continue his run of Samsons at the Met.

"Where are you from?" he asked me before we parted. When I answered, "Romania," he smiled and said, "Mama care te-a făcut!" which basically means, "Your mother!" and which is by far not an expression of ethnic admiration for anything maternally related. I stared at him, wondering if he had ever spent time in the Bucharest markets bargaining over onions or beets with the truly ethnically expressive vendors. He smiled at my puzzled expression and explained, "We have a Romanian maid."

It was about a week after this encounter that I found myself even less articulate—answerless, actually—when faced with José Cura's unexpected question of what I wanted to do with my life. His secretary had arranged for us to meet at the Metropolitan Opera on that March afternoon. I had waited for him outside the backstage door and saw him coming from far away—the unmistakable mane of hair bouncing up and down to the rhythm of his energetic yet smooth walk. He was smiling as he approached me and kissed me on both cheeks. I let some words out of my mouth before the process of thinking actually took place. "I'm ready for you!" I said, grinning. "Well, I'm ready for *you*!" he retorted.

Bewildered by the encounter, no wonder I could not tell Mr. Cura what I wanted to do with my life. "Admire you," I thought of replying, but fortunately restrained myself. After a few minutes, someone came to collect us and lead us to one of the rooms in the Met Press Office. As we walked, I commented to Mr. Cura, "So you just returned from Madrid and performed right away?! Wow!" I had seen that performance, too. "You were really amazing—with the jet lag and everything—it was incredible!" "That's because I have no technique, as some like to say," he replied.

We settled into the Met Press Office. I turned on the tape recorder and was instantly hypnotized by the story and personality of the artist and the man.

After the interview, I had two more opportunities to see José Cura onstage: one in 2005 as Roberto in Puccini's *Le villi*, at the Vienna State Opera; and the second, as Mario Cavaradossi in *Tosca*, again on the Metropolitan Opera stage. Each performance was, for me, another chance to discover the world of this complex artist, a world that encompasses wide artistic and personal horizons.

In the fall of 2008, Mr. Cura graciously sent me a complimentary copy of the newly released book of his photographs, entitled *Espontáneas*. The book offers yet another of his talents to the public through his passion as a photographer and sensitive observer of the world.

As for his million-dollar question to me, "What do you want to do with your life?" I can now say that it evokes different answers from me at different times. The only consistent factor in all my possible replies, the sole constant answer I could give is, "Live it fearlessly to the fullest and contribute my best to the world." After all, aren't José Cura's life and career illustrations of that very credo? And what an inspiration they provide!

Magically . . . Diana!

I had never heard anything like it. Diana Damrau's *Arie di bravura* CD played over and over on my car stereo and I couldn't get enough. The brilliant coloratura, the passion, the immediacy of her sound, her nuances, her depth, her lower register, her high register, *all* her registers! Everything about Diana Damrau's voice and artistry grabbed me and proved highly addictive.

So I wanted to know more about Diana, and visited her Web site. Her fun personality radiated off the pages. You could practically feel it bubbling all around cyberspace.

I had never seen her onstage. The closest I had come was during a rehearsal of *The Barber of Seville* with Juan Diego Flórez. But that rehearsal had taken place in a studio at the Metropolitan Opera, a sneak peek for members of the press, of the new 2006 production. Diana didn't sing full voice during that rehearsal, but what struck me right away were her physical agility and sparkling energy.

In the summer of 2008, as I planned my trip to Salzburg to interview Anna Netrebko for this book, I discovered that Diana Damrau would be performing in Vienna as Pamina in *The Magic Flute* at Theater an der Wien during the time I would be in Austria. I was thrilled at the opportunity to see her onstage and planned to ask her for an interview after her performance.

And so on a mild August evening, drunk with admiration for Ms. Damrau's highly nuanced Pamina, I made my way to the Theater an der Wien's stage door. I planted myself there, all ready to meet Diana and ask her to grant me an interview for this book. Watching people coming out the stage door, my thoughts toward *The Magic Flute*'s director got less and less friendly, as it dawned on me that because of the clownish face paint and wigs the singers had to wear in this production, it was a daunting task to recognize who was who as they walked out. I reassured myself, thinking

I'd seen Ms. Damrau's photo enough times and I would recognize her. Besides, she's got blond hair. It would be obvious.

Suddenly, a mass of blond curls appeared in the doorway and a whirlwind of golden radiance, laughter, and energy flew past me into a group of people, twirling them around in a mini-hurricane of hugs and kisses. My brain strained under the pressure of decision making: "That must be her! Blond, bubbly, with all these fans waiting." Before allowing the slightest doubt to arise in my mind regarding what looked like a totally new hairdo for Ms. Damrau, my feet took action and brought me to the group surrounding the blonde. "*Hallo!*" I yelled, grinning widely and extending my hand. The blond woman grabbed my hand and, in a very *German* German—with no Austrian touch whatsoever, said: "And who are you?" "I'm a writer. I've come from New York, and would really like to interview you for my book." The woman smiled, surprised: "A writer? From New York?! Wow!" She looked at her surrounding friends, who nodded in admiration. I continued: "So, I am in Vienna only until Sunday. Do you have time to meet for an interview one of these days?" "Yes," she said, "let's meet on Thursday at eleven in the morning, in the Theater Café here." Then, in a pirouette of golden curls and crystal laughter, she spiraled out of sight, followed by her adoring group.

"That was so easy!" I thought for a second, before freezing in dumb stillness and staring at the place where the blonde had held court. "Wait." A shadow of doubt gnawed at my neurons. I returned to my former waiting place by the stage door and continued to stare at the people, coming out with decreasing frequency. I walked inside to the security guard's booth. "Hello? Could you please tell me if Frau Damrau has come out yet?" The security guard, ruddy and mustached, looked slightly annoyed, and in a muddled Wienerisch, he mumbled: "I don't know." I felt compelled to explain: "You see, I just talked to someone outside. A woman. I thought she was Frau Damrau, but now I'm not so sure." "*Und?*" said the man. "Well, is there any other blond woman in the cast that might look like Frau Damrau?" The man leaned forward on his desk, his eyes bulging out so close to the window that his eyelashes were acting like up-and-down windshield wipers, as he blinked furiously: "Look, lady, they don't pay me enough to keep track of who looks like who in the cast!" Behind his looming, indignant figure I spotted some photos: of the singers, I presumed. "Aha, you have pictures!" I exclaimed. The man turned a subtle shade of red, but quickly sighed in relief as he realized I was referring to the artists' photos taped to the wall. "*Ja wohl!*" he nodded toward the pictures, then jerked upward startled to suddenly see me inside the booth with him. "Please," I pleaded, "can I just look at them? I have to see if there are any other blondes in the cast." The man scoffed and stepped aside, unblocking my view of the photos. Of course the photos were black-and-white— and the only white-looking hair was Diana Damrau's. "Thanks for your help," I sighed, stepping out of the booth. "*Ausländer!*" [Foreigner!] muttered the guard.

Increasingly doubtful that the woman I spoke to was Ms. Damrau, I walked outside and took in the lingering fans talking to one another, and to cast or orchestra members. I turned toward a short, middle-aged man whose loud, confident, Wienerisch-tinged rant somehow endowed him with an air of stage-door expertise. "*Grüss Gott!*" I ventured. "*Bitte schön,* have you noticed if Frau Diana Damrau has come out yet?" The man evaluated me and my Romanian–New Yorkese–accented German. "Hmm . . . who knows?" he offered, philosophically. "But I just spoke to a woman who I thought was her." "Maybe it was her, then," said the man, looking at his female companion. "But," I insisted, "she really didn't look like Frau Damrau's photo!" "Ha!" exclaimed the man, then turned to face me straight on. "They *never* look like their photos! Never. They always look so nice in their photos, but when you see them out here, they're ugly! They're all ugly!" By this point, his volume had gone up to an alarming level. "*Ugly!*" An older woman stared at us and patted my arm as she passed by: "Don't listen to him, *Kind* [child], we are all beautiful in God's eyes!" Slowly, I started to back away from the indignant man, who turned his rant to his companion: "Ugly, all of them! Except Domingo. He always looks like his photo," he acquiesced. I made my escape bumping into another middle-aged man who was holding a huge photo in his hand. "I overheard you," he said. "You are waiting for Diana Damrau?" "Yes," I whispered. "So am I," he said. "See?" and he held the photo up to my face. It was the same black-and-white rendition of Damrau I had seen in the security guard's booth, but in a much larger version. I nodded sympathetically, and continued to back away, thinking, "Theater an der Wien certainly has an original cast of characters, and they're not onstage. They're all out here. Waiting for Damrau. And me with them, in my cameo appearance."

I decided on one last attempt and approached a group of what seemed like people who worked at the theater. "Uh . . . excuse me," I said. "I have a dumb question. Do you know if Frau Damrau has changed her hairstyle?" The four pondered the question with a seriousness that impressed me. One of them answered: "No. It's the same as in her photo." I began my story: "Look, I talked to a blond woman tonight, and even set up an interview with her, but now I am not sure she is Diana Damrau. She is definitely a singer. Who could it be?" "Did she speak with a German or Austrian accent?" asked the only man in the group. "German." "Well, it could be *die zweite Dame* [the Second Lady], Hermine Haselböck. She is from Germany and speaks *German* German." "Oh, no!" I said, my heart sinking. The man looked at me sympathetically. "Diana may have gone out another way. There are other exits here, you know."

I thanked the man, and made my way to the street, formulating a plan about how I would handle this interview appointment on Thursday. I'd feel bad telling her I confused her with Diana Damrau. Maybe I could interview her anyway, and offer it to *Classical Singer*? As various thoughts were fighting for supremacy in my overwhelmed brain, Ms. Damrau's photo popped in front of my eyes again. "What . . . " I stopped. The owner of the photo was standing next to me: "Hello again! So the woman you talked to wasn't Frau Damrau, right?" "No." He smiled reassuringly: "We'll find her." Inspired by his enthusiasm, I followed him. As we came near the Theater Café, he went up close to the huge windows of the café. With an abrupt movement, he plastered Damrau's photo on the window and started pointing to various blond-haired women seated inside the café while his gaze moved rapidly from the women to the photo and back. "*Ach, nein*, not her . . . hmmm . . . maybe it's her . . . no! *Ach*, that one, *ja*, looks like the photo, hmmm . . . *nein*, perhaps *nicht* . . . " As the curious glances of the male diners started to focus on the man pointing at their blond wives, girlfriends, female companions, I felt it was an opportune moment for me to withdraw from what had been the most original stage-door-waiting experience of my life. "It's okay," I said to my gesticulating, muttering, photo-carrying companion, "she's not there. Thanks for your help." "*Nein, komm, komm!*" he yelled after me, wanting to pull me into the view of the increasingly alarmed diners. "No, really, it's fine," I said, taking my leave. He removed his act from the window and followed me: "*Komm, bitte*, one more try, please, *komm* . . . inside." Despite my better judgment, I actually followed him inside the café. He headed straight for the maître d' and shoved the photo in his face. To my surprise, the maître d' politely invited him to look around the dining area. I backed toward the door and left the Theater Café, carrying with me the image of my detective-like companion standing in the middle of the room with a huge photo of Diana Damrau, scrutinizing all blond females in sight and shaking his head in disappointment.

Thursday morning rolled over me with a flavor of nervousness. There I was, getting ready to meet a singer who was probably not Diana Damrau, but whom I had so confidently convinced I was dying to interview. And yet, in my mind, she couldn't be Hermine Haselböck, either, because Frau Haselböck was not German. I had researched her on the Internet, and found out she was Austrian, so her German should have sounded more Austrian, I thought. Then who was it that I was meeting?

In my tormented state of doubt, I had spent hours the day before in the Internet café, reading everything I could find on Diana Damrau. I prepared the interview questions as if I would be meeting with Ms. Damrau herself the next day. An act of faith, as my mother would say.

At 10:45 a.m., I arrived at the Theater Café, which was closed. Fortunately, Naschmarkt—Vienna's number one market—was sprawled right across the street and offered plenty of places to sit and talk, so that part did not worry me. The fact that I did not know who I was meeting, did. Just a tiny bit.

As I fidgeted in place, a petite blond-haired woman passed by me and I was struck by a flash of lightning. "This is Diana Damrau!" I recognized the face from her photo. After all, my sleuth-companion from two nights ago had offered me plenty of glances at Diana's photo. "Can't be!" I thought. Should I run after her? "This would be too unreal!" I wavered. Suddenly, from the opposite direction, I saw her walking toward me: tall and curly-haired: the blonde I had actually talked to that night. In a few seconds, it all came together. The petite blonde who passed by me stopped to talk to the curly-haired blonde. *Bam!* "If she stopped to talk to my blonde, then she *must* be Damrau, 'cause they know each other, 'cause they're colleagues!" Before my flustered thought could make its way to a logical conclusion, I found myself galloping down the street toward the two blondes. I underestimated either my speed or my braking skills and, when I stopped beside them, I almost made contact. Physical contact, and not in a nice way. The two blondes jumped, startled out of their conversation, and stared at me. I spoke rapidly, my words competing with gasps for air: "*Hello!* It's me . . . for the interview . . . with you." The curly-haired blonde saved me: "*Ja, hello!* I was just coming to you." I looked at the petite blonde and extended my hand, introducing myself. She took my hand, smiling and said: "Damrau." Bingo! Sighing in relief, I let it all out about my faux pas in mistaking identities. I confessed everything. To my delight, the curly-haired blonde let out a refreshing laugh: "I was so shocked! Someone from New York coming to interview me?! Why? I have not even been there that much, but I thought I'd do it. Why not?"

The three of us stood there staring at one another and laughing in the middle of Linke Wienzeile. Finally, the curly-haired blonde—who was indeed mezzo-soprano Hermine Haselböck—told Diana: "Why don't you go? Go do the interview. Since we all met like this . . . How fun!" I turned to Ms. Damrau: "Would you do it now? I mean, of course, I can wait until you come to New York." Diana thought for a minute: "Well, I am very busy . . . but . . . okay." I wanted to hug her with the awe, excitement, and relief I felt all at once, but channeled everything into a handshake and a quite loud, "Thank you so much!"

We said good-bye to the gracious Hermine Haselböck, who interrupted my attempts at apologizing, saying it was better for her not to do the interview now and that she was happy it worked out this way. I followed Diana Damrau into a café within Naschmarkt. We settled in a quiet corner. I turned on my recorder, and all the way to the end of the interview stared at her enthralled, as much by her personality and words as for realizing the incredible synchronicity of this encounter, when not even a case of mistaken identity could stop me from meeting Diana!

A Lesson in Profundity

There are those once-in-a-lifetime moments at the opera that keep you suspended in emotion and wonder; moments so incredibly moving that they're almost unbearable and yet highly addictive. You want more, long after the curtain has gone down. You want more as you board the plane to go back home. You want more for days and weeks later. You just want more. Period. That's how it was in Chicago Lyric Opera's October 2008 production of Massenet's *Manon* with Natalie Dessay in the title role and Jonas Kaufmann as Des Grieux.

From the moment Natalie Dessay stepped onstage until the very end, she weaved an enthralling theatrical, vocal, and artistic spell over the audience. In her scenes with Jonas Kaufmann, that spell intensified to the point that the audience unified in a collective riveted silence, racked periodically by gasps of sheer emotion. "Performances like this—this utterly complete experience of perfect cast and production—happen once every ten years!" commented an enchanted audience member, as I walked outside at the end.

I had connected with Natalie Dessay via e-mail and set up an interview on the day following her performance. Still under the hypnotic effect of the evening's performance, I met Ms. Dessay at her hotel and we sat down in a corner of the lobby. Initially I worried that the lobby background noise would prove somewhat distracting. However, right after I asked the first question, the surrounding environment melted away as Ms. Dessay's intelligence, thoughtfulness, charm, and humor obliterated everything in sight and sound except for her and her answers.

At one point during the conversation, I asked her if she has a favorite quote from an operatic libretto. "Why?" she inquired. I explained that my original intention for the opening of each chapter in this book was to add a quote from a role. "Meaning what?" she asked. I mentioned about the quote I had thought of for Dwayne Croft, from Verdi's *La traviata*: "Pura siccome un angelo, Iddio mi diè una figlia" (Pure as an angel, God gave me a daughter). "The reason for that quote," I explained, "was that at the time I did the interview with him, he had recently welcomed the birth of his daughter, and he was singing Germont at the Met. So, I'm using quotes that have some sort of a connection—in my mind—with the interviewee at the time of the interview." Ms. Dessay thought for a moment and said, "I am studying *Pelléas et Mélisande* now. And there is a quote I really love . . . " She began singing in a soft voice: "Laissez-moi, laissez-moi . . . " and suddenly stopped and looked at me: "But without the music, it's not the same. Opera means both the music and the words, for me. The quote without music means nothing!"

And there it was: the "aha" moment I was subconsciously longing for— the answer to my quote dilemma, which had begun as a fun experiment but somehow got stuck along the way. I realized that if I cannot have the music jumping off the page from the libretto quotes, those quotes have no complete meaning; they become simply a superficial ornament. By the sheer force of her commitment to the completeness of her art form, Natalie Dessay taught me a lesson in profundity.

In Sync and In Love

The morning shimmered with the promise of a gorgeous day, as I walked on the banks of the Salzach River on my way to the press conference at the Salzburg Sacher Hotel. Focused on EMI's launching of a new *Il trovatore* recording, the press conference's main attraction was the much-awaited presence of the recording's three stars: Angela Gheorghiu, Roberto Alagna, and Thomas Hampson.

Members of the international press assembled in the Sacher's conference room and, as the artists walked in, the thrill of anticipation burst out in spontaneous applause.

An avalanche of questions unfolded toward the center table where the three singers sat patiently and answered one by one.

When the conference was over, I approached Angela and Roberto, who immediately started speaking to me in Romanian. "You are Romanian, aren't you?" he asked, and she added, "We noticed you in the crowd and we said, 'she's so beautiful, she must be Romanian!'" In the chaos of requests for interviews that surrounded them, they agreed to an interview with me right away.

I followed Angela and Roberto to a niche in the lobby, a pleasant corner with a couch, two armchairs, and a table. As I set up my tape recorder, the bartender came to bring us orange juice.

"Is this natural?" Angela asked the bartender examining the liquid in the glass. "Yes, of course," he said. "Does it come from a bottle?" asked the diva. "Yes, but it is natural," insisted the bartender. "The bottle is not natural!" declared Angela. "I would like freshly squeezed orange juice, please." She smiled sweetly.

The bartender appeared embarrassed. "But we only have this one. I assure you that it is natural." "No, no. I would like fresh orange juice," insisted the diva. "You take two oranges, like this," she said, demonstrating by making two dangerous-looking fists, "and you squeeze. Like this, you see? Easy." The bartender turned around with the speed of a whirling dreidel and disappeared.

Ten minutes into the interview he reappeared with a shy smile, holding on to an enormous wineglass filled with what looked like freshly squeezed orange juice. Angela smiled. "Ah! This is it. You know what I want. Thank you."

It was my greatest pleasure to conduct this interview in my native language. I found that not only did Roberto speak Romanian flawlessly, but he also knew many of the particular ethnic expressions. I also sensed, in Angela and Roberto's voices and in their body language, the unique harmony of two people in love. I found them deeply connected by a spirit of youthfulness, optimism, an open-minded view of the world and their art, and a constant hunger for knowledge, development, and perfection. They radiated passion for each other and passion for their art. Not to mention a playful and refreshing sense of humor.

Seeing them together conjured up images from their recent opera film, *Tosca*. Directed by French filmmaker Benoît Jacquot, the film immortalizes Angela and Roberto as the timeless lovers, Tosca and Mario Cavaradossi. It was this film that led me to interview first Mr. Jacquot, and then its two stars. On screen and off, onstage and in real life, Angela and Roberto, seem to complete and complement each other in song as in dialogue.

My next encounter with the couple took place almost a year after the interview, after one of their March 2003 performances of *Faust* at the Metropolitan Opera. As Faust and Marguerite, Roberto and Angela gave the much-needed credibility and complexity to the two characters' interaction, which oftentimes can come across as one-dimensional and affected. In all the performances of *Faust* I've ever seen, there had been no soprano who so clearly portrayed Marguerite's metamorphosis from modest innocence to sensual awakening and finally, repentance. For me, *Faust* had never been one of those operas during which sniffles were guaranteed, no matter who sang. But Angela's Marguerite should have inspired the Met to write a warning on their calendar listing for *Faust*, "An adequate supply of Kleenex or handkerchiefs is highly recommended." This Marguerite's plight moved me and other fellow handkerchief-lacking spectators to tears.

Backstage, post-*Faust*, the two stars greeted their fans and welcomed me warmly, remembering our Salzburg encounter. As my mother, who had accompanied me, drifted into French during our chat with Roberto— which had begun in Romanian—a voice from the other end of the room admonished us, "Speak Romanian!" It was Angela, who in the middle of her conversation with an admiring young singer, somehow overheard the switch of languages and reminded us that Roberto needed to practice his Romanian. And we obeyed. As I left, I told Angela, "You made me cry tonight." "Oh . . . that bad?" she said, and we both burst out laughing.

A year after *Faust*, I had the opportunity to attend my first performance at the Opéra National de Paris, at the invitation of Ioan Holender, the general director of the Vienna State Opera. This invitation was initiated in Paris's oldest prison, the Conciergerie. I did some time there . . . touristically . . . and as I was leaving Marie Antoinette's cell, I bumped into Mr. Holender, who had decided to visit the Conciergerie that same afternoon. I had already interviewed the man they called "the czar of Vienna." And I couldn't help thinking, "Of all the gin joints, in all the towns, in all the world . . . " he had to walk into the Conciergerie to meet me at Marie Antoinette's cell. One of his goals during that visit to Paris was to see the performance of Massenet's *Manon* at the Paris National Opera, starring Alexia Cousin and . . . Roberto Alagna. He asked me to join him.

The evening after the prison encounter, I was taking my seat next to Mr. Holender, in eager anticipation of the performance, when a resplendent Angela made her way through the crowd to the seat right in front of me. She greeted Mr. Holender and smiled at me: "Ah, the girl from Salzburg."

During the performance, Mr. Holender frequently expressed his admiration for Alexia Cousin; he was in awe of her dramatic commitment to Manon. Yet we both remarked the visibly trembling jaw of the French singer who at times seemed dangerously close to bursting of too much dramatic weight invested in each sound. I asked Mr. Holender in a whisper, "Why is her jaw doing that?" Before he had a chance to answer, Angela whose sense of hearing never ceased to astound me, turned around to me and declared, "It is what happens when the technique is inadequate. It is very dangerous to sing like that." She then turned back to watch the performance. Mr. Holender remained wrapped in silence.

At the end of the performance, Mr. Holender and I joined Angela and Roberto backstage. As I walked alongside Angela, I told her, "You are the most wonderful, the best, the most magnificent; there is no other like you on the opera stage today!" She seemed to relish every word and affectionately grabbed me by the waist. Roberto was deep in conversation with Mr. Holender. All I heard was the name "Andrei Şerban."

That name would cross my path yet another year later, when a new production of *Faust* opened at the Met in April 2005, directed by Andrei Șerban—the Romanian theater and opera director. The title role was, again, sung by Roberto, but this time, his Marguerite was Soile Isokoski, as Angela was performing elsewhere. I reconnected with Roberto backstage, and the next day I joined him and other guests at the home of pianist Eugene Kohn for what turned into a very entertaining dinner. Sitting around the dinner table, occasional fragments of songs floated up from the guests. I was asked to sing. So I lunged into my favorite tango, Carlos Gardel's "Por una cabeza," followed by a gypsy song, as Roberto and some of the other guests provided me with excellent percussion by banging their hands on the table. And as the dinner came to its conclusion, Eugene Kohn said to Roberto, "So, your wife is arriving tomorrow . . ." Roberto leaned back with a glowing smile wrapped around a subtle sigh and whispered, "*Finalmente!*" (Finally!)

"And the Oscar Goes To . . ."

The letter that started it all came from Avatar Films. It was a press release on the new opera film *Tosca*, accompanied by an invitation to interview the film's director, Benoît Jacquot.

I was familiar with the director's name but not with his work. After watching the enclosed videotape of *Tosca*, I immediately rushed to the local Blockbuster to rent everything I could find by Benoît Jacquot. Only two of his films were available—*L'école de la chair* and *La fille seule*—but they were enough to pull me deeply into the cinematic world and enigmatic vision of the Paris-born film director.

Soon after, Avatar Films set up the interview date—my first interview over the phone. I called Mr. Jacquot at his home in Paris and launched into my best French. He declared I had the same accent as Angela Gheorghiu. "It must be the Romanian touch," I replied. He agreed.

After the interview was over, I was still enchanted by the filmmaker's melodious French-speaking tones, and I began having hallucinations and delusions of grandeur. "What if I send him my picture? What if he likes me and puts me in one of his films? What if he makes me a movie star?" The adolescent dreams of Hollywood fame came back as vividly as they had at thirteen, only this time the dream location was Cannes, the language had turned from English to French, and Paris was suddenly calling my name. I knew I had to do my best to meet Benoît Jacquot in person, for if I were to ever have a chance at coming close to the film world and getting my five minutes of fame, this was it!

So I wrote a "*merci*" note to Mr. Jacquot and very conveniently enclosed my headshot with what I thought was a valid excuse for sending him my photo: "I usually do my interviews face to face. I have seen what you look like, but you haven't seen me, so at least to maintain the semblance of an in person interview, I am sending you my photo."

It was a daring act and when I did not hear from him at all, I assumed it was just one of those crazy things one tries at least once in a lifetime. However, about two months later, *Classical Singer* contacted me for photos of Mr. Jacquot. Naturally I jumped on this pretext to contact him again. After asking him for photos, I inquired timidly about my letter. Yes, he had received it. "If you come to Paris, call me, and we will meet."

That was all I needed to hear—the decisive factor behind my first-ever trip to Paris. I had always wanted to visit the City of Lights and I had been saving for a trip to Europe. So on New Year's Day 2003 I flew to Paris to become a movie star. Or so I thought.

I finally met Benoît Jacquot in the middle of a snowstorm—a phenomenon Parisians hadn't seen in years. He invited me for coffee and we talked for a long time. The interview was already published and I handed him his issue of the magazine. I knew that this was my only chance to be direct with him, so I gathered my courage and told him that I want to be on camera; that if he could use me for any role , I would love to have such an amazing opportunity. He seemed taken aback. He found it unusual but somehow interesting that a journalist was asking him for a role.

There is no substitute for actually asking for what you want. It is still the best way to get what you want, or at least some semblance of it. The risk of rejection is high, and often frequent, but sometimes surprises do happen. In my case, the biggest surprise would be waiting for me in Vienna.

In May 2003, I embarked on my scheduled trip to Vienna, earlier than planned. Mr. Jacquot was filming a miniseries there—*Princesse Marie*—and he had told me I could stop by and visit the set. He had made no promises of any roles but at least I would be able to come close to his world and, to top it off, I would see the magnificent Catherine Deneuve in action, as she created the title role.

When I arrived in Vienna, I called Jacquot's assistant Antoine, as instructed. For a few moments I thought I was having jet-lag-induced hallucinations as Antoine instantly told me, "Welcome to Vienna! Your scheduled shoot is on Friday." The receiver fell out of my hands, right on top of the small turtle at my feet (my hosts had an army of turtles, which made walking through the apartment a bit hazardous). I retrieved the receiver, silently apologized to the turtle, and barely managed to find my words in French: "You mean, I am in the film?" "Yes, of course," came his reply.

I spent the following two days in a trance, getting fitted for my costume and learning my text. I had four lines, yet I felt as if Shakespeare himself had come down to Earth and blessed me with a deeply psychological material. I spent hours trying to capture the state of mind of this extremely minor character. I finally understood the significance of being a Method actor. Five minutes (actually three) minutes of movie stardom were better than nothing so I was going to give it my everything. As if my jet-lagged emotions were not stretched enough, I also had to handle the fact that my first-ever spoken movie scene would be with Catherine Deneuve. Walking around a bomb-searching Anthony Hopkins in Grand Central as an extra in the film *Bad Company* was a piece of cake compared to the mere thought of facing Deneuve on camera.

The day of the shoot opened its gates in brilliant sunshine and idyllic temperatures. A van picked me up and drove me to a castle on the outskirts of Vienna. I jumped from the car into another world, watching the elegant extras and open carriages making their way slowly up a tree-lined alley. It was a striking sight but I had to abandon it quickly to get my makeup and hair done.

I was certainly living out my movie-star fantasies, with makeup artists, hairdresser, and wardrobe mistress fussing over me until a 1930s provincial Russian woman emerged from their skillful hands.

"It's great to be an actress, isn't it?" asked Benoît, coming in to check the final result. "I love it!" I exclaimed. "Well, we'll see . . ." he told me, but I refused to let any doubts enter my mind. If I would never be on a movie set again, I was going to enjoy every second of the experience.

When I was finally ready, I walked to the back of the castle, where a table had been set up on the lusciously green lawn bordered by hedges. There was an intoxicating joie de vivre all around, from the countless bird trills to the frolicking butterflies. The sky was a perfect blue.

Benoît asked me to sit down at the table to rehearse my motions. I had to pick out a sugar cube and, being a quite provincial character, I supposedly had no idea of how to use sugar tongs. I grabbed the silver tongs clumsily and banged around in the sugar bowl until Benoît laughed. Then we proceeded to film my walk down the path toward the table.

I had to walk a bit hesitantly, notice my fiancé (played by the very young Jowan Le Besco), and continue toward him with a more decisive gait. However, my enthusiasm to display the perfect walk did not meet with Benoît's approval. "You are bouncing up and down like you are dancing. Just walk steady. And slow down!" I did, and just like that, my first scene was over.

As the crew was preparing the set for the next scene, Benoît's assistant gestured for me to take a seat in the director's chair. I sat and watched, hardly believing that I had come to be part of this production. A huge smile imprinted on my lips and the words "Benoît Jacquot" on the back of my chair, I got so absorbed in the improbability of it all that I didn't even notice when Catherine Deneuve had made her appearance.

I awoke from my revelry to catch a glimpse of her already sitting at the table. Benoît came to me and dragged me out of his chair, pushing me toward the great actress. I realized I hadn't even said, *"Bonjour,"* so I excused myself and shook her hand. She welcomed me with a sweet smile and I sat down opposite her. We spoke briefly. She asked me if I was actually Russian.

When I rehearsed my Russian accent for Benoît, he said, "Try the Romanian one. It sounds more natural in your French." So the accent turned from Russian to Romanian.

Take one. Catherine Deneuve delivered her lines in a calm, steady tone painted with subtle nuances of expression. She was beautiful to look at and she made me believe it was all real. I felt I was actually a Russian woman desperately eager to marry her son.

I was so infused by my purpose that I began delivering my lines with slightly too much conviction until I heard the dreaded word, "Cut!"

Benoît walked to me: "Why are you yelling?" *"Ah, non!"* I said. "I didn't realize it. Am I really yelling?" "Almost," he said, "you are very loud!" My cheeks burned in embarrassment: "I'm sorry. This is not theater, is it?" Benoît smiled. "No. It's not theater. The microphone is right here." He pointed toward the mike held by the sound man whose solid frame was shaking with laughter. "Do you know how loud you sound when you talk like that?" Benoît asked. "Do much less that you are doing." So I held back and fortunately did not cost Benoît too many takes.

It was all over in a flash. And difficult to believe it had actually happened. I had a hard time leaving the set and saying good-bye to a spectacularly unusual day. Later, I found out from Benoît that my scene would stay in the film. Thus in the spring of 2004, my three minutes of movie stardom circulated on the Arte Channel in Europe.

It was a beautiful surprise ending to what had begun as a phone interview.

The encounter with Benoît Jacquot had a profound impact on my life. Not only did he allow me to experience his world for a day, but he also took the time to read a synopsis of one of my stories and encouraged me to write a novel based on it.

When I saw him last in New York at the French film festival in October

2004, he asked me, "Is your novel published yet?" "No. Not yet. I am slow." I answered. "Well, you better hurry up!" he said. "Everyone says they are writing a book, but only a few ever finish."

Synchronicity, Modigliani, and a Dog Named Lenny

I was walking down Kärtnerstrasse in Vienna, with my friend Rosi Pritz of the Kupfer Agency when suddenly, I saw him: Thomas Hampson, sitting at a café table, engaged in a lively discussion. I turned to Rosi: "Wouldn't it be amazing to interview him?"

We kept on walking past the animated table that was drawing admiring glances from passersby. In front of the Staatsoper, we stopped and Rosi searched through her purse. "I have the number for his personal office, his secretary, if you want it. Just call and ask for an interview."

After I said good-bye to Rosi, I continued my stroll back to the Seventh Bezirk (district) where I was staying. As I walked down Neustiftgasse, a phone booth materialized in front of me. "I'm going to call right now," I decided. I dialed the number Rosi had given me. A man's voice answered. In my best German, I began to state the purpose of my call until I thought maybe it would be faster if I switched to English—save time on deciding between all those grammatical cases.

"So, if Mr. Hampson is available . . . " I ventured.

"This is Mr. Hampson," declared the voice.

Silence.

"Oh . . . " I uttered, gripping the phone like a handlebar of my favorite, rapidly swaying, Grinzing-bound Strassenbahn (electric streetcar) 37. "But I just saw you on Kärtnerstrasse!"

"I just came in, and walked into the office when the phone was ringing. So I picked it up."

And there it was again. Synchronicity. First time I heard the word was from the founder and former editor in chief of *Classical Singer*, CJ Williamson. When I looked it up, I came across Carl Jung's definition: "temporally coincident occurrences of acausal events"; in less words: "meaningful coincidences." But I preferred the metaphor that was one of Jung's favorite quotes indirectly hinting at synchronicity, from Lewis Carroll's *Through the Looking-Glass*: "It's a poor sort of memory that only works backwards" (the White Queen's reply to Alice's statement, "I can't remember things before they happen.")

Like Alice, I couldn't remember forward; fortunately my backward memory is still intact, especially when it comes to momentous encounters. A few days after that phone call, I was sitting face to face with Thomas Hampson in a beautiful room—that resembled a library—in his Viennese home. A third party joined us in that room, whose wise and affectionate presence never left us once during the three-hour conversation. He spent most of the time lounging at Thomas Hampson's feet, and occasionally, he would stroll over to where I was sitting with a friendly glance and an encouraging brush of golden fur against my knees. Lenny, the baritone's beloved golden retriever, was a supportive presence as I asked my questions; his occasional looks in my direction seemed to say, "You're doing all right!" As I later found out, Lenny's positive influence extended far. "It would never occur to him that he is a dog," writes multimedia artist Catherine Herberstein on the Web site of her design company, Lenny's Studio. Thus, Catherine, Thomas Hampson's stepdaughter, pays homage to Lenny, as a source of inspiration and love, naming her company after him and posting endearing photos of the golden eight-year-old in the "Who we are/Who is Lenny?" section of the Web site.

Somewhere in the middle of the interview, Thomas Hampson remarked, "I would be curious to know what your voice is like, because you have a very long neck."

"A Modigliani neck!" I blurted out, having only recently discovered the Livorno-born, Paris-based painter's signature long-necked portraits.

The baritone smiled in surprise. "Yes. I would think it must be challenging to sing out of a Modigliani neck, but the color of the voice is probably very interesting and unique."

He never heard me sing but his words registered. He was right: it had always been challenging to negotiate the freedom of sound when the path from the vocal cords to the resonators was so long. Over time, I've received many comments along the lines of: "That's a beautifully unique voice, but it's not really operatic. What is it?" I have been asked over and over again, "What would you define your voice as?" Now I always smile and think of Thomas Hampson, who unwittingly gave me my own "label"—a "label" that had always eluded me and those trying to define my voice. When asked what type of voice I have, my favorite answer is: "Modiglianesque."

The Miraculous Principles:
The Gift from
Ramón Vargas

"Give yourself permission to sing."

I looked at Ramón Vargas incredulously and blurted out, "But I don't need to give myself permission. I love singing, so why should I . . ."

"You don't love it. You command it. You look to the final result and demand absolute control." Ramón got up from his seat by the piano and pressed Play on the paused CD player. Jussi Björling's smooth sound floated around the room, spinning out its honeyed brilliance and freedom in "Ah! lève-toi soleil!"

We listened in silence for a few minutes, Ramón's face a portrait of awe and joy. "Do you hear what he does?" he said, pausing the recording again. "The sound exists. He gives himself permission to let the sound travel through him. He is humble."

I wanted to hide my face so Ramón would not see my glowing cheeks, burning in shame at the instant realization that humility was not part of my approach to singing. He sat down at the piano and said: "Now we start over," then took me back to the beginning of the lesson, seemingly unfazed that he had spent the last fifteen minutes trying to refocus my altered vision of singing into a single, luminous ray of truth.

Between 1999 and 2002, I had the privilege of studying voice with Ramón Vargas—all in all, I had six lessons in three years. The lessons did not last longer than twenty minutes or half an hour each. But they were for me the most intense revelations on the act of singing.

A lesson with Ramón was not just a voice lesson. It was a breakdown of all barriers, pretense, and hidden agendas, among other obstacles that blocked the natural path of the voice. The lesson began as an intense focalization on the present moment and turned into a direct attack on ego and insecurities. Whenever I faced Ramón in a lesson, I knew there were no psychological corners to hide in, no tricks I could use to impress him; there was no escape from being exactly what I was at that given moment. Basically, I was there to "face the music"—no pun intended.

Unlike any of my previous teachers, Ramón did not employ a method of specific vocalizing with me. He began very simply: With a sigh. Just letting out the breath in a deep sigh and allowing a very relaxed, vague v sound to form on that sigh. The v was practically subconscious, unforced; the lips didn't even have to come all the way together; it emerged from somewhere deep down, triggered by the sigh. Sometimes I would sigh and the v sound did not come. "That's okay," Ramón would tell me, "don't force. The idea is important."

He would take me up the scale on these v sighs, a half step at a time, starting very low—on an A-flat or G below middle C—and going up about one and a half octaves, ending at C above middle C. Then he would have me do the v sighs on two notes, whole step between them, like a slow trill, gradually increasing in speed. "Give it movement. A light, feathery movement like the stroke of a painter's brush," he would say.

Another exercise consisted of arpeggios in various combinations of five, three, one or one, three, five on the sound of "swa," staccato and then legato. He asked me to maintain the principle of the sigh but this time, the s gave the sigh more propulsion and the "wa" following the s released the sound.

I always fell into the trap here of focusing on sound, and trying to "produce" sound out of every "swa." Ramón would remind me constantly that it is the breath—its depth, flexibility, and spontaneous release—we were looking for in this exercise. The sound came second. We would begin these "swa" arpeggios at a faster pace, then he would slow down, urging me to maintain the same intention and spontaneity in the slow arpeggio as in the fast one. "Don't make it rigid to add more color. Do not confuse yourself. Stick with the principle, not the end result."

Since the exercises always began so low, I had the tendency to keep everything in the chest, and as we traveled higher on the keyboard, I would press these sighs downward to maintain the breath low. Ramón would then ask me to envision a vast expanse of light in front of my eyes. As I looked at this light, the eyes radiating outward, my head opened, helping the "swa"s distribute their focus evenly between chest and head. But when we took the "swa"s higher than an E-flat, moving into the soprano passaggio, sometimes my breath would rise high into the chest. In desperation to produce a sound, I would focus again on the end result, and the whole principle would evaporate into thin air, along with my high breath. Ramón would then stop me and we would return to the low *v* sighs until my breath was deep and flowing and my desperation soothed.

Afterward we would go back up the scale again, and in those rare moments when I managed to stay true to the principle, I could sing a high C or D as if they were floating on an ethereal thread, spinning out of nowhere, riding on release, energy, and awareness of being in the moment. I immediately fell into the trap of trying to recapture that same sound, so the focus shifted on the wrong objective and I would lose the principle again. So it was back to the basics. I was in awe of Ramón's patience.

Whenever I found the ideal sigh or "swa" and everything was in balance, I felt a natural flow of energy being released spontaneously. In the middle of this flow, the sound simply existed. This wondrous coming together of breath, depth, balance, and spontaneity would anchor me so profoundly in the moment that I had no room for judgment, manipulation, or control. That was the miracle of Ramón's principle of singing.

It never ceased to amaze me how the path leading to understanding this principle lay within the deceptively simple combination of sighs and "swa"s. Whenever I fully experienced this principle and transferred it to singing, my whole system of preconceived ideas about sound and singing dissembled. For brief moments, I could glimpse infinite freedom within singing, which was at times so scary that I immediately returned to the antiprinciple: holding and manipulating.

"Don't think of the voice, or of the sound; don't think of anything. Let it be what it is. Let it come as it does." My brain registered his words, and I would try and try until he would stop and throw me a frightening stare. "You are still afraid! You are afraid of making mistakes, you're afraid of the sound. You're afraid of everything! Is it true or not?" Well, even if it is painfully difficult to admit fear, the voice is a traitor. It reflects everything. When the voice wants to hide because of fear, it slides into every nook, every position that the mind creates to hold it, eschewing freedom.

"Sometimes you wonder why somebody's high notes sound so good, while the rest of the voice is dubious. You may hear a tenor whose middle voice is inward and tense or opaque, but when he goes to the high notes, the voice just opens freely and beautifully. That is because this tenor manages to free himself in his high notes. Do you see what I mean?" I nodded, grateful for the fact that I didn't have to discuss fear, at least for the next few minutes.

Ramón continued: "Your body and your intentions must be in agreement with your sound, but we can only begin to free our voices by starting with the small volume of our sound. If you make the sound bigger before you free yourself at the small level of sound, that sound will remain forced and rigid because it has never experienced freedom when it was small."

In other words, I thought, free the sound when it is a "newborn." When we want to sing, the sound is born as a result of intention, breath, energy—the whole mechanism being put into action. This baby sound must take its first steps into the world in freedom, otherwise it will have a hard time growing up to an expressive volume and maturity. If not freed, it will become an "adult" shackled by fear and manipulation. So how could I expect to fully serve music, when the chains of fear were weighing me down? Ramón's principle would lead me back to the sound as a baby, so I could then reteach it to walk—or rather, to float—freely in the present moment.

"The sound is small but spacious," Ramón would tell me. "You make the space, and the sound enters. Everyone has their own space. A good singer knows how to fill his space with sound naturally, so that the sound fits just right into that space and the singer doesn't need to force anything. Some singers may make the space too large, and they will never succeed in filling it with sound, so they push and darken. Others may make the space too small and squeeze the sound to fit it in. But this labor of discovering the right proportion of space and sound comes after finding the freedom. You can do this by yourself, too. You just have to give your body the natural principles and the body will find its way to sing because it is wiser than us."

Whenever Ramón told me I had found the right balance, I realized I was making less effort. "If you give too much, the body doesn't know where to take more energy from, to carry the huge sound. You will maintain your balance by staying with a smaller sound for now." I felt a tinge of disappointment, as my Romanian temperament claimed the right to express itself in a bigger, darker sound. But the maestro knew best. "When you sing, you do what I call 'movimenti paralleli' (parallel movements). That is: you give more energy/more tension, less energy/less tension. No! You have to find the right proportion of energy and tension, and when you sing louder, you add more energy but not more tension!" I would dutifully try to apply this principle until I didn't know anymore whether I had turned into a ball of tense energy or energetic tension!

"Do not sing!" Ramón would often tell me before I even started to open my mouth. It was as if he knew that in the process of getting ready to sing, a thousand watchful radars blinked feverishly in my brain, already plotting a course of action for my voice, which was by far not the healthiest path. Somewhere in my psyche, the premise of "Who do I need to impress next?" had become so associated with the action of singing that the verb *to sing*, itself, carried this loaded connotation. Throughout the lesson, Ramón would combat that false agenda by telling me not to sing at the beginning of each series of "swa"s or *v* sighs.

"Before singers initiate the act of singing, they are already committed to it," he would explain. "But *you* start singing without any kind of commitment and maybe, if you feel like it, you will casually decide to commit to your singing on the way, as the phrase unrolls. It does not work that way! That is already too late! Start already committed!"

I would then pull myself together and attempt to commit so intensely that I would overdo it, and I longed to sink into the earth at the sound of Ramón's exasperated sigh.

"Don't make the sound feel obligated to come. Ask it. Ask the universe. Ask God. Ask yourself for the sound. It is an act of humility."

The Unforgettable Gentleman

I left the euphoric crowd behind and walked dejectedly toward the parking lot. Commencement was over and its honorary doctorate recipient nowhere to be found. I had frantically wandered among the cheery graduates and their crowds of loved ones but soon realized Joseph Volpe must have taken another way out. His inspiring commencement address had both stirred and lifted the spirit of the 2002 Purchase College graduates.

As I walked by the Neuberger Museum, brooding over the missed chance to interview the Met's general manager, a familiar voice interrupted my mental rambling. "What's wrong?" I must have looked quite a sight, for the president of Purchase, Thomas Schwarz, was standing in front of me, looking genuinely concerned.

All of a sudden, I heard myself speak in the tones of a five-year-old: "Volpe! I lost him! I want Volpe!" Then immediately aware of whom I was speaking to, I quickly attempted to catch up with my age: "I mean, I knew Mr. Volpe was receiving an honorary doctorate here and I really wanted to use this opportunity to interview him. I had counted on meeting him after commencement but now he is gone."

President Schwarz smiled. "Cheer up! He's in the Neuberger right now. Do you want to meet him?" Beaming with gratitude, I followed the president into the museum. Joseph Volpe and his wife were just finishing up paying at the counter. After Thomas Schwarz introduced us, I asked Mr. Volpe for an interview. "Anything you want, dear," he said handing me his card and instructing me to set the interview date through his secretary.

Needless to say, I was in heaven. The first thing I did when I got home was to write CJ Williamson about this thrilling development. In anticipation of the interview, a great flurry of activity and e-mails followed at

Classical Singer as we decided to invite the readers of the magazine to send me the questions they had always wanted to ask of Mr. Volpe.

Throughout the weeks prior to the interview I was bombarded with e-mails from singers of various levels and ages. Many questions were brilliant, some very incisive, others challenging, but overall they were very helpful.

And then there was the million-dollar question "Please ask Mr. Volpe: Why am I not singing at the Met?"

The interview itself was a marvelous experience. I arrived at Mr. Volpe's office a few minutes early and he asked me in precisely on time. As soon as I sat down, he disconnected his phone, making it clear that he would give me his undivided attention for the full hour of the interview. And he did, focusing on each question with great care. I was utterly impressed receiving such consideration and respect from someone in his position, who obviously did not need another interview. Mr. Volpe's generosity with his time and attention made this interview one of the most memorable encounters of my life.

About a year and a half after the interview I ran into Joseph Volpe again at the Austrian Cultural Center, as the Met was celebrating its collaboration with the Vienna State Opera in Halévy's *La Juive*. I asked Mr. Volpe if he remembered me. He flashed his winning smile and said, "Of course I remember you. Are you still writing?" "Yes, actually I am writing a lot these days," I bragged.

He looked straight in my eyes, dead serious, and said, "Well, I don't see you writing about me!" I could not utter a word until he gave me another reassuring smile. I promised, "But I will. I will write about you again!"

Little did I know that several years later, Mr. Volpe would become a member of the School of the Arts Council at Purchase College. When the Purchase School of the Arts celebrated the fortieth anniversary of the founding of the college with a special gala in New York City in November 2007, I ran into Mr. Volpe again and gave him a few of my various business cards. In December 2008 as I wrapped up this book, I located Mr. Volpe and called his office. His assistant put me through right away. After his youthful, resounding hello, I asked my favorite question: "Do you remember me?" "Of course, I remember you!" he said. "I have about eight of your cards here for all the eight businesses you handle!" I laughed: "It's more a medical condition than anything else, really."

And so in the middle of a pre-Christmas snowstorm, Mr. Volpe took the time to come see me to give me an update on his life for this book.

Gracious, active, and positive as always, he continues to remain involved in the performing arts through Theatre Projects Consultants, contributing his expertise to the construction and development of theaters around the world.

James Conlon: Pursuing the Renaissance Ideal

Published in Classical Singer, *November 2004.*

"What's your passion?"

With that question, conductor James Conlon turned the tables on his interviewer, causing yours truly to be at a complete loss for coherent answers and simply blurt out, "Everything!"

I attempted to clarify, as much for the maestro as for myself, the exact definition of my life's passion—but somewhere between writing, singing, acting, and languages, the idea of a single-focus passion disintegrated. I told Mr. Conlon that I simply love everything and that this equal distribution of passion in several fields is precisely my problem.

"That's not a problem," said the celebrated conductor. "That's your gift. The greatest gift you can have is passion."

"But don't you believe in the idea that you have to do one thing in order to be excellent at it?"

"I don't believe in that idea. But our times do," replied the maestro without hesitation. "And all creative human beings who are thinking in terms of profession have to be clear about that. There is no question that we live in a world of specialists, and people need to have a well-defined job. That applies to every domain."

Singing included. What better illustration of the need to specialize than the well-contoured Fach system? Struggling, unknown singers hardly dare to cross Fach boundaries. They mold themselves into specific categories, weeding out of their repertoire all the Fach-defying roles, even if those roles might fit their voices better than some parts that lie strictly in their particular Fach.

On the way up the slippery staircase of auditions, most singers learn to play by the rules. They avoid crossing into "illegal" vocal territory, at least officially, in the hope that once established, they will be able to cross all boundaries as it suits them best, not guided solely by the dictates of a Fach guide.

Specialization of the singing voice may make things more practical for agents and opera companies. James Conlon, however, sees this phenomenon as both the effect and the cause of today's lack of the Renaissance ideal, as professionals are forced to be single-minded. The phrase *Renaissance man* or *Renaissance woman* refers to a well-rounded creative thinker with many talents and skills as well as a thirst for knowledge in various fields. Today such an individual may be called "a jack of all trades," a term that in a world of professional specialization bears a nuance of insult rather than admiration.

Conlon admits that the Renaissance ideal would be impossible to realize today, because there is simply too much data. At the time of the Renaissance, you could master almost everything there was to be known. Take Leonardo da Vinci, considered the ideal Renaissance man. Leonardo was a painter, sculptor, architect, engineer, and scientist. He studied anatomy, and even had knowledge of singing as well as an attractive voice. Throughout his life, Leonardo nurtured his immense love of knowledge.

It is true that no one can master everything today, as Conlon says. It is this love of knowledge that can carry the torch of the "Renaissance ideal" into our modern times.

"Even if you cannot be a Renaissance man or woman today, you can still be attracted to the Renaissance ideal," says Conlon. "And if you are attracted to that, I assure you that your entire life, you'll never lose the gift of passion. I say this to all singers, to all musicians: Your passion doesn't have to be just your voice or your music. You can be passionate and want to know many things in life, and that will only make you more fulfilled. Where is it going to lead you? You don't know that—but that's the exciting part. You just have to be true to your gift of passion and follow its direction."

What if you don't know what direction to follow? What if you enjoy singing, teaching, writing, and dealing with the business side of art equally? What if you love organizing concerts, running your own opera company, advising and guiding singers on their path? What if you like experimenting with different styles of music, and even write your own songs?

The maestro's reply is enthusiastic. "Do it! Do it all! If there is one specific thing that you are meant to do, it will develop as life goes along. But do not cut off avenues that appeal to you deeply because you feel obligated to focus on one thing only. Every single thing you do feeds on the other and grows and pushes you further, especially if it's something you truly love."

James Conlon's first love within the music realm was opera. He grew up in New York City, in a nonmusical family, and attended his first opera at the age of eleven. It quickly became his passion and he envisioned himself singing absolutely everything, from Boris Godunov to Rodolfo to . . . Carmen!

"Of course, I realized I was never going to grow up and be a mezzo," confesses the maestro, "so I employed a type of logic that only children can understand. There's only one way to do everything and be part of it all—the singing, the orchestra, the scenery—and that is to conduct!"

Once the thirteen-year-old Conlon made that decision, he threw himself into studying piano and violin, and devoured every book he could find on conducting and related topics. He was accepted into the High School of Music and Art (now La Guardia) as a singer with a baritone voice, but he rapidly emerged as a good pianist and became a regular accompanist in the lieder classes. He continued his voice lessons, spent a lot of time watching singers coach, and developed a thorough understanding of singing and the vocal mechanism.

Conlon's outstanding talent, musicianship and complete dedication brought him to Juilliard where fate—bearing the name of Maria Callas—stepped in to speed things along. The legendary diva was giving master classes at Juilliard when the school's president at the time, Peter Mennin, asked her to take a look at the young conductor and give her recommendation, as he was doubtful about allowing a student to conduct a Juilliard production. Callas watched Conlon on the podium for fifteen minutes, went right back to Mennin, and gave her enthusiastic approval—which led to Conlon's New York debut, conducting *La bohème*.

Conlon remembers Callas with gratitude and affection.

"We all thought of her—and rightfully so—as this great stage personality. We saw her as someone superpassionate and all over the place dramatically. But you could see from the master classes that she had absolute precision of the musical material before anything else. Nothing was by chance. It all seemed like an outburst of drama and emotion, but the foundation was guided by the strictest, most meticulous knowledge of the music. I learned that from her."

The Callas influence on Conlon's development was only the beginning of a series of encounters with the surviving phenomena of a "golden" generation in the opera world. The maestro gets teary-eyed when he remembers the brothers-in-law Tito Gobbi and Boris Christoff. Conlon's first *Don Carlo* was Christoff's last Philip.

"Can you imagine starting your life like that? I was petrified by this image I had of [Christoff], but I discovered a man of warmth and genius with an unbelievable spirit. I had the fortune to spend entire days with him at his villa, immersed in discussions about music . . . I met Tito [Gobbi] at about the same time. He would talk to me about Tullio Serafin and that whole generation of singers and conductors who knew every meaning of every note in the scores. Tito knew Tosca inside out, and it was inspiring to watch him when he directed it at the Met . . .

"It was unbelievable: just sitting with all these amazing artists and talking to them. I learned so much. These were people who knew opera and its culture. Despite all the stories that they were sometimes terrible colleagues, they were completely serious about their art. Their devotion to it was 100 percent."

Conlon's nostalgic description of the walks and meals enjoyed in the company of Boris Christoff made me think back to the few days I was fortunate to spend with Virginia Zeani, diva of the Golden Age featured in the December 2003 issue of *Classical Singer* and a hit with singers in the recent *Classical Singer* convention master classes.

Zeani shared her wisdom with her students beyond the span of a lesson. The more you were around her, taking part in her daily activities—such as going to the post office or helping her prepare one of her fabulous lunches—the more you learned about her art. Knowledge poured out of her throughout the day, at the most unexpected moments, and those students who simply spent time with her learned more than they would have in a lesson. Zeani is one of the very few remaining teachers of the "old school" of teaching. Conlon calls them "the endangered species."

What distinguishes the endangered species?

"A holistic approach to music-making—not just singing, but music-making in general," says Conlon. "Italy had this tradition of teaching by spending time with the masters, by apprenticeship. This goes back to the painters. Botticelli and Michelangelo became apprentices when they were children. They didn't do anything but bring the paints—and watch. So, the Italian tradition was based on observation and absorption of the masters' skills—and that also became the basis of the singing and teaching tradition.

"Spending time around the great singers and teachers gave students this holistic approach to music. Their art became a way of life. They understood that it's not just about the notes, or the correct use of technique. That's only the beginning. It's about culture. It's about all the things between the notes which you can't write down in a book on singing. It's about emotional, physical, intellectual, and spiritual commitment to music-making. But today it's really difficult to teach that, once a week for one hour in a voice studio. And we live an increasingly technological lifestyle, so we tend to think that there's a technique for everything."

As Conlon believes, today we are faced with an endangered species of music-making in a technological, information-saturated, fast-paced world, in which the Renaissance ideal is impossible to attain, and singers try to squeeze their spirits into the tight reins of the Fach system. We do admire the singers of the Golden Age. But we cannot possibly lead their lives and follow their recipes of development, because we are a product of our times, in which ironically, life expectancy is longer, but time seems scarce under the pressure of doing everything faster and sooner.

"As a singer today, you have to be very smart to know how to navigate this modern system of life without harming yourself," declares Conlon. "Don't rush, no matter what anyone tells you. Believe me, you can maintain your own healthy pace of development in a high-speed world, but it takes a lot of discipline and saying no to the many temptations out there, which sometimes look like opportunities. Wait, wait, wait . . . You'd be better off singing Mozart for ten years. And one other very important factor to your development is culture."

Conlon offers his own experience as an example.

"I was born and bred in the United States. I started traveling when I was twenty. I had a choice: to become music director of an orchestra in America or in Europe. I chose Europe, because I knew that if I stayed in America, I was really not going to learn anything new in terms of culture. I'd learn more repertoire, gain more experience, but that's it.

"It was the best decision I ever made."

The decision brought Conlon several remarkable tenures: from 1989 to 2002 as general music director of the German city of Cologne and its opera, as music director of the Rotterdam Philharmonic between 1983 and 1991—and the longest tenure of any conductor since 1939, as principal conductor of the Paris Opera from 1995 to 2004.

"I spent over twenty years living in Europe. The minute you leave one country and go to another, automatically you know twice as much as everybody at home. As soon as you have to learn a second language, and work with people in their country, on their terms, in their culture, you are already more advanced than anyone who stayed in one place.

"Of course, you can start a career in America. We have our own generations of musicians and there is an 'American voice.' But we're talking about opera, a classical art form that has its roots in other centuries, other languages, and other places. The more you are able to walk back in time and in the culture of opera spiritually, the better your music-making will be. I say this to every American singer: 'You have to go to Europe, somehow!' Of course, you won't be going to the Germany of Beethoven or the Italy of Verdi, but those countries are still closer to the root of your art by direct link with the languages, the cultures, the expression of emotions . . . You can do it all here, but you won't be a complete artist if you don't experience Europe.

"Go to Germany and get a job in a theater, because you will learn how to be a professional in a way you will find nowhere else in the world. However, don't stay too long and don't get yourself in a situation where you are required to accept repertoire that is not good for you. This is going back to specialization. You have to a pick a Fach that's safe for you and stick with it, at least until you get your experience. I personally don't believe the human voice is made in categories, but in the beginning you have to navigate the system."

How did James Conlon navigate the system of politics and power plays during his remarkable tenure at the Paris Opera?

"My attitude was to stay completely focused on my art."

Conlon admits there is no such thing as immunity to politics, because when an artist and an administrator come into conflict, the administrator always wins—in the short run!

"In the short run, they will get what they want, they will change the policy, they will get rid of you, they will make your life miserable. You can't fight a politician; you can't fight an administration, not if you are a serious artist. If you're not a serious artist, then you have the time to get involved in all those power games. Over the years, I learned not to participate, and to become a force of my own."

Conlon believes that the only power artists have is the power to convince by devotion to their work, in their daily performance, not just while they're in public or on the podium, or on the stage, but also behind the scenes. Then, work is always fundamental; it is an artist's greatest weapon and no one can contest that. He often advises singers not to get into politics to gain attention, outlining the difference between celebrity and quality.

"What's the first quality of a celebrity? People know about them. But the question is: *What* do people know about them? Criminals are known! Anybody can be famous. You want to make money, then make money; you want to be famous, then be famous; but don't confuse these with being an artist. There are all those things around being an artist that can distract you from the art itself. You should keep your devotion to your art, as if it were a religious vocation. Everyday, keep your focus on the art and do what you need to do for your art, day after day after day."

That focus includes self-analysis and the willingness to change personal traits that may be obstacles to the development of a career. During one of the orchestra and chorus rehearsals at this year's Cincinnati May Festival, the maestro stopped during a tricky succession of phrases and addressed the chorus: "Chorus, very well. A-minus! Now let's try it like this." He followed with a series of praises for the different sections of chorus and orchestra alike. By taking care to compliment the positive aspects and only afterward moving on to correcting the mistakes, Conlon held the Festival chorus and the Cincinnati Symphony spellbound and inspired them to work harder.

I was witness to what I believe is one of the keys to Conlon's success: the personable touch and ability to connect to people, even sharing inside-jokes with the various sections of the orchestra. He wasn't just a brilliant conductor at work, he was also a human being trying to communicate his ideas and create a harmonious environment around him. No wonder his tenures are long lasting—he just celebrated his twenty-fifth year with the Cincinnati May Festival. I complimented the maestro on this positive and gentle approach to collaboration, only to find out to my surprise that this was not a natural trait.

"Sometimes the things you get to be the best at are the things you were the worst at when you were young. I learned to be like I am now—very slowly!" admits Conlon. "I was brought up a very critical nature: self-critical, critical of others, exigent, and very impatient."

He remembers being very inspired by Pope John XXIII, who had declared that the biggest obstacle he'd had to overcome was arrogance. "That was amazing! People loved him because he was very simple and accessible, and he wasn't caught up in the trappings of the Vatican. You would never ever imagine he could be arrogant. But he overcame that!

"You *can* gain the qualities which seem impossible to you at first. It took me years and years to surmount impatience and my critical nature, and to figure out how to put those traits to good use. So, you're seeing the results of a long road. I truly believe that the things that are the most difficult for you are often your biggest gains when you surmount them."

The 2004–2005 season will bring James Conlon back to the United States, where he will conduct most of his home country's leading orchestras, also returning to the Met for *Tosca* and *Un ballo in maschera*. A longtime champion of composers whose lives were affected by the Holocaust, Conlon will continue to devote his time to performing their music throughout America and Europe. His busy schedule also includes teaching annually at the Tanglewood Music Center and the Aspen Music Festival, as well as a seven-year association with the Van Cliburn International Piano Competition, both as conductor and master teacher. In the 2005 season, he is slated to become music director of the Ravinia Festival and plans to work with the Steans Institute for Young Artists, focusing on expanding the Festival's education goals.

This past June, Conlon returned to Juilliard to receive an honorary doctorate. Facing the sea of singers, musicians, actors, and dancers, the maestro offered a rousing commencement address. His concluding words prevail as inspiring advice to *Classical Singer* readers as well:

"The only lasting values to be found in the life of a professional artist are those to be found in the drama, the dance, and the music themselves, and in the constant love and giving which those art forms demand of us all. Competition is a reality in an artist's survival in the real world, but when it comes to art, the real competition should be within yourself, with your potential: the struggle to draw the best from your spiritual, intellectual, and emotional wealth. Ultimately, there is only one competition in life, and that is the race with time to realize your potential in only one lifetime."

Leonardo da Vinci would agree.

An Encounter with
Virginia Zeani

Published in Classical Singer, *December 2003.*

Virginia Zeani has sung Violetta more than six hundred times, a feat unequaled by any soprano in operatic history. Luciano Pavarotti tackled his first Alfredo alongside this "ideal Violetta." She was considered one of the most beautiful women in the world and one of the greatest singing actresses on the lyric stage. Zeani's career covered a repertoire from bel canto to verismo as well as contemporary operas. She created the role of Blanche in the world premiere of Poulenc's *The Dialogues of the Carmelites* at La Scala in 1957.

Blessed with raw musical talent and a phenomenal instrument, Zeani manifested an innate wisdom in handling her talent. She was able to carry and mold her voice through three different Fachs, in a logical progression from lyric coloratura through lyric to lirico-spinto. This vocal evolvement is perhaps best captured by the opera that allowed her to show this transformation during the course of a performance. From the coloratura of Olympia, the lyricism of Antonia, and the seductive vocal darkness of Giulietta, Zeani always performed these three roles together, creating a metaphor for her own career out of the challenging vocalism required in Offenbach's *The Tales of Hoffmann*.

The longevity of her career was a matter of "intelligence, sensibility, and good taste," says Zeani.

"I never sang anything too early! Even my debut as Violetta, at twenty-two, was not too soon, because my voice had matured by sixteen, and I had studied for eight years with Lucia Anghel and Lydia Lipkowska in Romania," she says. "Then when I came to Italy, I already knew four roles by heart. But for the first fifteen years of my career, I stuck to lyric coloratura. I did not attempt roles like Aida, Tosca, Butterfly, or Puccini's Manon before the age of thirty-seven."

Opera audiences around the world have Zeani's inner sensible career guide to thank, as they were able to revel in her performances for more than thirty-four years. She lent her voice, musicality, theatrical temperament, and beautiful stage presence to seventy operatic characters, from her debut role as Violetta in Bologna, in May 1948, to her last role, Mother Marie in Poulenc's *The Dialogues of the Carmelites* in San Francisco, in November 1982.

Zeani's marriage to the late, celebrated Italian bass Nicola Rossi-Lemeni led to a fruitful and rewarding musical partnership. The two often performed and recorded together. It also brought along the inevitable compromises a singer faces when married to a famous colleague. Married at thirty-one, while in full swing of her ascension to stardom, Zeani became a mother at thirty-two. She returned to the stage three months after the birth of her son. She admits it was not an easy life.

"When you marry a singer of my husband's renown, you have to know how to give him part of your activities, your time, your energy; and when you also have a child, your career will subtly take second place. And if you want a career, you have to find that balance, to devote time to it as well.

"I am exhausted just thinking back on my life. I really don't know how I handled it all. It was a struggle."

Undoubtedly, part of the struggle was living in an age where certain preconceived notions were intrinsic to the culture and social expectations. Zeani was an exceptionally modern woman for the fifties, juggling family and motherhood with the increasingly challenging demands of her career.

The tumult of Zeani's first "two lives"—childhood and adolescence in Romania, youth and career in Italy—mellowed with her move to the United States and her transformation from singer to teacher. Indiana University offered both Zeani and Rossi-Lemeni teaching positions in 1980. The arrival of the two glamorous opera stars in Bloomington was earth shattering, as some students described it.

The two threw themselves passionately and generously into shaping young voices and sculpting budding singers into accomplished artists. Results followed quickly. More and more of their students began winning the Met National Council Auditions as well as other international competitions. Sylvia McNair, Elizabeth Futral, Patricia Risley, Stephen Mark Brown, Angela Brown, and Marilyn Mims are a few among the successful singers who have been enriched by their encounter with Virginia Zeani.

"It is this encounter between the teacher and the student that determines how productive their work together is going to be," says Zeani. "I call it 'encounter,' most call it 'chemistry,' but if it is good, it establishes trust. Many people study with teachers they don't trust, and they end up changing teachers quickly. But I believe the more you change, the more lost you are, because you change ideas. While new ideas might be refreshing for a moment, you won't know where you are anymore."

Zeani's passion for teaching, coupled with her natural generosity and warmth, transcends the teaching experience as vocal diagnosis and remedy, encouragement, and guidance within the confines of a limited time. I had the chance to observe voice lessons with three of Florida Grand Opera Studio's young artists—Christina Pier, Chad Johnson, and Tim Kuhn—at Zeani's home in West Palm Beach, Florida. Technical and artistic issues took precedence—but the promise of a home-cooked meal was no weak incentive to hard work.

The three hours of productive morning singing melted into an afternoon discussion over Zeani's delicious pasta specialties. The topic? Countless variations of singers' hopes and struggles, whys and hows, ifs and whens, mingled with gossip, frustrations, joys, and Zeani's own special brand of humor, advice, and wisdom.

Christina Pier, a winner in this year's Met National Council Auditions, has been studying with Zeani since 1999. A young, impressive dramatic soprano, Pier refers to Zeani as a mother figure, friend, and mentor.

"Studying voice with her has changed my life. First of all, she transformed me from a mezzo to a soprano, and gave me the confidence to sing all of this great repertoire."

Tenor Chad Johnson marvels at Zeani's wealth of knowledge and experience.

"She studied with Aureliano Pertile! Both Pavarotti and Domingo made some debuts with her! She just knows so much about the stage, about artistry!"

Tim Kuhn, a former tenor Zeani changed to a booming baritone, agrees, adding that his teacher cares not just about the technical development of her students but also about their spiritual and emotional well-being. He offers a moving tribute.

"A voice lesson with Virginia Zeani is not just a voice lesson. It is a life lesson!"

One of Zeani's priorities in teaching is being able to "understand the psychology of a voice." She believes it is important for teachers to mentally transpose themselves into a student's physical structure—the head, the neck, the body—to understand and guide each individual voice. Keeping the physical characteristics in mind, Zeani then applies the same basic principles to all her students.

"You should start with the breath and the projection of the sound. I think of the breath as intracostal, which means the ribs expand, as they do when you are yawning. You need to maintain that expansion as you sing the phrase, and help it by tucking the lower abdomen in. Not forcing it in! It is all very subtle and elegant, as if you were a dancer. Whenever you feel the chest or ribs collapse on you, help them reexpand through the breath."

This should not be misunderstood as a recommendation to take a breath during a long phrase or vocalise to maintain the expansion. I observed that placing two hands laterally on the ribs, and creating a mental image of gently pushing the hands away with the outward movement of the ribs while singing, illustrated Zeani's point.

"It is not a violent movement of the ribs outward. That can create problems. It is elasticity; gymnastics of the breath, and this image of expansion prevents collapsing," says Zeani. "I maintain the elasticity of the breath in my students through agility exercises. It doesn't matter if you are a bass or a mezzo, or if you have a big dramatic voice, not inclined toward coloratura. I believe in agility and take all my students through fast scales and arpeggios, legato, and staccato.

"That was very important for me as a singer, too. I had studied as a mezzo. Lydia Lipkowska, who was a lyric soprano with high agility, made me do lots of agility vocalises and in three months, I had a high F! Before, I could only get to a G below high C. This change opened up my life! That is why I insist on this. Of course, I won't have a huge voice do excessive agility, but just enough to keep it flexible."

Another aspect of elasticity is economy of breath. Zeani insists on "economizing the breath and not giving too much." She demonstrates by whistling like a bird up and down a scale, and then purposely loses the whistle by blowing too much air.

"You see what happens if I give too much air? It's the same in singing!" Inexperienced students may have some difficulty in giving very little breath and yet avoiding the rigid physical feeling that inevitably comes with any mental command involving 'hold.' In this case, the emphasis was placed on holding back on the stream of air.

"I know the word *hold* is tricky, because you can get rigid," declares Zeani. "Of course, you still have to remain flexible while not giving too much breath. That is one of the most difficult processes to understand. It is also a question of language. Some words may trigger the right idea into a singer's mind, while others may not. If someone studies with me longer, throughout the year, I will use different imagery to help them understand."

Zeani believes in the methodical development of a singer's technique. She starts her new, beginner-level students with easy vocalises on vowels, and then adds consonants to the vowels.

"The consonant has to be hooked up high, and it leads the way for the vowel into this resonance space we call the mask. The mask position is vital for the projection of the sound. This position must be the same throughout all of your registers."

To demonstrate, Zeani proceeds to hum randomly ascending arpeggios to a high D, and back down—to the second A below middle C!

"I can do that so easily because every note is in that same position, in the mask!"

This position is the secret behind Zeani's fearless approach to her rich chest voice. A matter of debate among teachers, the indulgence in the chest voice, when it comes to high voices, can become a subject of endless disagreement. Some teachers believe in avoiding the occasional temptation to bask in the chest voice when the singer has to linger mostly in high tessituras. Others believe the lower voice to be an anchor to the rest of the voice, so they allow their soprano students to plant their vocal feet firmly on chest soil, in proportion to their Fach.

Zeani, however, presents it differently.

"I don't see it as a question of chest. That is a big mistake people make, thinking that the chest voice is somehow different or that you have to avoid it or not avoid it," she says. "Every vocalise has the mask position, whether you start low or high. When you go low, you still have to maintain this position. But the resonance will move from the head to the chest by itself. You don't have to do anything other than maintain the position, and the voice will resonate in the chest naturally, as much or as little as your physical structure allows it to."

She exemplifies by singing a five note scale ascending and descending from G below middle C, on "ah." Then she sings the same scale attempting to avoid the chest resonance. The sound loses color and strength.

"You see what happens. It is a mistake to avoid that resonance I just found for fear of not being able to sing high. Avoiding the resonance will misplace your position, and then you truly won't be able to sing high correctly! If you maintain the position, and go high" [she demonstrates by ascending to a high D], "the resonance will move more and more into the head. That's just normal."

Zeani could not be more emphatic about keeping the position of the sound in the mask. Yet she accentuates the difference between position and resonance, as confusion between the two may lead to trouble.

For those unfamiliar with the term, the *mask* refers to the resonating chambers above the upper teeth, behind the nose, in the sinus cavities, extending up to the forehead, and including the dome created by the hard palate. Zeani helps singers to locate the mask by emphasizing the complete relaxation of the lower jaw, which she uses only to accompany the articulation of the words. She creates a mental image of the upper teeth as a boundary, above which a singer should sing and articulate. The sensation of inhalation through open, flaring nostrils further helps in locating the resonating space behind the nose; the space which is the core of the mask.

Yet one should be leery of too-vivid, behind-the nose imagery. Observing several beginning students, I found that too much emphasis on the opening of the nose could lead to a nasal sound, while persistent wiggling attempts to relax the jaw might create more tension or pain. Zeani herself warns against excessive zeal.

"In teaching, as in life, it is a question of balance, sometimes very delicate balance!"

She agrees that you should not go overboard with any teacher's suggestions. They are only means to help illustrate principles, but technique is the sum of all its great and small parts.

"Technique is everything together. The artistic and the technical. You should never ignore one for the other."

With her more advanced students, Zeani simply becomes the characters her students bring to her, transforming herself from Germont to Edgardo to Leonora to Rosina in the span of four hours. To illustrate her points, she sings the phrases being studied, in the right key. Breaking the student's awed silence, she jokingly declares, "I would make a great tenor! And an acceptable bass, but only in the morning!"

The emotion, phrasing, messa di voce, accents, and characterizations pour out of her—and she can switch from demanding technical perfection to offering moments of intensely emotional artistry that leave her students—and her master class audiences—spellbound.

A beautiful, warm, intelligent, humorous woman; complete artist; and generous teacher, Virginia Zeani was a phenomenon on the stage and is a force of nature in real life. Former, current, and prospective students from all over the world come to her door. She is a tireless worker in helping those who touch her with their talent and devotion to singing, and she also finds the time and energy to travel and give master classes.

The Bucharest Opera
Résistance

Published in Classical Singer, *November 2004.*

The Bucharest National Opera has a special significance in my life, because it became a refuge for my mother and me during the two and a half years we were separated from my father.

My father escaped from Romania in 1985, and was immediately declared a traitor. My mother and I were left to suffer the repercussions during the peak years of dictator Nicolae Ceauşescu's communist regime, until my father managed to get us out of the country.

During those years of oppression, there was hardly anything to do in the evening. My mother and I lived in just one room of our home, since the *securitate* (the dreaded security militia) had confiscated most of the furniture, and cut off the heat and electricity regularly as a form of terror. To get us out of the house during those freezing, candle-lit evenings, my mother took me to the opera. The opera house opened its doors to us and became a place of refuge, an oasis.

The Bucharest Opera is a simple version of the Garnier Opera, very Parisian in style, echoing Bucharest's nickname from the 1930s, "little Paris" or "the Paris of the East." It has about one thousand seats, and no specified spaces for standing room. During the worst communist years, sets, costumes, and funding were scarce, and so was the heating during the winter. People attended the opera wrapped in coats, scarves, and hats—and only took their gloves off to make sure that the sound of the applause reached the singers onstage.

Singing under those circumstances was a miracle. The repertoire at that time included the standard works, such as *Rigoletto, La traviata, Lucia di Lammermoor, The Magic Flute,* all performed in Romanian with the company's own singers. The occasional guest singers—all from the Eastern Bloc—meant the house would be a little warmer, and there would be toilet paper in the restrooms!

The audience was always generous with their applause, but sometimes in the winter, I wondered if they sincerely expressed their enthusiasm for all singers, even for the comprimarios, or they were simply jumping at every opportunity to warm themselves up by clapping their hands.

During those years of persecution and dictatorship, I had the feeling that the Bucharest Opera became a refuge for many, regardless of their personal situation. Obviously, the opera had to bow to the "supreme leader" and would throw the occasional gala in which the soloists were obliged to sing patriotic songs, hymns to Ceaușescu, and odes to the party. But a subversive undercurrent lived behind those Parisian-style doors.

I particularly remember a performance of *The Abduction from the Seraglio*. At the end, when the Pasha Selim decides to allow the lovers to leave freely, the Pasha appeared onstage out of his costume, dressed in a suit and sunglasses, the customary attire of the feared *securitate* agents. Then he handed a huge passport to Belmonte. Since the text was in Romanian, the singer playing the Pasha role cleverly manipulated the words to parody the practically impossible process of obtaining the much-coveted passport, which allowed access to the West. (Most Romanians did not own a passport.)

In any other venue or institution, or even in private gatherings, people would have been arrested merely for daring to laugh at a subversive joke, much less to ridicule the regime openly. But there it was on the stage, defiance in operatic form, greeted with laughter, applause, and a few tears.

Throughout their long history of oppression, Romanians have mastered the ability to laugh at their own woes, and the opera offered them that opportunity.

Another similar moment happened during one winter performance of *Il trovatore*. In the final scene, Manrico asks Azucena if the chilly air of the jail cell doesn't harm her bones. "No," she replies, "all I want is to get out of here because I'm suffocating."

The singers directed their exchange toward the audience, transforming the "chilly air" into a more sarcastic "cooling breeze," and the unforgettable vision of hundreds of bundled-up, hat and glove-wearing spectators shaking with laughter still lives vividly in my mind.

I remember a performance of *Carmen* with a special Russian guest in the title role. The rest of the cast was Romanian, while our bullying, Big

Brother–Soviet neighbor required that its mezzo sing in Russian. In the cacophony of Romanian and Russian phrases that ensued—which would have made Bizet turn over in his grave—the Romanians did not miss the opportunity for taking another stab at the Iron Curtain. After his entrance aria, Escamillo asks Carmen: "What would you say if I told you that I loved you?" She replies that he shouldn't love her, to which Escamillo responds, "Your answer is not very tender."

That evening, when Carmen's reply came in heavy Russian, Escamillo faced the audience and substituted the "approved" Romanian translation of the French text with: "Your language is poisoning my brain!" The Soviet propaganda–indoctrinated audience exploded in roars of laughter, causing the flabbergasted Russian guest to later return to Leningrad and report the strange, unruly behavior of the Romanian audience.

Whenever the Bucharest Opera's curtain rose, the Iron Curtain seemed to go up with it, and you could allow yourself to think and laugh freely, even if at the end of the performances you returned home to harsh reality. There was a tacit agreement of solidarity and resistance between the audience and the performers that defied the omnipresent fear, suspicions, and general paranoia that ruled outside the opera house. The buffet would open every night even if all it could offer were boxes of stale crackers. Hardships notwithstanding, people maintained their opera-going customs dating from 1921, when the first Romanian Opera House opened in Bucharest. Part of these customs included a visit to the buffet for socializing, discussions, and champagne or snacks.

Sixty-five years later, the public frequented the buffet in their winter coats, sometimes munching on the sole delicacy of a dubious expiration date, but mostly just feasting on one another's courage and determination in maintaining their cultural tradition despite the harsh conditions.

After the fall of the Iron Curtain, the Bucharest National Opera underwent a difficult phase. Romanians were intoxicated with the freedom as well as the subsequent Westernization brought on by the 1989 Revolution. Attendance at the opera diminished drastically until the late 1990s when, after a few changes in administration and marketing resources, there was a surge of interest in the opera. Thanks to privatization, the concept of the sponsor opened a door to opportunities for renovation.

Today, the company's repertoire still consists of both opera and ballet. The season runs from October to June, with performances starting at 6:30 p.m., and the occasional ballet matinee on Sundays. Each year, BNO offers about twenty-four opera productions and ten to fourteen different ballets, with no apparent pattern of repetition. The most expensive ticket costs about six dollars.

The company still has its own fixed roster of singers, though many more guests appear regularly. Romanian singers established in careers abroad donate their time and give up large fees to perform on the Bucharest stage.

In recent years, very young singers have had the chance to make their debuts at the National Opera, through the opera's close collaboration with the Bucharest University of Music. The performances are exciting, brimming with the energy and enthusiasm of outstanding graduates who are grateful to gain experience on the stage.

Through the George Enescu International Festival and with the help of the Vienna State Opera, as well as some Covent Garden productions, the Bucharest Opera has attracted more attention in the past few years. Despite the increase in sponsors, funding is still scarce and the opera can afford only one premiere a year, but there is still a very knowledgeable audience infused by the energy of the new generation of opera-goers, eager to discover in the many young voices the next Angela Gheorghiu, Haricleea Darclée, Virginia Zeani, Maria Cebotari, Nicolae Herlea, Alexandru Agache, Leontina Vaduva, Stella Roman, Eugenia Moldoveanu, and so on.

As I watch today's productions in the top opera houses, I am in awe of their technological prowess, which grows from season to season, striving to outdo itself by developing the visual aspect of opera, sometimes to an extreme. But I often think back to those evenings at the Bucharest Opera, where among the most rudimentary sets and antique productions, I had some of the most thrilling experiences of my entire opera-going life. In the freezing darkness, the voices and the music alone wrapped the audience in beauty, emotion, and fantasy. The singing soothed, stirred, and seduced until you were madly in love, and became addicted.

That was opera in its purest, most sincere form.

Recommended Discography and Videography

JAMES CONLON
Web site: www.jamesconlon.com
CDs
Bruch, Max, *Symphonien 1–3*, 2004. Gürzenich-Orchester, Kölner Philharmoniker. EMI Classics B000005GKJ.

Sumi Jo: Prayers, 2001. Sumi Jo; Gürzenich-Orchester, Kölner Philharmoniker. Erato B0000560N6.

DVDs
Encore! with James Conlon, 2006. The Takács Quartet. A film by Andy Sommer. B000FILUNI. (A six-part television series featuring the finalists of the Twelfth Van Cliburn International Piano Competition.)

Rossini, Gioacchino, *Semiramide*, 2000. June Anderson, Marilyn Horne; Metropolitan Opera Orchestra and Chorus. Image Entertainment B00004Z4W9.

DWAYNE CROFT
CDs
En concierto, 2000. Dwayne Croft, Ainhoa Arteta; Max Bragado-Darman. Rtve Classics Import B00004ZBFH. (Arias and duets of Mozart, Rossini, Verdi, and others.)

Puccini, Giacomo, *Manon Lescaut*, 1992. Mirella Freni, Luciano Pavarotti; James Levine, Metropolitan Opera Chorus and Orchestra. London Decca B00000418G.

DVDs

Puccini, Giacomo, *Manon Lescaut*, 2008. Karita Mattila, Marcello Giordani; James Levine, Metropolitan Opera. Metropolitan Opera HD Live Series. EMI Classics B001DHE9KQ.

Verdi, Giuseppe, *Don Carlo*, 2005. Rolando Villazón, Amanda Roocroft, Violetta Urmana; Riccardo Chailly, Royal Concertgebouw Orchestra, Nederlanse Opera Chorus, Amsterdam Opera. BBC/Opus Arte B000AOGMHG.

JOSÉ CURA

Web site: www.josecura.com

CDs

Anhelo: Argentinian Songs, 1998. Assorted accompanists. Erato B00000DGWU. (Songs by Cardoso, Cura, Ginastera, Guastavino, Piazzolla, Ramírez, and others.)

José Cura: Artist Portrait, 2004. Sir Colin Davis, London Symphony Orchestra; Plácido Domingo, Philharmonia Orchestra. Warner Classics B00006L724. (Arias by Cilea, Leoncavallo, Mascagni, Puccini, Verdi and others.)

DVDs

Puccini, Giacomo, *Manon Lescaut*, 2005. Maria Guleghina, Lucio Gallo; Riccardo Muti, La Scala Orchestra and Chorus. TDK DVD Video B000AMMSQW.

Verdi, Giuseppe, *Otello*, 2006. Krassimira Stoyanova, Lado Ataneli; Antoni Ros-Marba. Opus Arte B000LSBMV2.

DIANA DAMRAU

Web site: www.diana-damrau.com

CDs

Arie di bravura 2007. Jérémie Rhorer; Le Cercle de l'Harmonie. Virgin Classics B000R20VM8. (Arias by Salieri, Mozart, and Righini.)

Mozart: Donna, 2008. Jérémie Rhorer; Le Cercle de l'Harmonie. Virgin Classics B0017IYWEE.

DVDs

Mozart, Wolfgang Amadeus, *Ascanio in Alba*, 2006. Iris Kupke, Charles Reid; Adam Fischer, Mannheim National Theater Orchestra and Chorus. Deutsche Grammophon B000I8OFLY.

————, *Die Zauberflöte*, 2006. Paul Groves, René Pape; Riccardo Muti, Wiener Philharmoniker/Salzburger Festspiele. Decca B000ICL3Q0.

NATALIE DESSAY

Web site: www.natalie-dessay.com

CDs

Airs d'opéras italiens, 2008. Evelino Pidó, Concerto Köln. Virgin Classics B000WPAGD4. (Arias by Verdi, Bellini, and Donizetti.)

Bach: Cantatas BWV 51, 82a, 199, 2008. Neil Brough, *trumpet;* Emmanuelle Haïm, Le Concert d'Astrée. *Virgin Classics* B001GAQR2S.

DVDs

Donizetti, Gaetano, *La fille du régiment*, 2007. Juan Diego Flórez; Bruno Campanella, Royal Opera House Orchestra and Chorus, Covent Garden. Virgin Classics B0013V33DG.

Massenet, Jules, *Manon*, 2007. Rolando Villazón, Manuel Lanza; Victor Pablo Pérez, Symphony Orchestra and Chorus of the Gran Teatre del Liceu. Virgin Classics B000VJ271A.

PLÁCIDO DOMINGO

Web site: www.placidodomingo.com

CDs

Amore infinito: Songs Inspired by the Poetry of John Paul II (Karol Wojtyla), 2009. Josh Groban, Andrea Bocelli, Katherine Jenkins, Vanessa Williams; London Symphony Orchestra. Deutsche Grammophon B001NXRDHG.

The Essential Plácido Domingo, 2004. Assorted conductors and orchestras. Sony BMG B00064AEYW. (Arias and songs by Bernstein, Verdi, and others.)

DVDs

Puccini, Giacomo, *Turandot*, 2003. Eva Marton, Leona Mitchell; James Levine, Metropolitan Opera Orchestra and Chorus. Deutsche Grammophon B000094HMU. (Filmed in 1988.)

Tan, Dun, *The First Emperor*, 2008. Elizabeth Futral, Paul Groves; Tan Dun, Metropolitan Opera Orchestra and Chorus. Metropolitan Opera HD Live Series. EMI Classics B001D6OKVK.

SIMON ESTES
CDs

Ol' Man River: Broadway's Greatest Hits, 1992. Munich Radio Orchestra. Polygram Records B00000E47N. (Songs by Kern, Rodgers, Weill, and others.)

Wagner, Richard, *Parsifal*, 1993. Waltraud Meier, Matti Salminen; James Levine, Orchestra and Chorus of the Bayreuther Festspiele. Philips Classics B00000414X. (Recorded live in Bayreuth July and August 1985.)

DVDs

Great Arias with Plácido Domingo and Friends, 2008. Barbara Hendricks, Shirley Verrett; Lorin Maazel, National Orchestra of France. View, Inc. B001GJ4U8C.

Wagner, Richard, *Der fliegende Holländer*, 2005. Matti Salminen; Woldemar Nelsson, Orchestra of the Bayreuther Festspiele. Deutsche Grammophon B0007Q6PBU. (Filmed in 1985.)

RENÉE FLEMING
Web site: www.reneefleming.com
CDs

Mozart, Wolfgang Amadeus, *Visions of Love: Mozart Arias* (1996). Charles Mackerras, Orchestra of St. Luke's. Decca B00000429M.

Strauss, Richard, *Four Last Songs*, 2008. Christian Thielemann, Münchner Philharmoniker. Decca B001D27GKQ.

DVDs

Sacred Songs: Live from Mainz Cathedral, 2006. Trevor Pinnock, Mainz Cathedral Choir, Deutsche Kammerphilharmonie Bremen. Decca B000E97HTE.

Strauss, Richard, *Arabella*, 2008. Morten Frank Larsen; Franz Welser-Möst, Orchestra and Chorus of Zurich Opera House. Decca B0012L0TG6.

ANGELA GHEORGHIU and ROBERTO ALAGNA
Web site: www.angelagheorghiu.com
CDs

Angela Gheorghiu: My Puccini, 2008. Antonio Pappano. Roberto Alagna; assorted conductors and orchestras. EMI Classics B001E1YVU4.

Angela Gheorghiu: My World, 1998. Malcolm Martineau. Decca Classics B0000069D9. (Arias by Martinů, Pergolesi, Leoncavallo, and others.)

C'est magnifique! Roberto Alagna Sings Luis Mariano, 2005. Yvan Cassar, Paris Symphony Orchestra. Deutsche Grammophon B000CQQGVO.

Roberto Alagna: French Arias, 2001. Bertrand de Billy, Orchestra of the Royal Opera House. EMI Classics B000058B1Y.

DVDs

Donizetti, Gaetano, *L'elisir d'amore*, 2005. Angela Gheorghiu, Roberto Alagna; Evelino Pidó, Orchestra and Chorus of the Opéra National de Lyon. Decca B00005V15Q. (Filmed in 1996.)

Puccini, Giacomo, *Tosca*, 2003.Angela Gheorghiu, Roberto Alagna, Ruggiero Raimondi; Antonio Pappano, Orchestra and Chorus of the Royal Opera House, Covent Garden. A film by Benoît Jacquot. Kultur B000BB1MH8.

Verdi, Giuseppe, *Don Carlos*, 1997. Roberto Alagna, Karita Mattila, Thomas Hampson, José Van Dam. Antonio Pappano, Théâtre du Châtelet, Paris. Kultur B00008DDRK.

———, *La traviata*, 2005. Angela Gheorghiu, Frank Lopardo,

Leo Nucci; Sir Georg Solti, Orchestra and Chorus of the Royal Opera House, Covent Garden. Decca B0009AM5I6. (Filmed in 1994; special edition with highlights CD.)

THOMAS HAMPSON

Web site: www.hampsong.com

CDs

Mahler, Gustav, *Das Lied von der Erde*, 2008. Michael Tilson Thomas; San Francisco Symphony. San Francisco Symphony B001DPC3Q0. (Hybrid SACD.)

Verdi: Opera Arias, 2006. Richard Armstrong, Orchestra of the Age of Enlightenment. EMI Classics B000F5GOKU.

DVDs

Massenet, Jules, *Werther*, 2006. Susan Graham; Michel Plasson, Toulouse National Orchestra/Théâtre du Châtelet. Paris. Virgin Classics B000EQHSDC. (Filmed live in concert, 2004.)

Verdi, Giuseppe, *Simon Boccanegra*, 2007. Cristina Gallardo-Domas, Ferruccio Furlanetto; Daniele Gatti, Wiener Philharmonkier and Wiener Staatsopernchor. TDK DVD Video B000MRP1Z0. (Filmed in 2002.)

BENOÎT JACQUOT

DVDs

La fille seule (A Single Girl), 1995. Virginie Ledoyen, Benoît Magimel. Fox Lorber B00004TBFS.

Princesse Marie, 2004. Catherine Deneuve, Heinz Bennent. Imavision B000FMQLGK. (French television series.)

VESSELINA KASAROVA

Web site: www.kasarova.com

CDs

Love Entranced: French Opera Arias, 2001. Frédéric Chaslin, Munich Radio Orchestra, RCA B00004STY1.

Massenet, Jules, *Werther*, 1999. Ramón Vargas, Christopher Schaldenbrand; Vladimir Jurowski, Deutsches Symphonie-Orchester Berlin. RCA B00000K4H0.

DVDs

Monteverdi, Claudio, *Il ritorno d'Ulisse in patria*, 2003. Dietrich Henschel, Malin Hartelius; Nikolaus Harnoncourt, Orchestra La Scintilla of the Zürich Opera. Arthaus Musik B00008OSEE.

Mozart, Wolfgang Amadeus, *La clemenza di Tito*, 2007. Jonas Kaufmann, Eva Mei; Franz Welser-Möst, Orchestra and Chorus of the Zürich Opera. EMI Video B000J20W7A. (Filmed in 2005.)

GREGORY KUNDE
Web site: www.gregorykunde.com
CDs

Bellini, Vincenzo, *Bianca e Fernando*, 1994. Young Ok Shin; Andrea Licata, Orchestra and Chorus of Teatro Massimo. Nuova Era B0000036BW.

Delibes, Léo, *Lakmé*, 1998. Natalie Dessay, José van Dam; Michel Plasson, Orchestra and Chorus of Capitole de Toulouse. EMI Classics B00000C2JP.

DVDs

Berlioz, Hector, *Les Troyens*, 2004. Susan Graham, Anna Caterina Antonacci; Sir John Eliot Gardiner, Orchestre Révolutionnaire et Romantique, Monteverdi Choir, Théâtre du Châtelet, Paris. BBC/Opus Arte B0002TTTHO.

Donizetti, Gaetano, *Don Pasquale*, 1994. Ferruccio Furlanetto, Nuccia Focile; Riccardo Muti, La Scala Orchestra and Chorus. TDK DVD Video B000OQDRZU.

ANNA NETREBKO
Web site: www.annanetrebko.com
CDs

Souvenirs, 2008. Emmanuel Villaume, Prague Philharmonia. Deutsche Grammophon B001GSV39W. (Works by Charpentier, Dvořák, Grieg, Kálmán, Lehár, Lloyd Webber, Offenbach, R. Strauss, and others.)

Anna Netrebko Sings Opera Arias, 2007. Umvd Import B000H5VDTK. (Works by Bellini, Puccini, Verdi, and others.)

DVDs

Prokofiev, Sergey, *Betrothal in a Monastery*, 2005. Sergei Alexashkin; Valery Gergiev, Kirov Opera. Philips B001LKLKGG.

Verdi, Giuseppe, *La traviata*, 2006. Rolando Villazón, Thomas Hampson; Carlo Rizzi, Wiener Philharmoniker/Salzburg Festival. Deutsche Grammophon B000F3TAOE.

SAMUEL RAMEY
Web site: www.samuelramey.com
CDs
A Date with the Devil, 2000. Julius Rudel, Münchner Rundfunk Orchester. Naxos B0000682W0.

Opera Arias, 1990. Donato Renzetti, Philharmonia Orchestra and Ambrosian Opera Chorus. Polygram Records B00000E3IX. (Arias by Bellini, Boito, Handel, Mozart, Rossini, and Verdi.)

DVDs

Boito, Arrigo, *Mefistofele*, 2001. Gabriela Beňačková; Maurizio Arena, San Francisco Opera Orchestra and Chorus. Kultur Video B00005N-GA8. (Filmed in 1989.)

Verdi, Giuseppe, *Attila*, 1998. Cheryl Studer, Giorgio Zancanaro; Riccardo Muti, Teatro alla Scala Orchestra and Chorus. BBC/Opus Arte B00066K2R4. (Filmed in 1991.)

JULIUS RUDEL
CDs
Handel, George Frideric, *Julius Caesar*, 1990. Beverly Sills, Norman Treigle; New York City Opera Orchestra and Chorus. RCA B000003EOP. (Originally recorded in 1966.)

Weill, Kurt, *Lost in the Stars*, 1993. Orchestra of St. Luke's. Musical Heritage Society B000000FRC.

DVDs

Donizetti, Gaetano, *Roberto Devereux*, 1999. Beverly Sills; New York City Opera Orchestra and Chorus. Video Artists Int'l B00005N5SJ. (Filmed in 1975.)

Saint-Saëns, Camille, *Samson et Dalila*, 2000. Plácido Domingo, Shirley Verrett; San Francisco Opera Orchestra and Chorus. Kultur Video B00004ZEQF. (Filmed in 1991.)

PATRICK SUMMERS
CDs

Catán, Daniel, *Florencia in the Amazon*, 2002. Ana María Martínez, Chad Shelton; Houston Grand Opera Orchestra and Chorus. Albany Records B00007IG3O.

Floyd, Carlisle, *Cold Sassy Tree*, 2005. Patricia Racette, Dean Peterson, Christopher Schaldenbrand, Oren Gradus; Houston Grand Opera Orchestra and Chorus. Albany Records B000A139DO.

DVDs

Bellini, Vincenzo, *I Puritani*, 2007. Anna Netrebko, Eric Cutler; Metropolitan Opera Orchestra and Chorus. Deutsche Grammophon B000Y9M09G.

Puccini, Giacomo, *Madama Butterfly*, 2008. Cheryl Barker, Jay Hunter Morris; Opera Australia/Australian Opera Orchestra and Chorus. Kultur Video B0015NR2F2. (Filmed in 1974.)

CAROL VANESS
CDs

Mozart, Wolfgang Amadeus, *Idomeneo*, 1996. Cecilia Bartoli, Plácido Domingo; James Levine, Metropolitan Opera Orchestra and Chorus. Deutsche Grammophon B000001GR8.

Verdi, Giuseppe, *Aroldo*, 2001. Neil Shicoff, Roberto Scandiuzzi; Fabio Luisi, Maggio Musicale Fiorentino Orchestra and Chorus. Philips B00005O83U.

DVDs

Albeniz, Isaac, *Merlin*, 2004. Eva Marton, David Wilson-Johnson; José de Eusebio, Teatro Real Madrid Orchestra and Chorus. BBC Opus Arte B0001RVRX6.

Mozart, Wolfgang Amadeus, *Don Giovanni*, 2000. Thomas Allen, Ferrucio Furlanetto, Andrea Rost; James Conlon, Gürzenich Orchestra Cologne, Cologne Opera. Arthaus Musik B00004UEE3. (Filmed in 1991.)

RAMÓN VARGAS

Web site: www.ramonvargas.com

CDs

Canzoni, 2000. Roberto Negri, piano. Delta B00000DDMG. (Neapolitan songs and other classical Italian songs.)

L'amour, l'amour, 1999. Marcello Viotti, Munich Radio Symphony Orchestra. Sony Classics B00000K4H4. (Arias by Donizetti, Gounod, Massenet, Puccini, Tchaikovsky, and Verdi.)

DVDs

Mozart, Wolfgang Amadeus, *Idomeneo*, 2007. Magdalena Kožena, Anja Harteros; Sir Roger Norrington, Camerata Salzburg. Decca B000ICL3R4.

Puccini, Giacomo, *La bohème*, 2008. Angela Gheorghiu, Ainhoa Arteta; Nicola Luisotti, Metropolitan Opera Orchestra and Chorus. Live from the Met. EMI Classics B001DHE9KG.

ROLANDO VILLAZÓN

Web site: www.rolandovillazon.com

CDs

Cielo e mar, 2008. Daniele Callegari, Orchestra Sinfonica e Coro di Milano Giuseppe Verdi. Deutsche Grammophon B000ZXSZFY. (Arias by Boito, Ciléa, Donizetti, Ponchielli, Verdi, and others.)

Gitano, 2007. Plácido Domingo, Orquesta de la Comunidad de Madrid. Virgin Classics B000FIHZLE. (Zarzuela arias.)

DVDs

Donizetti, Gaetano, *L'elisir d'amore*, 2006. Anna Netrebko, Leo Nucci, Ildebrando D'Arcangelo; Alfred Eschwé, Vienna State Opera Orchestra and Chorus. Virgin Classics B000F3T3CS. (Filmed in 2005.)

Massenet, Jules, *Manon*, 2008. Anna Netrebko, Alfredo Daza; Daniel Barenboim, Staatskapelle Berlin. Deutsche Grammophon B0012UQ-IW6.

VIRGINIA ZEANI

CDs

Il mito dell'opera: *Virginia Zeani*, 1995. Alfredo Kraus; assorted conductors and orchestras. Bongiovanni B00000447J. (Arias and duets by Bellini, Donizetti, Verdi, and others.)

Verdi, Giuseppe, *La traviata*, 1995. Nicolae Herlea, Ion Buzea; Jean Bobescu, Bucharest State Opera Orchestra. Vox B00008FZZW. (Highlights from the opera.)